Oracle Press™

Oracle Business Intelligence Applications

Deliver Value Through Rapid Implementations

Simon Miller
William Hutchinson

New York   Chicago   San Francisco
Lisbon   London   Madrid   Mexico City   Milan
New Delhi   San Juan   Seoul   Singapore   Sydney   Toronto

Cataloging-in-Publication Data is on file with the Library of Congress

McGraw-Hill Education books are available at special quantity discounts to use as premiums and sales promotions, or for use in corporate training programs. To contact a representative, please visit the Contact Us pages at www.mhprofessional.com.

Oracle Business Intelligence Applications: Deliver Value Through Rapid Implementations

1 2 3 4 5 6 7 8 9 0   DOC DOC   1 0 9 8 7 6 5 4 3

ISBN   978-0-07-180414-1
MHID   0-07-180414-5

Sponsoring Editor	**Technical Editor**	**Production Supervisor**
Paul Carlstroem	Florian Schouten	Jean Bodeaux
Editorial Supervisor	**Copy Editor**	**Composition**
Jody McKenzie	Bart Reed	Cenveo Publisher Services
Project Manager	**Proofreader**	**Art Director, Cover**
Sandhya Gola, Cenveo® Publisher Services	Claire Splan	Jeff Weeks
Acquisitions Coordinator	**Indexer**	
Amanda Russell	Jack Lewis	

Isaac Newton said, "If I have seen further, it is by standing on the shoulders of giants." This book is dedicated to all the giants on whose shoulders I have stood.

Also to my wife, Meg.

—Will Hutchinson

This book is dedicated to my four children—Libby, Zeke, Ivy, and Tate—even though they're calling this "the most boring book ever." This book is also dedicated to my wife, Lori, who supported and encouraged me every step of the way through this process.

—Simon Miller

About the Authors

Simon Miller (Toronto, Canada) is a Master Principal Sales Consultant at Oracle, specializing in Oracle's prebuilt BI Applications. Over the past 15 years he has worked exclusively in the BI Technology, Architecture, and Analytics space across North America and parts of Europe. Simon was originally trained on what is now Oracle's prebuilt BI Applications in April 2002.

Simon is responsible for working with one of Oracle's largest customers, supporting both evaluations and implementations of Oracle BI Applications. Prior to Oracle, Simon worked at Siebel and was the first Siebel Analytics Master Certified resource in Canada. Simon has won numerous awards, including Oracle BI Sales Consultant of the Year for North America in 2008, and a Global Leadership Award from his primary customer in 2012.

Simon has a BS degree from McMaster University in Hamilton, Ontario.

William Hutchinson (Chicago) is a Master Principal Sales Consultant at Oracle, specializing in Oracle's BI tools and applications. He has worked in business intelligence and data warehousing for more than 25 years. He started building data warehouses in 1986 at Metaphor, advancing to running Metaphor UK's sales consulting area. He also worked in A.T. Kearney's business intelligence practice for over four years, running projects and providing training to new consultants in the IT practice. In addition, he worked at Informatica and then Siebel, before coming to Oracle with the Siebel acquisition. He became Master Principal Sales Consultant in 2009. He has worked on developing ROI and TCO models for business intelligence for more than 10 years.

Will has a BS degree in chemical engineering from Princeton University and an MBA in finance from the University of Chicago.

About the Technical Editor

Florian Schouten has more than 15 years of experience with ERP, BI, analytics, and decision support. Florian is responsible for the product management and strategy for Oracle's BI Applications, a suite of prebuilt analytic solutions across the various front-office and back-office functions in CRM and ERP systems. Prior to this role, Florian ran the development organization focused on building real-time analytic solutions for Oracle Fusion Applications called Oracle Transactional Business Intelligence. He came to Oracle via the PeopleSoft acquisition, where he held various product management and development roles related to analytics and performance management.

Florian has a PDEng degree (professional doctorate in engineering) in mathematical decision support models from Delft University and an MA degree in operations research from Tilburg University.

Contents

Foreword

Have you recently met a business analyst satisfied with the speed of deployment of business intelligence solutions in their organization? If so, you are in the minority.

For years, the lines of business and information technology (IT) have seemingly been at odds. Lines of business have a notion as to what they need, yet IT efforts have often fallen short in delivering comprehensive solutions or have not met desired time windows for delivery. Certainly, building the back-end data warehouse has always been a challenge, and understanding what key performance indicators (KPIs) are and which ones will be important to the lines of business is an art as much as a science. IT folks also point to the difficulty in understanding the meaning and quality of data in the source systems that feed the desired data model. In fact, building the extraction, transformation, and loading (ETL) scripts is often the most time consuming part in the build-out of these solutions.

Over a period of years, vendors and consultants have positioned industry data models as an ideal starting point. These help greatly in identifying needed KPIs and gaps that remain. However, building ETL scripts remains a challenge even where these are deployed. Part of the issue is the wide variety of source systems present in most organizations, many of which are custom built.

Where ERP and CRM systems are well defined by applications vendors, there is another solution. Horizontal data models that align to modules in these applications can deliver business intelligence solutions to these frustrated lines of business in much less time. Because the sources are well understood, the ETL scripts can also be pre-defined. Business intelligence tools can be pre-populated with business metadata and exposed as part of intuitive dashboards. Oracle's Business Intelligence Applications, the subject of this book, follow this paradigm.

Oracle's Business Intelligence Applications reached their current maturity through steady evolution, beginning as part of the Siebel business intelligence solutions prior to Oracle's acquisition. Since that acquisition, Oracle invested heavily in extending the data models, the lines of business covered, and KPIs presented within those areas. A wide variety of source systems are now supported including Oracle's Fusion Applications, E-Business Suite, PeopleSoft, JD Edwards, Siebel, and SAP.

Make no mistake about it, though. Like most pre-defined solutions of this type, the BI Applications likely deliver a subset of the business intelligence that your lines of business are looking for. Some additional work will be needed as you are asked to provide additional KPIs, access to other data sources, and find a need to continue to address the challenges of data quality. But, the BI Applications can quickly deliver a core set of KPIs providing intelligence about the business and speeding time to positive return on investment for projects of this type. And, in organizations where the ability to acquire consulting or other skilled talent is more limited, they can deliver a solution that might have been thought of as outside the realm of possibility.

The continued popularity of these solutions provides proof that organizations find much value in this approach. The two authors of this book, Will Hutchinson and Simon Miller, worked more than 10 years with the BI Applications as they evolved and share their experiences here. Because of that, I am confident this book will help you better understand the how and why of Oracle's BI Applications and will help assure your own success in delivering critical business information.

Best wishes for your success and I hope you enjoy this book.

Robert Stackowiak
Vice President of Big Data
and Analytics Architecture
Oracle Enterprise Solutions Group

Acknowledgments

W e'd like to thank our management for supporting us, including Ken McMullen, John Duda, and Adam Driver. We'd also like to thank Paul Rodwick, Florian Schouten, and his entire product management staff (Rao Adivikolanu, Hari Cherukupally, Manmohit Saggi, Ashwin Warrier, Manuel Puyana, Anand Dodd, Ling Xiang, and everyone else). We'd also like to thank the staff at McGraw-Hill for their enthusiasm, professionalism, and guidance.

From Simon Miller

I'd also like to thank Erica and Lauren from my local Starbucks, who kept me well caffeinated and fed during my long writing sessions. I'd also like to thank my Oracle business partner Janice Zajchowski for her support, encouragement, and patience. I'd also like to thank my co-author Will Hutchinson for introducing me first to Oracle BI Applications 12 years ago and then to Siebel eight years ago. It was his wisdom and experience that has led to a career I could never have dreamed of.

From Will Hutchinson

I'd also like to thank Sandra Tice, who introduced me to analytic applications when she lured me to Informatica in 2001. She convinced me customers wanted this type of product and that together we could sell it.

Introduction

O racle BI Applications provide a prebuilt data warehouse to complement Oracle and non-Oracle CRM and ERP data sources, using multiple Oracle technologies. They provide a comprehensive suite of end-user-focused prebuilt dashboards, subject areas for ad-hoc analysis, prebuilt best-practice architecture, and are actively supported and maintained by Oracle for future releases.

Oracle BI Applications have a long history of development, with hundreds of millions of research and development dollars invested, over more than a decade. Out of the box, Oracle provides prebuilt ETL, an enterprise data warehouse data model, an Oracle Business Intelligence semantic layer with logical metric and dimension definitions, and prebuilt dashboards.

Thousands of customers around the world are in production today with Oracle BI Applications, with hundreds more joining the customer base each year. This is a strategic and long-term application for Oracle, who continues to invest and grow the solution. This book is geared toward everyone touched by an Oracle BI Applications purchase and implementation, including the functional end users, implementers, IT support, and data warehouse professionals. This is intended to be a supplement to the official Oracle installation and configuration documentation, from the perspective of a business user and project manager.

This book gives you the opportunity to see Oracle BI Applications through the eyes of two tenured individuals who have built their careers around explaining what the BI Applications are and how they can help an organization.

With this book, you will learn the following:

- Why you would consider purchasing a prebuilt BI Application
- The challenges and risks of building a data warehouse from scratch
- Whether Oracle BI Applications are applicable for your needs
- What to be aware of when implementing
- How to extend and make the implementation your own
- How Exalytics can help with your deployments
- What each of the different components are from a technical perspective
- What the out-of-the-box content is for each application

This book contains 15 chapters.

Chapter 1: Crash Course in Data Warehouse Survival

In this chapter, we cover the basics of data warehousing and Business Intelligence, for those who are new to the industry. We lay down the foundation and context to help you understand how a solid Analytics foundation needs to be in place to scale to an enterprise and stand the test of time.

Chapter 2: Don't Reinvent Any Wheels

In this chapter, we explain what a prebuilt BI Application is and why it might matter to you. Organizations don't build their own GL and payroll systems anymore, but rather purchase proven packages from software vendors. BI Applications are no different—when you find the right fit for your needs.

Chapter 3: Oracle BI Applications Architecture

This chapter is a deep dive into all the moving parts and pieces of the BI Applications architecture, to help you understand the scope of content that has been prebuilt.

Chapter 4: Exalytics: Go Fast, Not Slow

In this chapter, we provide an overview of Exalytics and how it can enhance your usage of Oracle BI Applications.

Chapter 5: Financial Analytics

This chapter is mainly a functional explanation of what Financial Analytics are. It details the business benefits, what's available out of the box, and what the intended use is. This chapter also provides a unique perspective on various options for financial reporting, including how Essbase can enhance your end-user experience.

Chapter 6: Order Management and Supply Chain Analytics

This chapter is mainly a functional explanation of what Order Management and Supply Chain Analytics provide, as well as the business benefits, what's available out of the box, and what the intended use is. There's also a detailed explanation around how some of the key metrics (bookings, billings, and backlogs) are derived.

Chapter 7: Manufacturing Analytics

This chapter is mainly a functional explanation of what Manufacturing Analytics provides, as well as the business benefits, what's available out of the box, and what the intended use is. This is some of the most recent content added to the Oracle BI Applications family, and this chapter provides the most detailed explanation of Manufacturing Analytics available today.

Chapter 8: Procurement and Spend Analytics

This chapter is mainly a functional explanation of what Procurement and Spend Analytics provide, as well as the business benefits, what's available out of the box, and what the intended use is. This chapter also covers an optional component called Spend Classification, which can help you better leverage your investment via better aggregations of spend into major categories using Oracle technologies such as data mining.

Chapter 9: HR Analytics

This chapter is mainly a functional explanation of what HR Analytics provides, as well as the business benefits, what's available out of the box, and what the intended use is. It also spends considerable time discussing the new features added for release 7.9.6, Absence Management, Recruitment, and Learning Enrollment and Completion. If your knowledge of HR Analytics is a few years old, it is worth the time to spend researching the new content.

Chapter 10: Enterprise Asset Management Analytics

This chapter is mainly a functional explanation of what Enterprise Asset Management Analytics provides, as well as the business benefits, what's available out of the box, and what the intended use is. It looks at maintenance from the point of view of the asset owner and maintenance organization. This chapter provides some of the most recent content added to the Oracle BI Applications family, as well as some of the most detailed explanation of Enterprise Asset Management Analytics available today.

Chapter 11: Project Analytics

This chapter is mainly a functional explanation of what Project Analytics provides, as well as the business benefits, what's available out of the box, and what the intended use is. It also covers when to select Oracle BI Project Analytics, Hyperion Project Planning Analytics, or Primavera P6 Analytics.

Chapter 12: Sales Analytics

This chapter is mainly a functional explanation of what Sales Analytics provides, as well as the business benefits, what's available out of the box, and what the intended use is. It also covers some of the vertical market sales analytics that are tied to vertical market versions of Siebel. In addition, it covers the boundaries between Sales Analytics and other products such as Price Analytics, Marketing Analytics, and Order Management and Supply Chain Analytics.

Chapter 13: Service Analytics and Contact Center Telephony Analytics

This chapter is mainly a functional explanation of what Service Analytics and Contact Center Telephony Analytics provides, as well as the business benefits, what's available out of the box, and what the intended use is. It covers how these analytics interact with sales cycles and with asset management functions. It also covers some of the issues in tying them into data coming from you IVR and CTI systems.

Chapter 14: Making It Yours Without Ruining the Foundation

This chapter is a natural extension to Chapter 3—once you understand the delivered architecture, you can transition to understanding and planning how to extend Oracle BI Applications without breaking them or hurting your ability to upgrade in the future.

Chapter 15: Conclusion

In this chapter, we summarize the key points of the book and encourage you in your success. We also touch on what to expect in the future with Oracle BI Applications.

We hope this book provides valuable information that not only helps the success of your implementation, but also helps to advance your career.

CHAPTER
1

Crash Course in Data
Warehouse Survival

Welcome to *Oracle Business Intelligence Applications: Deliver Value Through Rapid Implementations*. This book is meant for anyone, functional or technical, who will either use or implement Oracle Business Intelligence (BI) Applications. It is also meant for those who are considering buying a BI Application, rather than building a data warehouse from scratch. The objective of this book is to provide trusted background information, tips and tricks, and best practices not found anywhere else. This information is based on more than 25 years of experience, from the perspective of those who sell the BI Applications, watch the implementations unfold, and seek references of success.

It's important to understand the underlying motivations behind this book. When an Oracle sales team sells a BI Application to a customer, there's a strong desire not only to see it implemented quickly, but to see it be successful. The measure of success is based on user adoption as well as on the financial benefit and/or process improvement the organization derives from the BI Application. Typically, the greater the number of users as a percentage of the overall organization who regularly use the application, the more successful the application will be, because more people will be making better and faster decisions. The personal goal of the authors is to get you promoted so that you can one day present your successes at Oracle OpenWorld.

This book gives you the basic foundation and understanding you need in order to know where to start, how to select trusted advisors, how to form your team, how to set user expectations, and what pitfalls to avoid.

In most data warehouse projects, you only get one chance to make a good first impression with end users. Once you've lost their confidence, it's nearly impossible to bring them back. Therefore, let us educate you on the business and technical sides of the BI Applications to ensure you only need to implement them once.

Data warehousing isn't for the faint of heart. Thousands of custom data warehouse projects have failed over the years, just as many projects have been highly successful. The investment is significant—in some cases more than an enterprise resource planning (ERP) implementation for small-to-midsize companies. However, the return on investment (ROI) is worth it. In some cases, you'll see instantaneous cost savings the day you go "live" and populate your first dashboard. Many people who have implemented successful data warehouses report internal rates of return of over 100 percent per year. Simply put, Oracle BI Applications reduce the risk, lower the cost, significantly lower the implementation time, and improve the quality of your deliverable compared to a custom data warehouse, as you'll see in this chapter.

Oracle BI Applications offer a prebuilt data warehouse solution that can be fed from multiple sources, providing high-quality and high-performance analytics. These analytics provide a high level of insight into your organization for understanding its underlying performance.

The History of BI Applications

Oracle BI Applications aren't new; there's a lot of history behind them and the overall prebuilt BI Application market. Understanding how we got here will help shed some light on the maturity and value of the applications through years of development and refinement. It's important to understand the many successes and failures that have resulted in your finding this book so that you end up on the right side of history with your company.

This section provides some of the experiences of the authors of this book, Simon Miller and Will Hutchinson.

Simon Miller's Experiences

Around September 2000, a healthcare business in Milwaukee, Wisconsin, decided to hire a contractor to be a temporary data warehouse manager at one of their billion-dollar divisions. The data warehouse manager at the parent healthcare company went through the alphabetical list of BusinessObjects (now acquired by SAP) partners. The first company to answer the phone was the one I worked for. It was a small firm, with only a few employees. I was told to commute to Milwaukee from Toronto on a weekly basis for a few months to do some Informatica and BusinessObjects programming. When I arrived, I was informed that I was actually a manager with four employees reporting to me and a yearly million-dollar budget for contractors—and all I had to do was take an existing implementation over the finish line. I was a junior programmer, analyst, and trainer, and not ready for this type of role.

The existing implementation was for a prepackaged BI Application from Decision Point Analytics, known as DPA. This healthcare company, along with a large telecommunications company, was probably their biggest client and was therefore able to call the shots with respect to product development. Almost a year had been invested in the implementation, with over a million dollars spent in contracting resources, and the expectation was that everything was working just fine. (The data source was EBS—Oracle eBusiness Suite version 9*i*—and the Oracle DB version 8*i*, to show just how far back this goes.)

Over the first month I realized I was in big trouble. The employees resented working for a clueless contractor half their age. Business users wouldn't show up to meetings, and it was clear they were never really involved. I tried to do some testing and quickly found the data was wrong on the reports. Duplicates kept showing up that were not in the source system. When I started asking difficult questions concerning the design of the data model, the data integrity of the custom/proprietary ETL (Extract, Transform, and Load) tool, and so on, I became more and more worried.

My first major task was to tell the CIO that that the project was dead on arrival: a year and a million dollars wasted. I had to duck and cover from the guy who hired me because this was his baby. Somehow I managed to not get fired. I was able to partner with a manager from the IT department, secure a new budget, and hire a new team of contractors. I wasn't able to use the employees who reported to me because they didn't have a BI and data warehouse background. They were scattered across the United States and weren't able to spend much face time with the end users in Milwaukee.

The smartest thing I did was to hire an architect by the name of Paul Scheibel. I doubt I would have been successful without him. He was an experienced DBA and BI Architect. He knew how to get data out of EBS. He was a skilled data warehouse data modeler, and a good analyst. Unfortunately, he later went on to be a competitor of mine at Oracle (more on that later). I hired approximately 12 contractors, all highly skilled, and each week we flew into Milwaukee to work together for the week. Paul mainly led the team; I was the project manager and liaison to the healthcare company. I educated the CIO and IT manager, and eventually transitioned the data warehouse management to the IT manager.

Early on we came up with ways to salvage what we could from DPA, but in reality it was just a paper proposal. We knew the application was badly designed, but that was hard to accept by the healthcare company, which had poured so much money into it. The parent company was using DPA, but had limited success.

At one point the parent company had 80 "onshore" consultants working full time just to deliver 25 custom dashboard reports with limited interaction or drilldown to senior management. We were also visited by Informatica, where I met Will Hutchinson. Informatica had a prepackaged BI Application they were selling, and I was tempted to purchase it. However, we were too far down the path of building a new custom data warehouse with the new team of contractors. Keep in mind that I was leading the fourth or fifth attempt to build something. First the healthcare company tried to create reports directly off EBS. Then they tried replicating EBS to create reports. Next they tried Noetix views, and then they tried a precursor to BusinessObjects Rapid Marts (Universes connected directly to EBS). Finally, they tried DPA. Not many people were tracking how much money had been spent and lost by these failed implementations.

Although the Informatica prebuilt BI Application was tempting, it was a version 1 product that needed a bit of work. It was a good start, but we made fun of the data model; it looked like Darth Vader's personal fighter from *Star Wars* when you looked at it from a distance. In fact, the model was so complex because it was one data model that encompassed many business processes of an organization, including procurement, order to cash, financials, HR, and several varieties of customer relationship management (CRM).

The other challenge was that Informatica was using their own BI tool (Power Analyzer) at the time. Although it was revolutionary and had functionality still not met by any BI tool today, it was doomed to failure because there was little architecture below the user interface (UI).

Later on, Informatica struggled to get their technical sales people to sell to their customers' business people, thereby speaking different languages, and were competing with IT staff who wanted to prebuild their own custom solutions with existing technology. The few customers who did purchase the tool, however, ended up using it for many years.

Informatica shut down that line of business in 2003, at which point Will Hutchinson went to Siebel, started working on their CRM BI Applications, and helped Siebel launch a line of ERP BI Applications in 2004.

The problem with pre-built BI Applications at the turn of the century was that ERP applications weren't as mature, and customers ended up customizing the physical tables. Customizations at the source meant customizations downstream in the data warehouse. In cases such as PeopleSoft, customers were actually encouraged to do lots of customizations. In other cases, functionality was either missing or companies weren't yet ready to abandon custom business processes dictated by legacy mainframe applications in favor of best practices offered by an ERP. This meant the buy-versus-build proposition was tricky for prebuilt BI Applications; it came down to a company's ability to custom build their own data warehouse. Most IT organizations thought they could do it themselves, when in reality 75 percent of data warehouse projects seemed to fail in one way or another.

Also, the makers of ERP and CRM systems had, with one exception, not realized that the online transaction processing (OLTP) systems would not provide the kind of analytic reporting their customers needed. They felt users would be content with static reporting delivered from the OLTP. Data warehousing was seen as a sideline.

Siebel was the one exception. They realized early on that unless sales and marketing people were provided analytic reporting to help them manage their territories, sales cycles, and marketing campaigns, they would not enter quality data into the CRM system. Siebel, therefore, built analytic applications tied to Siebel CRM.

Over a period of nine months, my team really delivered, both in quantity and quality. We delivered 12 data marts, which 10 years later were still in use and in production. The adoption rate increased over time—the key indicator of success.

Once my contract was over in 2001 (I terminated it early because my wife was expecting our first child), I went to work closer to home for a small Canadian company based out of Montreal, Quebec. I was hired to lead the implementation of a prebuilt BI Application for the insurance industry. I was trained on a horizontal prebuilt BI Application for JD Edwards, which used Informatica and MicroStrategy. I was sent into a coal mining company to implement it, and was caught in the middle when the customer thought they had bought a vertical application. They blindly made their purchase without a proper fit/gap analysis. Needless to say, it probably never left the shelf. I was also trained on the prebuilt BI Applications from Informatica, which by then had invested (I was told verbally) between 100 and 150 million dollars of R&D into their design.

While working at a property and casualty (P&C) insurance company, I led a team that implemented the prebuilt Insurance BI Application. It was a really rough time for many reasons. The product was being built "just in time" for delivery, and at one point the customer realized this. The product was well designed by a team with deep insurance knowledge. However, this was our first P&C customer, and we were loading real data for the first time. Much of the delivery was similar to implementing a custom data warehouse.

I badly estimated the work effort, and many deadlines were missed. There were many change requests, and it was hard to separate a client-requested change in scope from a reasonable request to fix a defect in the product design.

This BI Application went into production and was approximately 1TB. At the time this was a big data warehouse. It took months to convert the historical data and ensure the accuracy. The maintenance and enhancements were managed by the company I worked for, and the insurance company felt they had overpaid for everything (they hadn't).

I still believe to this day the insurance company could have spent a small fortune and many years of failed implementations if they had tried to get off their legacy mainframe data warehouse on their own. Over time, the insurance company tried to replace it, but quite frankly, a better solution wasn't readily available at that time at a lower cost.

Since then, other products have evolved, such as Skywire, purchased by Oracle. I took my lumps on that project and still carry the battle scars today. The insurance company benefitted, but not the short-term careers of the project teams—at either my company or the insurance company.

I had a number of other interesting experiences with prebuilt BI Applications in the early pioneering days. For example, at one point I partnered back up with Will Hutchinson and Informatica to compete against Siebel Analytics at a pharmaceutical company in Toronto. It was an apples-to-oranges competition because the main data source was a Siebel CRM vertical.

Informatica's offering was for ERP sources horizontally (useful across the industry for order management, inventory, procurement, and so on), whereas Siebel Analytics was for CRM sources both horizontally and vertically. The pharmaceutical company chose Siebel Analytics. Ironically, Will and I ended up working together later at Siebel, then at Oracle. Through a series of wise acquisitions and wise investments, both products ended up being consolidated and merged under what are now Oracle BI Applications.

Another example shows what often happens when a customer buys only a data model rather than a full end-to-end prebuilt BI Application. At another P&C insurance company I was hired to be a project manager to implement IBM's insurance industry model. It quickly became clear to me that this was at least a five-year implementation. Once again I found myself telling senior executives that many more years and millions of dollars were required to build what they thought they had bought. The IBM prebuilt data model was logical and looked nothing like the physical model. The data model assumed you'd have to spin off data marts, which would be custom built. There was no pre-built ETL. There was nothing wrong with the IBM model, other than the fact that expectations had not been set properly with the business.

I had to form a breakout team to deliver a stovepipe custom claims data mart in nine months, just to keep the business happy. Everyone thought it would be a temporary stop gap, but I knew better. The primary data modeler on my team was a Canadian P&C insurance industry expert by the name of Hassan Yousry, who went on to compete with me later on at another insurance company (he won, sort of).

I was morbidly satisfied when three years later that same insurance company came to me for help because they couldn't build the ETL to populate Hassan's data model. At that point, all I could say was, "I told you so." Again, nothing was wrong with the data model. The mistake the company made was to think a data model was enough.

One day in 2005 I received a phone call from Informatica that led to a job offer. Will Hutchinson convinced me to work for Siebel instead, to follow the BI Applications. When I was asked in my final interview at Siebel why I wanted to work there, the answer was simple: I was tired of reinventing the same wheel.

At Oracle, I had similar competitions with Teradata's logical data model, having to explain the importance of a fully baked solution over a logical reference model you can only print and look at.

Remember Paul Scheibel from my first crack at a BI Application at the healthcare company? When he was finished, he took the team and data marts we built (with permission) and started selling Jaros Analytics, which was later bought by Noetix.

Before the Siebel acquisition, Oracle had PeopleSoft EPM. The horizontal part of EPM was eventually archived because it didn't make sense to have two completely overlapping products after the acquisition. Some of the verticals (such as Campus Solutions) are still being maintained with support and small incremental enhancements. It could also be argued that PeopleSoft EPM was overly engineered, hard to implement, and difficult to maintain.

I've also competed with BusinessObjects Rapid Marts and Analytical Applications (now owned by SAP) as well as Cognos Analytical Applications (both new and old architectural approaches).

I've never seen or heard of a successful long-term implementation of those competing products.

At Oracle, I partnered with a company that builds applications for the hotel industry. They were an early adopter of Oracle Business Intelligence Enterprise Edition (OBIEE) and an Oracle OLAP combined solution. I helped them design OperaBI, a corresponding prebuilt BI Application. Oracle OLAP was an important part of the solution, given the online analytical processing nature of the analysis (metrics by dimensions without many textual attributes) and the overwhelming number of transactions that needed to be processed and summarized.

Imagine a single 300-room hotel, 365 days per year, and every transaction on a hotel bill plus every reservation. Now spread that out over many years across a chain of hotels, large and small. We're talking about billions of rows of data with an expectation of a subsecond response.

One of the biggest eye-openers for me was when Oracle lost a sales cycle to a competitor who offered a stovepipe HR Analytics application to a pharmaceutical company. This company did a rapid superficial evaluation, believing at face value what the competitor BI sales rep proposed to them. (Note that part of my job is to ensure my sales reps convey accurate messaging that I can back up at a very detailed level.) The sales pitch went as follows:

> Oracle is still using the old and now-obsolete method of data warehousing, where you need prewritten ETL. Our way is to provide you a wizard that automatically generates the ETL you need based on what you put into the wizard, and based on the wizard's discovery of your source system.

This sounded great in theory. However, the customer failed to get an implementation estimate before the software purchase. Only the vendor could provide implementation support. There were very few customers (if any) who had done this before, and they only found out the true implementation cost after they made the software purchase. The implementation price tag came in at over $1 million, and this was not a fixed bid—just for a single stovepipe HR data mart that was supposed to be prebuilt.

Siebel produced prebuilt BI Applications for CRM and acquired intellectual property, including a data model and ETL adapters to EBS and PeopleSoft. Initially these products were completely separate, although Siebel replaced the existing BI tool with Siebel Analytics, which later became OBIEE. Oracle acquired Siebel and dedicated extensive time and resources to merge the products together with a common data model, ETL, and OBIEE semantic layer.

At this time of writing, customers can expect a number of exciting developments, both short and long term. Fusion Applications have OBIEE deeply embedded, and the prebuilt BI Applications continue to serve up content. Fusion customers have access to both real time and historical data from the same user interface. Engineered systems are now available, and when you combine various options, such as Exadata, Exalytics, Oracle Database, Oracle OLAP, Essbase, TimesTen, and so on, you're no longer restricted in performance capabilities.

To sum things up, here are the morals of my story:

- Oracle's prebuilt BI Applications have been around for a very long time and have evolved to a much higher level of technical maturity than any other in the market.

- Companies that try to build a custom data warehouse typically fail 75 percent of the time, unless they have the time, patience, skill set, and deep pockets to do it right.

- Not all pre-built BI Applications are the same. Some are good, but most are badly designed. Well-designed BI Applications can be defined by strictly adhering to data warehouse best-practice methodologies (discussed later on).

- A solution isn't prebuilt unless it comes with prebuilt ETL, a *physical* data model you can actually implement using conformed (shared) dimensions (no disconnected stovepipes), a BI tool semantic layer, and at least a starter set of interactive dashboards.

- It's really hard to find good data warehousing data modelers. This is usually the Achilles heel of most projects if you're trying to build your own.

- Many BI/DW implementations are IT driven, and without business user involvement they seem to fail—or at least fail to grow over time.

- Only one prebuilt BI Application on the market has evolved and matured over the years and continues to have investment far into the future with Oracle and SAP data sources, and that's Oracle's BI Applications.

- Oracle's technology footprint has grown via engineered systems to handle the ever-increasing amounts of data that companies are generating and need to be analyzed.

Will Hutchinson's Experiences

I started in what was then known as Decision Support in 1986 with a startup called Metaphor. There I had the pleasure of working with many of the people who would shape this industry, including Larry Barbetta, Jorgen and Katherine Edholm, Liz Geiger, Bob Haas, Ralph Kimball, John

Morley, Ramesh Nair, Laura Reeves, Margy Ross, Bill Schmarzo, Warren Thornthwaite, and many others. In addition to some amazing hardware, we also worked with clients to design what would be called "data marts" to solve single function problems for them, initially mostly in the areas of sales and marketing. After a while, we noticed commonalities among schemas; for example, that a shipments schema for one company looked remarkably like a shipments schema for another company. Laura Reeves used to keep screenshots of generic schemas in her appointment book. We helped many organizations with their query and reporting problems, making or saving our clients many tens of millions of dollars.

I participated in a study in 1988 and 1989 where Metaphor commissioned a market research firm to tell us how our customers were deriving value from their decision support systems. This was my first exposure to the ROI of data warehousing. In it, we found that the vast majority of benefit came not, as everyone had assumed, from saving money. Instead, 94 percent of the benefit came from increasing revenue. The balance came from business cost savings. Virtually none came from IT cost savings. In hindsight, part of this lopsided split between revenue generation and cost saving was due to so many of our installations (and therefore, the people we surveyed) being in sales or marketing departments. However, I still find that much of the benefit of better BI comes not from operational efficiency but from increasing the strategic options available to organizations or their ability to respond to the unexpected.

After a stint in consulting, I took a job at Sequent, where I became acquainted with the work done at DPA, and ended up at Informatica. Sandy Tice, also formerly of Metaphor, lured me there with the promise of something radically new: BI Applications. These had the four components we still associate with BI Applications

- An enterprise-conformed bus architecture schema spanning many subject areas that supports many leading merchant databases.

- Prebuilt ETL connectors. (Informatica had connectors to Oracle, PeopleSoft, and Siebel, with connectors to SAP and JD Edwards in the wings.)

- Prebuilt metadata in an ETL tool to insulate users from the underlying physical schema.

- Prebuilt reports and dashboards.

These BI Applications comprised the biggest data model I had ever seen, all conformed and built around a Kimball-style bus architecture. Sandy had known Ralph Kimball at Metaphor and understood the power of dimensional modeling and the ability of a bus architecture to provide predictable response times to many different types of queries on a variety of database platforms. Ralph is widely recognized as one of the grandfathers of data warehousing and is one of the key sources of inspiration and education for both Will and Simon. For more information, you can refer to one of Ralph's many books, such as *The Data Warehouse Lifecycle Toolkit*.

At Informatica, we tried to sell these BI Applications. However, the market was not ready for them, and Informatica understood how to sell tools, not applications. Informatica exited this business in 2003. This experience taught me several lessons that may not make sense to the novice reader but will be explained in detail later on:

- One could build an enterprise-class data model that comprised many different subject areas.

- One could build ETL connectors to commercial OLTP systems that did drastically cut customers' time to implement that actually worked.

- The separation of the source-dependent extract from the source-independent load was a useful abstraction that maximized reuse and maintainability.

- One could keep up with OLTP systems vendors' changes to these data models.

- Existing BI tools could not handle the complexity of enterprise-class data models. A new class of tools was needed. Informatica realized this and built PowerAnalyzer. Although it could handle large data models and keep users from constructing queries that did not make sense, its web-based front end was rather clunky.

- The reduction in total cost of ownership (TCO) between building a data warehouse and buying and extending one was astounding. Also, I discovered that because almost all the costs in the TCO model were IT costs, they did not depend on the customer's industry or whether I was selling Financial Analytics, CRM Analytics, HR Analytics, or any of the other BI Applications Informatica was selling. Therefore, I built a reusable model for this.

While with Informatica, Sandy and I called on Simon in Milwaukee. One of our Canadian reps and I also worked with Simon and the consulting firm he worked with in Toronto, as he has described earlier. Also, shortly after I joined Informatica, I ran into Larry Barbetta and other Metaphor people I knew (such as Duane Cologne and Doug Pippert) at a trade show. Larry had founded a company called nQuire to develop a better BI tool. Larry tried to hire me, but I was not interested.

While I was at Informatica, Siebel had bought nQuire and replaced its existing BI tool, BusinessObjects, with nQuire. Siebel renamed nQuire "Siebel Analytics." Siebel had had a line of analytic applications for Sales Force Automation Analytics, Marketing Analytics, and Call Center Analytics. They realized that it is much more difficult to get people to enter high-quality and timely data into a CRM system than it is into an ERP system. Sales people and marketers need to get something back that used that data and delivered value. Siebel believed that "something" was dashboards, so they built analytic applications for their CRM OLTP systems.

Siebel bought nQuire because they had run into the same limits on data model size that Informatica had with BusinessObjects. After acquiring nQuire, Siebel then released versions of its CRM Applications with an nQuire front end about 60 days after the acquisition closed.

After Informatica closed down the BI Applications business, I e-mailed Larry Barbetta and asked him whether he remembered our conversation from over two years ago and whether he was hiring. He replied that he did remember the conversation and was hiring.

After I joined Siebel, Larry asked me whether, given my background at Informatica, I would help him launch a line of ERP Analytic Applications. He wanted to extend Siebel's reach beyond just CRM. I became the product manager of Supply Chain Analytics, as we called it then. Siebel acquired much of the non-CRM intellectual property from Informatica for its BI Applications. Larry was willing to hire aggressively to realize this goal. I recruited several of my old Informatica and Metaphor colleagues to join me at Siebel. Many of these people persuaded others to join Siebel. I also persuaded Simon to join Siebel. Siebel shipped the first version of the ERP BI Applications four months after acquiring the Informatica IP.

In 2006, when Oracle's acquisition of Siebel was complete, Siebel was shipping more analytics than it was any of its CRM products. At the last Siebel users' conference, Charles Phillips, the president of Oracle at the time, described Siebel Analytics as "the hidden gem of the acquisition." Shortly after the acquisition, I ran a lunchtime seminar for many of the technical people in the Chicago office and showed them the ERP Analytic Applications and Siebel Analytics, which had been renamed OBIEE. After the demo, one of the ERP sales consultants said to me, "You have better connectivity to E-Business Suite than we do. I want to sell that."

Oracle BI Applications have grown immensely since that time. As Simon said, we unified the CRM and ERP data models. We finally got connectors to JD Edwards and SAP. We have kept up with release schedules for PeopleSoft, E-Business Suite, and Siebel. We have added content to many of the applications (HR Analytics, in particular). We have added many new analytics over the years, including Financial Management Analytics, Manufacturing Analytics, and Enterprise Asset Management Analytics.

Requirements for a BI Application
At this point, hopefully you're convinced that based on the thousands of implementations and history of this product, there's something substantial to evaluate and seriously consider for your business and technical needs. What we still need to convince you of is why you might need a data warehouse and why a prebuilt data warehouse in the form of Oracle BI Applications could make sense to meet your requirements.

Types of BI Applications (Kimball vs. Inmon)
BI Applications, whether prebuilt or custom built, should in theory look exactly the same. The requirements and design of BI Applications are affected by the following:

- The data model design approach
- Horizontal (for example, Financials) or vertical (industry specific)
- The type of data sources (ERP, CRM, industry-specific OLTP)

What it all boils down to, however, is the data model design. There are two well-established and documented best-approach practices: one pioneered by Ralph Kimball and the other by Bill Inmon. When evaluating a prebuilt solution or a custom build, this topic of Kimball versus Inmon often comes up. These are two very different approaches, namely in two areas:

- **Data model design**   The Inmon design includes a normalized data model (smaller data sets across many tables with little redundancy) for the core data warehouse plus separate physical spun-off summarized data marts. Kimball requires a denormalized data model (think of Excel download of data) with conformed (shared, common) dimensions (what you see metrics "by") at the lowest possible granularity.

- **Layers of data**   Inmon requires multiple transformations of data, from source to temporary staging to data warehouse to data marts, whereas Kimball requires fewer transformations, from source to temporary staging to data warehouse

Both have different ideas for what a data warehouse should look like. In the case of horizontal BI Applications (Order Management, Procurement, Financials, Sales, and so on), you can use either. In the case of some verticals (Insurance, Financial Services, and so on), it can be hard to apply a Kimball data model, especially when items such as "products" have so many unique types and sets of attributes. Figures 1-1 and 1-2 illustrate the two different designs you'll commonly find. Figure 1-1 is an example of the data marts being

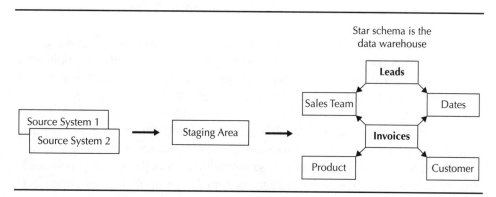

FIGURE 1-1.   *An enterprise star schema model*

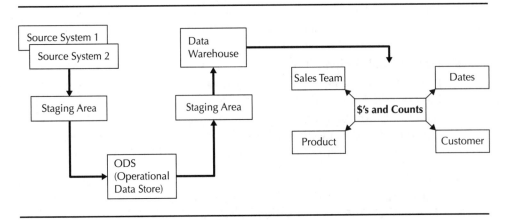

FIGURE 1-2. *An enterprise data warehouse with data marts spun off*

the actual data warehouse, all as one layer. Figure 1-2 has two layers, with subsets of the data exposed to the end users and Business Intelligence Tool.

What's the difference for horizontal applications? It could be argued that the Inmon approach is simply overkill for otherwise simple structures. Extra layers of data and extra data hops means longer processing times, additional maintenance and overhead, and an application that's harder to learn. Oracle's prebuilt BI Applications take the Kimball approach, which provides faster implementation times for relatively simple horizontal BI Applications (bread-and-butter analytics).

There's room for both. The Inmon approach is occasionally necessary, especially when you're building an industry-specific vertical with a complicated data model and various products with completely different descriptive attributes (for example, a car and a loan). However, be aware this can take years to implement.

A question I often ask is, "Would you rather spend your time implementing something that's specific to your industry that differentiates your company, or would you rather spend your time custom building something that you should already have in place today for industry best-practices analytical functionality?" In other words, get the prebuilt BI Applications in place quickly to level set your organization to your peers before you look at your vertical BI needs. A subject area such as Financial Analytics, for example, is the same as comparing your Payroll Application. You can't run the business without it, but it's not going to differentiate you in the marketplace. You're already behind, so it's time to catch up to your peers. Just because you're a bank, for example, doesn't mean you'll do things any differently in the area of HR. Spend your time on what will differentiate you in the marketplace.

Although two approaches have been discussed so far, there's actually a third, which is a hybrid approach. Bill Inmon believed you needed to take the time to design a full enterprise data model before implementing anything to ensure that as you rolled out more and more stuff, the parts would fit together. Ralph Kimball believed you needed to build a subject area and deliver value. Inmon was right about what would happen if someone following Kimball's methodology did a less than rigorous design. However, if one followed Inmon's dictum, design would take several years, by which time everyone on the project might be fired. Of course there are always exceptions; however this is based on our personal experiences. We like to characterize the difference as follows:

- Kimball's approach is feasible, but suboptimal.

- Inmon's approach is optimal, but infeasible.

Part of the beauty of Oracle's approach is that you get the broad data model Inmon advocated with the relatively quick time to market Kimball realized is needed to get and keep business sponsorship.

Top-Down vs. Bottom-Up Approach

Two different approaches are commonly taken to manage an overall data warehouse project: top down and bottom up. It's important to be able to compare and contrast these approaches. When custom building an app, you'll inevitably choose one approach and have to live with the consequences of your choice for many years. By comparing the two approaches, you can make the most informed decision.

A top-down approach involves gathering Phase 1 requirements (for example, 25 reports or metrics), building and implementing them, and then moving on to the next round of requirements. Only the data needed for those requirements would be sourced and delivered to end users. Phase 2 would then be kicked off, and so on. A bottom-up approach involves acquiring all possible data from a data source (or more) and populating a data warehouse at a detailed level. Then reports are built for end users, which would utilize a subset of the loaded data.

On one hand, the top-down approach is more agile and can deliver more quickly (at least at first); on the other hand, every time there's a need to drill into more details, you're at risk of having to build again from scratch. Similarly, the bottoms-up approach, on one hand, means you don't need to redesign and long term you have a more agile solution; on the other hand, you have to ask end users to fund a large project for a long time with no deliverables—and their needs can't change while they're waiting.

Which is better? A cynic would say "neither on its own." The good news is the BI Applications provide the benefit of both approaches without the drawbacks. You can take the bottoms-up approach with a fast implementation, and you have the flexibility of focusing on specific report deliverables without having to be concerned about the underlying architecture.

Occasionally, there's pushback from a data warehouse team, with concerns that an Inmon approach provides more flexibility to changes down the road. We've had those conversations countless times and have come to the following conclusions:

- We've yet to hear of or see a practical example of a data source change that would break the Kimball approach once in production; this is more of a fear of a theoretical unknown.

- The Inmon approach can take (from experience) anywhere from three to five times longer to implement. The Kimball approach seems to have a faster ROI. Even if a change to a dimension were to be required down the road, the ROI would have long been passed and therefore there shouldn't be a financial disadvantage here. An example might be the IBM Information Warehouse methodology put forth in the late 1980s. To execute that methodology, one had to build an enterprise data model and then build out the data warehouse from there. IBM and its clients soon realized that this approach would take three to five years to deliver anything useful. By that time, the people working at the client company would have lost interest and funding.

- The Inmon approach requires data profiling. The Kimball approach does not. Data profiling has a deep impact on implementation times and work efforts. Data profiling involves looking at counts of various types of codes and records to help determine how to best normalize a data structure to avoid redundant data. It's also used to determine just how much Master Data Management (MDM) work might be required to be implemented first, before starting your data warehouse project.

- In just about every case we've come across, you need to spin off a data mart from an Inmon data warehouse that looks like what you needed in the first place with a Kimball data warehouse. Therefore, any changes required down the road would be needed either way.

- The party model with the Inmon approach allows you to model all entities and their relationships irrespective of transactions, which is good; however, it uses recursive joins, which is bad for BI tools. The Kimball approach only provides reporting for relationships where there's a transaction to begin with, which is okay for most (if not all) analytical reporting requirements, but a challenge for MDM projects where the data warehouse becomes the source of record rather than the underlying transactional applications.

NOTE
A party model *is a generic set of tables that stores customers, suppliers, partners, and so on in the same set of physical tables.*

Operational Reporting vs. Analytical Applications

BI Applications are not meant to provide operational reporting. Ralph Kimball often talked about the concept of "real time enough," by which he meant "latency low enough that lower latency does not result in substantially better decisions." They're meant to support analytical needs. It's not always black and white which bucket some requirements fall into. If the data needs to come directly from the data source in real time, for example, that's operational. Caution should be taken if users are looking for mostly non-aggregatable data attributes (fax number, source keys, and so on) so they can download the reports into Excel. It's a red flag that they don't intend to summarize information to identify trends and patterns in a visual manner. Before adding new attributes to Oracle BI Applications, it's important to be clear on the analytical need for that information. Sometimes it helps to break this down into chunks:

- Does the reporting have to be real time or from a data warehouse?

- If it has to be real time, can it be near real time with trickle feed ETL?

- Do you understand the implications of one approach over the other? For example, you can't use views to store historical inventory balances; you need to put the data into a reporting database to keep track of each snapshot.

- Do you need to combine data from multiple sources?

- Have you loaded the data into Endeca for a short period of time to validate and prove the value of adding to your data warehouse?

The following table compares and contrasts the different types of reporting requirements, based on a number of comparison criteria:

	Transactional	**Operational**	**Analytical**
Storage type	ERP/CRM Direct.	ODS, Cube.	Data Warehouse, Cube.
History	None.	Limited number of snapshots.	As much as required.
Volatility	High.	Medium.	Low.
Purpose	Review list of specific transactions and current statuses.	Tactical, one-time views of data.	Start with summary views and then drill to details.
Records processed	Few (for example, a pick list) that are returned in a row/ column report.	Depends. Also typically row/ column reports.	Can be millions (or more). Ideally summarized at the database level for performance.
Unique features	Real-time data.	Can be whatever you want it to be.	Ad-hoc, slice and dice, drill, constant DB or Cube interrogation.

Oracle provides the following options for operational reporting (note that this is not an exhaustive list):

■ **OTBI**   Oracle Transactional BI with Fusion Applications (using OBIEE)

■ **BI Publisher Reports**   Report directly against EBS

■ **BAM**   Business Activity Monitoring directly against EBS, which provides a "twinkling" effect, where you watch the data change on your screen in real time

■ **Golden Gate**   Replicate data with some minor transformations for operational reporting

You'll find many other options in Chapter 5, which covers financial analytics. A handful of software companies actively promote the approach of reporting directly off the source systems using a combination of real-time and materialized database views, even though countless customers have failed at this approach. We use the diagram shown in Figure 1-3 to explain

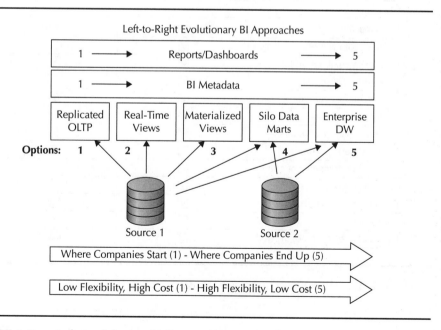

FIGURE 1-3. *Left-to-right evolutionary BI approaches*

to customers what happens when they look for shortcuts, and why many companies have to go through multiple reimplementation cycles of their data warehouse.

Although it may seem to be more cost effective at first to try to use these views for data exploration, alerting, and analysis, in the end the costs are much higher when you consider the implementation time and lost opportunities to otherwise benefit from the data. If we're convinced a data warehouse is the right solution for a customer's needs, yet they think they can start with views, we usually tell them they're only going to have to invite us back in a couple of years and we'll have to start all over again. To be clear, Oracle BI Applications start with Approach 5 in the diagram.

What you can't do with an operational reporting approach, with or without views, is outlined in Figure 1-4. Approach 5 is a data warehouse approach, whereas a combination of Approaches 1 through 3 is a database views approach. Approach 4, by the way, is simply a poor man's version of approach 5: you can't span multiple subject areas and dimensions aren't conformed.

End users need to:	Approach 5	Approaches 1–3
Rapidly prototype requirements	☑	⃠
Change calculations ad-hoc	☑	⃠
View historical snapshots	☑	⃠
View trending over time	☑	⃠
Query multiple data sources	☑	⃠
Compare to corp. objectives	☑	⃠
View restated data on the fly	☑	⃠
Have fast performance of queries	☑	⃠
Perform ad-hoc analysis	☑	⃠
Build their own dashboards	☑	⃠
Query multiple subject areas	☑	⃠
Have a single version of the truth	☑	⃠

FIGURE 1-4. *When you need a data warehouse*

Here are some other examples of types of analyses requiring a data warehouse approach:

- Inventory daily balances for three months and then store monthly balances in a full star schema data model, allowing slicing and dicing by any relevant dimension

- Cycle Time Management using order-to-ship or procure-to-pay type of queries

- Net Bookings by netting out the current bookings and backlog based on order line changes on a daily basis

- Provide an entry point to deliver cross-functional content, including Procurement, Financials, Manufacturing, Supply Chain, and so on, using conformed (common and shared) dimensions such as Product, Supplier, and Time.

Conclusion

Far too many companies stumble when they try to do data-warehouse-type reporting directly off their source systems. In fact, the systems integrators we speak to say that when they are brought into clients who are complaining of performance problems in their source systems, they start by looking at what reporting they do directly from the source system. Inevitably, when they identify reporting that can be done from a data warehouse and move that reporting off the source system, performance improves. Maintenance costs on the transactional side typically fall because the BI tools run against separate data stores are typically easier to use than reporting tools provided with source systems.

So if you think you might need a data warehouse, and you are looking for a prebuilt solution, this book should help you decide if Oracle BI Applications are right for your organization.

CHAPTER
2

Don't Reinvent
Any Wheels

B ecause data warehouses (DWs), Business Intelligence (BI), analytical applications, and so on mean different things to different people, it's important to set the frame of reference used in this book. Bill Inmon's widely accepted definition of a data warehouse is as follows:

A data warehouse is a subject-oriented, integrated, time-variant, and non-volatile collection of data in support of management's decision-making process.

Data Warehouse Primer

For a quick recap, here are some key points (in layman's terms) about how a data warehouse is defined:

- It's used for storage of both current and historical perspectives.

- Data is taken out of transactional applications and databases.

- It's designed by BI/DW experts using industry-accepted approaches.

- Data is put into an environment designed for reporting, ad-hoc analysis, and performance measurement.

- It's designed for easy integration of multiple sources.

- The creation of "a single source of the truth," although cliché, simply means having a single place to provide data rather than having different data stores that don't match or reconcile.

- Data is transformed and stored along the way to calculate metrics.

- It's used for storage of snapshots (for example, Daily Inventory Balances and AR/AP Balances).

- It's designed to get data out (display data) rather than in (enter data).

- It involves proper data-modeling techniques, with limited table joins.

- It has multiple data sources feeding multiple subject areas using conformed dimensions.

■ It's optimized with aggregate tables based on end-user needs.

■ It always has some sort of ETL (Extract, Transform, Load) or ELT (Extract, Load, Transform) mechanism (the difference being where and how the data is transformed).

Although data warehousing and Business Intelligence might seem like the same thing, the key difference is in the focus areas. Data warehousing in the context of this book is related to getting data into a data store, whereas Business Intelligence is related to getting the data out and using it for analytical purposes. Business Intelligence is a broad topic and needs some context to help explain it. However, for a quick recap, here's how Business Intelligence is defined (in no particular order):

■ It's a single place to retrieve information, for actionable insight.

■ It's tied to corporate objectives, from the contributor level to chief executive.

■ It provides better and more timely decision-making capability.

■ It's a self-service environment with full ad-hoc capabilities.

■ It provides exception-based reporting (more than just static reports).

■ It has the ability to handle any security model.

■ It's drillable back to line items in transactional applications.

■ It's another tab in your transactional application. In other words, your users who spend the bulk of their time in a transaction-processing system should be able to satisfy their analytical needs without having to log in to a separate BI system.

■ It provides automation and input into business processes.

■ It's an environment where everyone can benefit from access to information.

■ It's an assembly line of information delivery to end users.

■ Its highly interactive dashboards are dynamically driven, based on end-user roles, responsibilities, and profiles.

■ It provides balanced contributions of both business and IT when defining requirements and delivering.

■ It offers predictive analytical techniques.

Just as BI and DW are similar but different concepts, we also need to differentiate analytical applications. BI is a general term that can mean a free for all, where users are employing information in a disconnected manner. Analytical applications apply some discipline in how, where, and when the information is used in a repeatable manner and who can use it. For a quick recap, here's how we're defining an analytical application:

■ It uses highly interactive, role-based dashboards, starting with a summary view of data and allowing for drill down into details.

■ It provides the ability to identify root-cause analyses with a small number of mouse clicks.

■ Its dashboards are designed by end users, in a tool intuitive enough to be used with little training.

■ It follows a defined business process, guiding a large number of users to perform root-cause analysis in the same way.

■ It is focused on exception-based reporting, with clear actions identified for end users to take to correct the business issue.

As one would expect from something designed according to the Ralph Kimball bus architecture (for those familiar with his methodologies and designs), Oracle BI Applications from a physical implementation perspective are made up of two primary types of tables used in queries for end users:

■ **Dimension tables**   These tables are used to store textual attributes about specific entities as well as for grouping at a report or dashboard level; they also contain information required for tracing back to the source system for testing/validation purposes.

■ **Fact tables**   These tables are used to store numerical values used to aggregate (sum, count, average, and so on) and trend over time; you can think of looking at a fact "by" something else (dimensions).

Figure 2-1 shows an example of an Oracle BI Application dimension table, and Figure 2-2 shows an example of an Oracle BI Application fact table.

Slowly changing dimensions are used to track the history of data over time. This is often required in any data warehouse and is therefore important to understand. An example could be separating the history of

Portion of W_CUSTOMER_ACCOUNT_D	
ROW_WID	Primary key of the table
CREATED_BY_WID	Various fields to keep track of when data has been modified and source of the change
CHANGED_BY_WID	
CREATED_ON_DT	
CHANGED_ON_DT	
EFFECTIVE_FROM_DT	Used to support slowly changing dimensions
EFFECTIVE_TO_DT	
CURRENT_FLG	
DELETE_FLG	(Optional) Used to soft delete records via filters
DATASOURCE_NUM_ID	Unique ID for particular source system, and concatenation of natural keys at source; forming unique natural key for table for ETL lookups
INTEGRATION_ID	
ETL_PROC_WID	Used to track specific ETL run
TENANT_ID	Supports a multitenant model
X_CUSTOM	Placeholder to show ETL mapping for extension fields
FLEX_ATTRIB_1_CHAR	Series of placeholder fields for custom extensions
NAME	Long list of attributes used for reporting and display purposes, where you can see corresponding metrics "by" and can aggregate "by" these attributes
ACCOUNT_TYPE_CODE	
ACCOUNT_TYPE_NAME	
ACCOUNT_NUM	
COMPANY_CODE	
COMPANY_NAME	

FIGURE 2-1. *Key fields on a sample Oracle BI Applications dimension table*

Portion of W_SALES_BACKLOG_LINE_F	
ACCOUNT_REP_WID	Numerous foreign key relationships to dimensions involved in the star schema.
BUSN_AREA_ORG_WID	
CHNL_TYPE_WID	
COMPANY_ORG_WID	Establishes the "grain" or level of detail for the table. Determines what you can see your metrics "by."
COST_CENTER_WID	
PROFIT_CENTER_WID	
CUSTOMER_BILL_TO_LOC_WID	
CUSTOMER_SHIP_TO_LOC_WID	
CUSTOMER_SOLD_TO_LOC_WID	
CUSTOMER_WID	
PRODUCT_WID	
ORDER_STATUS_WID	
PLANT_LOC_WID	
SUPPLIER_WID	
SCH_BACKLOG_FLG	Various flags for deriving calculations and applying filters at the semantic layer.
UNSCH_BACKLOG_FLG	
FIN_BACKLOG_FLG	
NET_AMT	Various raw metrics available, amounts, quantities, counts, etc.
OPEN_QTY	
SALES_UOM_CODE	Unit of measure information.
DOC_CURR_CODE	Supporting fields for multi-currency conversions. Allows for row-by-row toggling from document to local to global currencies, as transactions all stored in document amounts.
LOC_CURR_CODE	
LOC_EXCHANGE_RATE	
GLOBAL1_EXCHANGE_RATE	

FIGURE 2-2. *Key fields on a sample Oracle BI Applications fact table*

a sales-rep-to-customer mapping from the current territory-to-customer mapping. You can track an effective start date and end date, along with a flag to show the current view. In this example, a practical application is to toggle between a territory view and a sales rep's personal sales attainment view.

One would be used to understand customer purchases over time based on either a historical or current territory view; the other shows the performance of the sales rep. When territory and sales rep changes occur, this often drives these types of analytical needs. Under the Kimball methodology, there are three basic types of slowly changing dimensions:

- **Type 1**   Only current "state" is maintained.

- **Type 2**   The full history is tracked, based on a set of attributes that need to be compared (for example, marital status, location, and territory).

- **Type 3**   The current and previous records are maintained (for example, previous surname).

Figure 2-3 shows an example of how they work. Note that this is a simplistic representation; in reality, there are also effective to/from dates available and a current record flag. For a more detailed description, and for other types, you can look up "slowly changing dimensions" in Wikipedia.

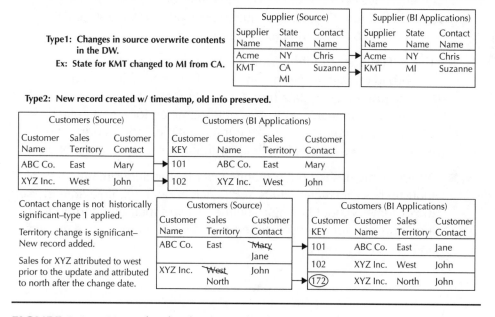

FIGURE 2-3.   *How slowly changing dimensions work*

What Is a BI Application?

BI Applications are the result of combining the data warehouse, Business Intelligence, and analytical applications terms that we just defined into a single solution. BI Applications don't need to be prebuilt to meet any sort of definition. In theory, custom built and prebuilt should result in similar designs—if they follow well-defined best practices. This is similar to the opening line from Tolstoy's novel *Anna Karenina*: "All happy families are alike. Each unhappy family is unhappy in its own way" (assuming, of course, you can hire dozens of the most highly skilled resources available for an indefinite amount of time, and ask your end users to be patient and not change their requirements for a couple of years). Unfortunately, this doesn't happen too often, especially in today's volatile business climate. To meet this need, Oracle has more than 80 BI Applications available, both horizontal and vertical. Some are more "prebuilt" than others, meaning most include prebuilt ETL components, but some do not.

A BI Application, by definition, should include the following:

- A flexible and scalable *physical* data model based on defined informational needs, industry and IT best practices, and the experience of thousands of customers of Oracle's lines of OLTP systems—and not just the first round of report requirements, optimized to store data for fast retrieval of large and flat data sets.

  This data model should permit modular deployment but also be rich and broad enough to permit analysis of cross-functional problems. Having just a logical data model is insufficient. A logical data model cannot be instantiated as is. It is not optimized for a particular database manager to minimize implementation and performance issues. It makes for great wallpaper, though, if you have a plotter.

- A thoroughly fleshed out semantic layer that includes many types of industry best-practice metrics and is rich enough to allow an end user to consume without having to define many of their own formulas at a report level (for example, time series metrics, comparative metrics, and rate of change).

■ ETL programming that's flexible enough to separate the source-specific movement of data from the source to a generic temporary location, from the final source-independent load into the target tables (data warehouse physical data model).

■ Interactive role-based dashboards defined by the business community based on a few revisions, testing, and data profiling. These should start with a summarized exception-based view of the data and allow for fast root-cause analysis and drill down into details.

■ A form of guided navigation for end users to help them find the "needle in the haystack," or the few transactions causing the biggest problems. This navigation should take a minimal number of mouse clicks, require little training to use, and provide a consistent analysis for a broad community.

■ A well-thought-out architecture that includes best practices, optimizations, reusable objects, naming conventions, tuning strategies, and documentation.

Oracle BI Applications meet these criteria, with a prebuilt end-to-end solution that allows an organization to quickly have insight into their transactional applications. Of course, no enterprise solution is expected to be used without customizations, which is why it's important to perform a fit-gap analysis before deciding whether to buy or build. Even if there's only a 40-percent fit out of the box, there may still be value. Here's a comparison of the two possible scenarios:

■ **Changing prebuilt** Value diminishes because it becomes harder to maintain as time goes on.

■ **Extending prebuilt** Value is maintained because you have a launching point and would have had to build this functionality anyway.

Therefore, when you're conducting a fit/gap analysis, it's important to differentiate whether work would be required to modify existing components, or if you're simply going to extend and leverage the out-of-the-box functionality as a starting point. Most likely you won't use any of the dashboards and reports out of the box, and there's no cause for alarm in this finding. The important areas to consider and compare are the source tables, where data is accessed from, and the target physical data model.

The semantic layer is also important to compare, but not as important as the ETL and physical data model. A fit gap is more accurate when you focus on a single list of attributes required before business metric calculations (ratios, percent formulas, and so on), rather than a collection of reports with overlapping/redundant attributes. Dragging and dropping attributes on a screen to create a report is a much different work effort compared to developing ETL to pull in new data fields.

Figures 2-4 through 2-10 provide an example of a cross–BI Application analytical workflow, using prebuilt content with relatively minor enhancements. It should be noted this type of flow is only possible with an enterprise data

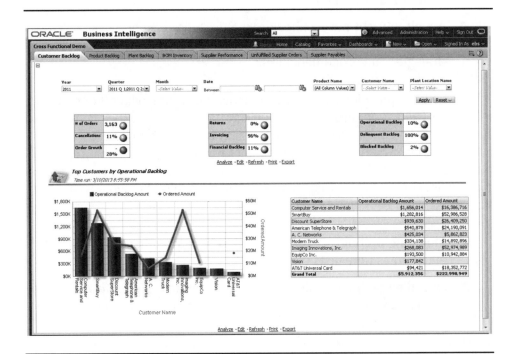

FIGURE 2-4. *Customer backlog example*

model made up of multiple subject areas, essentially linking different transaction types with common dimensions. This is very difficult to build in real life, which is why most companies taking a build-from-scratch approach end up designing multiple disconnected data stores. This example is not out of the box, but was built by Simon Miller (for a demonstration) over a period of two to three days, using the BI Applications as a base. The underlying data is from an Oracle internal sample data set (originally sourced from an EBS R12 demo instance called "Vision").

The base assumption is that this is an interactive role-based dashboard, that could be used to monitor the throughput of orders to ensure timely revenue recognition.

Figure 2-4 shows which customers have the largest backorders, and compares that as a ratio of what they've ordered. Figure 2-5 answers the question "what product/part/assembly is driving the backorders for the chosen customer," once you've drilled down from the first dashboard tab.

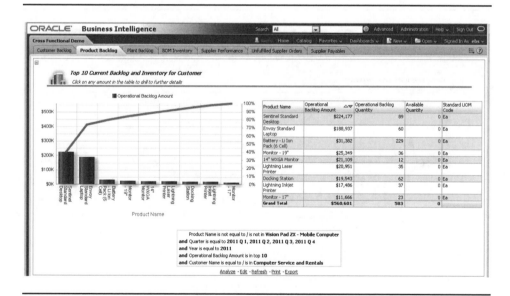

FIGURE 2-5. *Product backlog example*

Figure 2-6 answers the following questions:

- What plant manufactures the top model?

- What is the current inventory on that model, and is it worth fulfilling from another location?

Next, Figure 2-7 answers these questions:

- What parts or components are required to manufacture and assemble that model?

- What is the inventory required to make the product?

Figure 2-8 shows which supplier provides the part, along with the history for that supplier. Assuming there's an urgent need to source the part, you

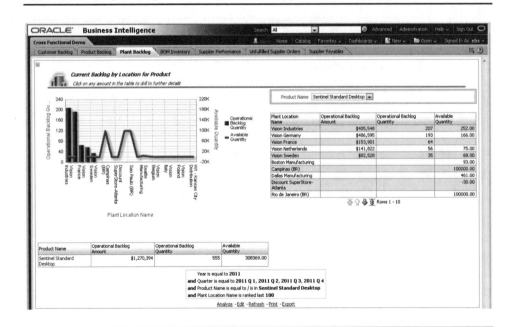

FIGURE 2-6. *Backlog location example*

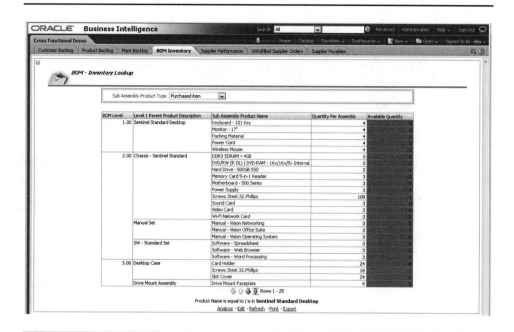

FIGURE 2-7. *BOM breakdown and inventory example*

may need help to identify the most trusted and reliable partner. Figure 2-9 shows whether requisitions or purchase orders are already in flight, so you don't order more than what's required. In this example there are a number of requisitions on hold, which could help indicate the root cause of the backlog. Finally, Figure 2-10 shows whether the supplier is being paid on time and whether it is possible to have a credit hold with that supplier. If so, no wonder there's a backlog!

The ability to string together this type of analysis allows end users to follow the problem they are analyzing wherever the data leads them. Without an enterprise data model as one would find in an Oracle BI Application, building this type of workflow either is impractical or leads to a solution that solves one problem but cannot easily be changed or extended when the problem changes.

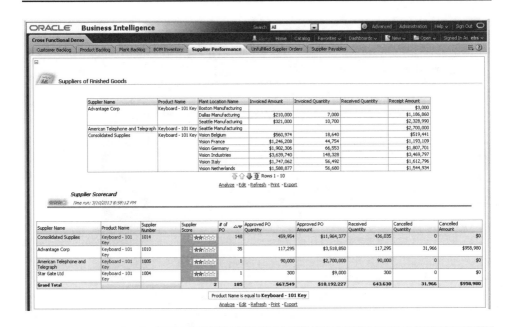

FIGURE 2-8. *Supplier performance tracking example*

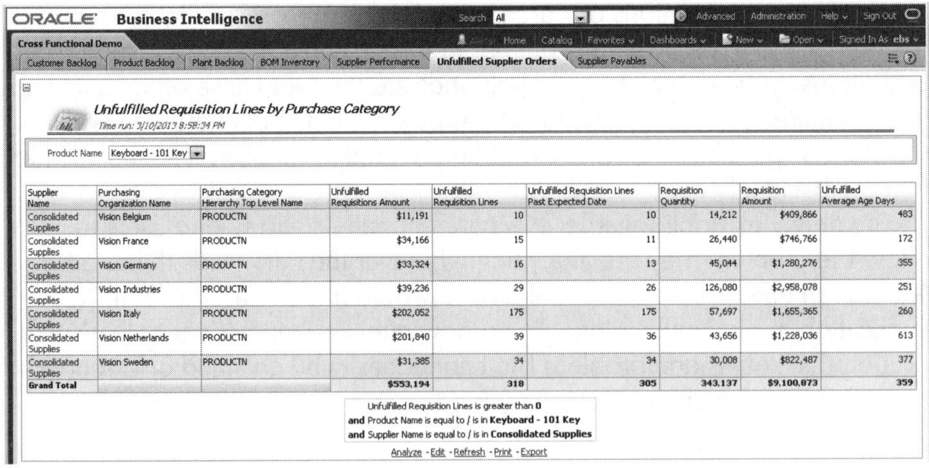

FIGURE 2-9. *Unfulfilled requisitions example*

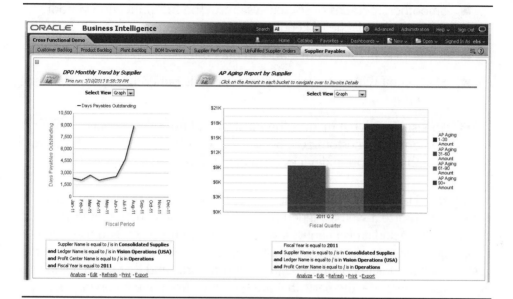

FIGURE 2-10. *Supplier payables example*

Why Buy, When You Can Build?

Companies with low maturity and experience with data warehousing tend to choose a solution based on software license price because they don't know how to evaluate the underlying technology and architecture. They do so, even though Gartner estimates that less than 25 percent of the total cost of ownership of a BI system is software license cost. It's important to know how to evaluate a prebuilt BI Application to understand if it meets your needs.

Many people ask, "Why buy, when you can build?" In some cases, the initial cost is the same. You choose between buying software and implementation services. The key advantages of a prebuilt solution are

- Dramatically reduced time to value.
- Lowered risk.
- Lower total cost of ownership (TCO).
- Easier maintenance.

- Smoother upgrades of source systems. (The BI Application vendor owns the headache of keeping the ETL connectors current.)

- Better overall engineering and architecture.

- Starting off with cross-subject area analysis rather than one data mart at a time.

- Focusing on what matters the most to end users—the delivery of content that's customized, personalized, role based, interactive, and portable to mobile devices, printers, e-mail, and so on.

Figure 2-11 outlines a typical implementation weighting of where you're likely to customize a well-designed BI Application. You can prebuild ETL, data models, metadata (semantic) layers, and so on; however, end users will always be asking for new types of dashboards and reports. We often tell our customers that Oracle could prebuild 10,000 reports, and that still wouldn't be enough! Therefore, the parts that are "generic" from one company to another, that are high risk to deliver, and take the longest time to build from

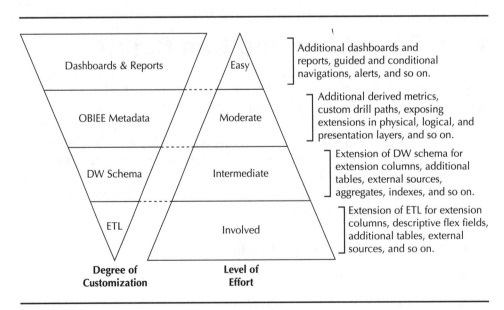

FIGURE 2-11. *Customization is inversely proportional to the level of effort.*

scratch should be prebuilt. During your implementation, you need to carry the ball down the last few yards of the field (that is, adapt the solution to the parts of your business that distinguish it from your competitors).

When customers ask us what a BI Application is, we tell them it's no different from what they can build themselves if they can find the right skill sets, hire dozens of developers, and spend a decade or so implementing with an unlimited budget—and by the way, user requirements can't change while during the building process. If you choose to do this, you're basically at risk of reinventing a wheel.

To add some perspective, in the early days of ERP rollouts, it was common to customize and therefore hard to prebuild ETL that would work out of the box. Also, from the point of view of the vendor, there were many more players with substantial market share, making the task of building out ETL adapters much more difficult to develop a business around. The consolidation of the ERP and CRM markets has made building and maintaining the adapters much more feasible. The buy-versus-build value proposition wasn't as strong a decade ago, due to the high degree of customizations and custom implementations on the source OLTP and CRM side.

Today, it's perfectly reasonable to expect to install the software, run an ETL load, troubleshoot for a day or two, and then look at some initial data on a dashboard from your source system. Of course, that's just a start—but you're already a year ahead of the game. Will the data in the dashboards be right? Not all of it. How safe will it be to start doing analysis after only a few days? Not at all. Now, though, you have something to show your users to get feedback on how your implementation and business differ from the generic case.

Again, you're already a year or more ahead of the game. Do not lose sight of how much of an impact you will have on your users when you deliver data—imperfect data, but data nonetheless—after only a few weeks. This initial view will let your users detect any issues in the data, thus further accelerating your time to deliver and their ownership of the solution.

Let's look at what you're getting yourself into if you decide to build from scratch. A good example is when Simon Miller was sent in as a consultant to his alma mater, McMaster University. He was a technology-agnostic data warehouse professional at that time. McMaster was about to sign a purchase of BusinessObjects, thinking this is exactly what they needed. After spending an hour at a whiteboard, they were able to quickly see they weren't even close to being ready to start using a BI tool. They needed a data model; they needed ETL designs; they needed an overall data architecture and data governance plan.

In hindsight, they may have been able to use the PeopleSoft EPM Campus Solutions prebuilt data warehouse, but at the time Simon wasn't aware of that product because he wasn't yet an Oracle employee. McMaster delayed the frontend purchase for a couple of years because this was such a minor part of what they needed to focus on. Instead, the focus was shifted to designing the overall physical data model that would meet their short- and long-term needs.

In 2003, Simon helped develop an Excel work effort estimation model for the purposes of calculating fixed-price bids for data warehouse and data mart implementations. It was initially built for an insurance customer that didn't believe Simon's assertions as to the "true" cost of the implementation they were planning. It was then repurposed by Simon's former employer, field tested, and was used to calculate budgetary amounts for planning purposes. In both cases, it was used to explain and justify just how involved and expensive even the smallest of custom-built BI Applications projects could be. You should plan on creating a similar model if you need to justify why a custom build is cost and time prohibitive.

Will Hutchinson has over the years built an overall TCO model that implementation efforts are a part of, and we've both found examples of how one can break down in fine detail all the moving parts and pieces, associate a cost, and roll up to obtain a better estimated cost. Most companies seem to just "wing it" when it comes to estimates.

Creating a Work Estimation Model

A work effort estimation model can assume a generic Business Intelligence development life cycle, with the following major steps (some are sequential, some parallel, not always in this order). This life cycle is based around what would be required for a completely custom-built approach. Oracle Consulting, for example, has developed a similar type of model that Simon built, and so have many of our implementers. Without a good estimating tool for a prebuilt BI Application project, you can expect to have to go back to the well numerous times asking for more money and time extensions.

Table 2-1 lists some of the inputs required to calculate the estimated costs and work efforts. With this information the math is simple; for example, if you know you have to build 420 simple ETL mappings, and on average each one takes one day to develop and a half day to unit test, then you have to plan for 420 days times 1.5 days, which equals 630 person days, plus project management overhead, plus contingency overhead, just for this one component.

Input	Description
Number of source tables	Number of tables that would be brought into the reporting environment. This is, most likely, a small fraction of the number of tables in the source system. These need to be documented and analyzed to determine SQL statements needed to extract the data in an optimal way.
Average number of fields/ source table	Average number of fields for each of the tables to be brought into the reporting environment.
Number of base-level fact tables	Number of transaction-level fact tables, not including snapshot, cycle time, and aggregate fact tables.
Number of dimensions	Number of dimensional tables for groupings, attributes, and hierarchies.
Percentage of fact aggregations/derivations	What percentage of the number of fact tables will result in an aggregate, cycle time, or snapshot table? Be sure to include "aggregates of an aggregate" in the total number.
Percentage of dimensional snowflaking	This is a data modeling design where hierarchies are either all folded into one physical table or stored in multiple tables. This is a technical decision/assumption. It's a judgement call made by the data modeler, and is determined by the number and complexities of the required hierarchies. Multiple hierarchies for the same dimension, for example, can often be snowflaked.

TABLE 2-1.   *Application-Specific Parameters*

Input	Description
Percentage of staging tables	Used where an intermediate data structure (between source and target) is used as a temporary holding area for ETL processing.
Number of reports	Number of static/drillable reports to be released as part of the scope. Definition of a report is one that can be mocked up on a single sheet of paper, as an example.
Number of reporting data elements requiring business rules	Number of reporting objects/data elements that will require some sort of formula to calculate a value to be displayed on *any* report. Do not double count if the reporting object is used on multiple reports.
Avg. number of non-key fields per fact table	This input is slightly technical and will be an assumption. Each fact table usually represents a process or transaction. A non-key field is a data element that could show up on a report and may or may not require a formula to calculate. The non-key fields are typically measures or numerical.
Avg. number of non-key fields per dimension table	This input is slightly technical and will be an assumption. Each dimension table usually represents a business entity and is used to group or roll up measures by some hierarchy or attribute. Examples include time, products, and geography.

TABLE 2-1. *Application-Specific Parameters* (continued)

Input	Description
Percentage of simple mappings	A simple mapping is one that passes the data from source to target without requiring complex or nested logic to transform or to cleanse. For example, if 65 percent are simple, then assume 35 percent are complex. If required, you can have an easy/medium/complex type of breakdown.
Percentage of simple reports	Of the total number of reports, what percentage will require simple displays to the users? Anything not considered easy should be reviewed to see what can be pushed back into the semantic layer instead of at the report level.
Number of dashboard tabs	How many tabs will need to be created, assuming a consistent amount of interaction for each tab? For example, two to three dashboard prompts, four to five queries/reports, and so on. You can also break this down into simple, medium, and complex.

TABLE 2-1.   *Application-Specific Parameters* (continued)

Roadmap to a Custom Built Solution

Later we will discuss how using a prebuilt BI Application allows one to shorten or eliminate some of the following steps while still meeting or exceeding project expectations. Here's a generic life cycle with the types of questions you need to ask to properly define a scope and project plan for a custom built data warehouse.

Design and Develop the Project Plan

The following questions should be answered when you are designing and developing your project plan:

- Who are all the required players?

- How long will it take to acquire the team you need?

- How are you going to estimate your work efforts? Are buffers required?

- How do you balance between reality and user expectations?

- What other projects will compete for resources?

- What development methodology will you use?

- What key milestones, bottlenecks, and such should be anticipated?

- How do you compensate for the high risk if this is your first time developing a data warehouse?

When you're done, you should at least double your work effort estimations. (In some cases, you may wish you had tripled them.) Also, you should break down the deliverables into manageable subject areas and strive for delivering new content every 90 days. Last but not least, you should assume you'll need to revisit the deliverables shortly after release.

Develop a Competency Center Around Design and Architecture Best Practices

A competency center can take months to develop properly, so don't be surprised. Also, the team needs to work well together, but you shouldn't assume they will. If your team is mostly contractors, you should expect competing, best-practice philosophies (even if they are with same firm), often with a battle of egos, religions, cricket rules, and varying experiences.

You'll need to define the following items:

- Naming conventions
- Architecture

- Documentation templates

- Approaches to testing

- Code migration

- Break fixes

Also, you'll need to determine how to coordinate the following items:

- Data model design changes in the data modeling tool

- Data model changes (DDL) from the data modeling tool

- ETL metadata, updated from DDL

- The BI tool semantic layer, updated from DDL

Gather Detailed Requirements

First, you need to decide how to gather requirements. Ideally, you should mock up dashboards in Excel with links for drilling into views such as charts and pivot tables. It's important to define a Kimball matrix, as described in any of Ralph Kimball's books. Users need visual diagrams to sign off on, not a 150-page IT document. Don't focus on reports, but rather the data elements required and the level of detail likely needed to determine root causes.

Assess priority based on use cases, with clear definition of how and why BI Application will be used. Ask "What are you going to do with the data and why?" rather than "What do you want?" Flow chart the business processes used to analyze the data, asking questions such as:

- Why is a process going wrong?

- How do you know?

- What is the impact?

- What should be done about it?

It helps to define role-based requirements, based on the various profiles of your end users. Remember that generic one-size dashboards don't fit all. These requirements are often based on job function and level within an organization (for example, district sales manager). Be clear early on concerning what the security requirements are, as they will need to map to your various application roles and therefore dashboard design. However, verify that "security requirements" are not driven by people's desire to protect their fiefdoms.

When gathering requirements, be prepared to ask the following questions:

- Where, when, and why you need to drill back to the source system? Is it to view detailed data, or is it to take action?

- How often does the data *really* need to be updated? Does it vary by day of the month or proximity to the financial close? Beware when users say they need "real-time" updates.

    - Ask what events drive the need for low-latency data.

    - Ask whether only certain data elements need low latency.

    - Ask what analyses cannot be performed well if data is "as of last night" or "as of the end of the last shift," for example. Variable update frequencies are acceptable.

Finally, be prepared to take a hard look at how much history will you need to maintain. It's almost always more than users think. For example, the University of Chicago keeps a database of monthly stock prices since 1926 (CRSP). People still look at that data today. Your users may not need 80 years of history, but they may easily need over five years of history.

Perform Source System Analysis

Source system analysis requires a detailed assessment of each source table needed as part of an ETL load; in some cases, you also need to look at stored procedures to retrieve required data (not immediately available in a table). You'll need to know the following:

- How will you detect changes to source system records?

    - Is there a Date Last Updated field?

    - What triggers that date to get changed?

- How do you categorize the source data (type of dimension, type of fact, and so on)?

- How does the source system fit into a business process (order lines, invoice lines, ship lines, backlog lines, and so on)?

- What can be hard-coded into your ETL versus what should be dynamically changed in parameter files (for example, should financial account grouping changes be performed at the source)?

- What data needs to be persisted in the staging area between ETL loads and why?

You also need to be sensitive to what SQL (or other retrieval language) is required to pull the data. Do you need to consider database hints, outer joins, recursive joins and so on? Do you need to modify the source system to facilitate change detection or increase performance? Are you legally permitted to access data directly or do you need to access the data via the application layer using APIs?

Perform Architectural Design

While your team may already have a bias, it's worth keeping an open mind when asking the following: Should you employ the Inmon or Kimball approach? If you choose the Inmon approach, ask how many layers of data you would require (ODS, DW, data marts, and so on), as this has a significant impact on timelines and environmental sizing guidelines.

You'll need to define how to exchange metadata between BI tools, from both a process and technology perspective. Consider how you will handle multiple data sources. How will you handle things when management announces an acquisition? Do not assume that the best answer is, "Wait for them (acquired company) to migrate to our (acquiring company) ERP."

Other questions you should be able to answer as part of your overall architecture include

- How will you handle ETL restartability?

- What is the hardware and data storage architecture?

- Will the BI system be on premise, in the public cloud, in a private cloud, or some combination?

- What is the design of the aggregation approach and strategy?

- How will you insulate the data warehouse from upgrades of the OLTP?

Ask yourself, how will you handle changing source system domain values used in business rules? For example, if new accounts are added to the GL, this affects the rollup to a financial statement. As another example, perhaps a new customer type is added or a sales stage is used to drive metric calculations and displays.

Finally, you'll need to design the target data warehouse database, parameters, settings, indexing strategy, etc. as part of your physical architectural footprint.

Design the Physical Data Model

There are a number of key tenets when designing your physical data warehouse model. The first is that this is best handled by someone experienced and who does this on a full-time basis rather than someone who does this on a casual or part-time basis. Another tenet is it's important that you ensure the design is source system agnostic. Again, think of how you would react when management announces an acquisition. Ensure you design using the lowest possible level of granularity. Your users will develop legitimate needs to drill to the lowest level of granularity at which the data is collected. Plan for it. Ensure you can practically aggregate data by using degenerate (or junk) dimensions. These are defined simply as "stuff" associated with a fact table that doesn't warrant a dimension on its own (for example, transaction type codes). Kimball describes these well. Here's a partial checklist you can work from, to ensure you have everything covered:

- Do you have consistent standards, naming conventions, and data types?

- What does the staging area need to look like?

- What does your Kimball matrix look like?

- What type of indexing strategy is required?

- What data profiling is required?

- What types and quantities of fact tables are required?

- How much snowflaking, if any, will be required?

- Do you collapse some dimensions into a common party dimension?

- How do you handle multiple currencies and languages?

- How do you identify source system soft deletes?

- How do you handle security and multitenant designs?

- How do you ensure traceability back to source transactions?

Finally, consider how you will handle time series metrics (YTD, LYTD, AGO, period rolling, and so on). Even if you do not calculate these in the data warehouse—and we do not recommend doing so—you should ensure the BI tool can calculate them easily. It doesn't hurt to initially define some aggregates, however, in reality you need to be in production for a bit before you can determine where your performance bottlenecks are based on actual usage.

Design the Logical Data Model and Review It with End Users

If this step isn't done right, nothing else matters. This is the heart and soul of your design, and your best chance of confirming you're going to meet the needs of your end users early on. This is accomplished by gathering your requirements, documenting a Kimball matrix based on what you've heard, then reviewing the Kimball matrix with the end users who are clear on their reporting requirements.

It doesn't hurt to stress test the design with known and future requirements. For example, look up some news stories in your industry about something going wrong for a company. If they had happened to your organization, how would the data warehouse have helped your organization cope more easily? While you need to meet the stated needs of your end users, you need to look beyond to what they don't yet know but may be interested in down the road.

Too often end users are fixated on row and column report designs. If possible, look beyond report needs to a cross-subject area type of analysis. End users need to understand the concept of having metrics "by" some dimension. The OBIFS (Oracle Business Intelligence Foundation Suite) presentation area, also called a subject area is a living version of a Kimball Matrix. It can also be thought of as a logical data model that forms the basis for ad-hoc subject areas and a user-friendly presentation. This step may require multiple iterations, but is worth the effort as it forms the core foundation of success over the long term.

This step is the key basis for signoff to start development of the ETL, that will reduce the risk of ETL rework later on, which is costly.

Define Security Integration Requirements

Security integration with source systems, authentication and authorization stores, and various portals is a step often overlooked early on, which can cause expensive rework later on and/or restrictions in the available functionality of your application. Some of the considerations include

- For your dashboards, how do you match security from the source system without re-creating a new or duplicate security model?

- How will you drill back to the underlying source system? Will your BI tool support this?

- How do you handle users not in the source system, where the security model and application roles are defined?

- What are the implications on security for a data warehouse with multiple source systems?

- Do you filter on facts or dimensions, or both—and when?

- Who gets what type of access to which folder of reports/dashboards?

- Who can see which dashboards?

- How do you ensure row-level security enforced at all times with all UIs?

Design Test Plan

Designing the test plan is often overlooked. It is a painful, although critical, exercise. Be sure to secure time in advance with the end users, and be accurate with the project timelines. Remember that this is your first and only chance to properly test data before your application's credibility is at risk. Once users lose confidence in the application, it is very hard to bring them back.

Users need to define the testing/validation they would otherwise do in production. Also, you should plan to test various scenarios, including the following:

- Entering, updating, and monitoring a handful of transactions entered
- Cross-footing from operational reports

- Cross-footing from custom SQL statements on source system tables

- Looking up a handful of records on a report to match to the source system

Don't try to cross-foot from a legacy data warehouse because this is often futile. Also, you need to ensure the source system is frozen after an ETL load while testing is underway. For example, you can take a snapshot and load it onto a test or disaster recovery server. Finally, you need to test both initial and incremental loads for proper inserts and updates.

Design the BI Semantic Layer

Depending on the quality of the chosen BI tool, designing the BI semantic layer can be a long or short exercise. OBIEE, for example, has a (thick) three-level semantic layer and takes longer to develop than other BI tools; however, the more you can put into your semantic layer up front, the more time you'll save in the long run on report development, and you'll allow more end-user report development without compromising the integrity of the figures they are reporting. Spending time on a thick semantic layer ensures a better end-user experience, better performance, and more flexibility.

Here are some questions you should consider while designing the BI semantic layer:

- How are you going to model slowly changing dimensions?

- How are you going to model time series metrics?

- How are you going to ensure security is dynamically applied?

- If you are not using OBIEE, how many different semantic designs will you need?

The semantic layer is the translation from what an end user sees to where the data physically lives and how it is retrieved. OBIEE provides the ability to have this defined in a single location, whereas other BI tools inevitably result in a fragmented design. Most other BI tools require different semantic designs and security models to provide the complete range of enterprise reporting needs; therefore, allow extra time to model this and document how you will handle changes to maintain some level of consistency.

Finally, it's important to work with end users on various design options for the organizing of attributes they can see in their ad-hoc environment. Too much and they'll drown in available attributes and will be challenged to find the attributes they need. Too few attributes and they'll be unable to create all the queries they need, and therefore will be frustrated.

Design ETL

Setting the right ETL architecture as a foundation is critical. You only get one chance to do this, and if it's not done correctly, you will be burdened by poor decisions for years. Most leading thinkers say that designing and implementing ETL is 60 to 80 percent of the total work efforts. Design the ETL improperly, and you will hobble your data warehouse until you redesign it, assuming you can afford to down the road.

Here are some questions to keep in mind while designing ETL:

■ How detailed do you need to document the ETL, and what templates will you need to first design and test out?

■ How will you update documentation when changes occur?

■ How will you line up documentation with a test plan?

■ What workflows do you need for approvals and signoffs?

Develop ETL

When developing ETL, you need to determine the impact of an outage of any of your development servers. For example, would it affect five developers for four hours? It can add up!

Although a project plan may look good on paper, it often doesn't reflect real life. Assumptions are made with respect to output of work by a well-functioning team. You need to be realistic about how efficient you really can be with so many inevitable bottlenecks, such as the following:

■ Regular team meetings

■ Daily distractions from e-mail and co-workers

■ Waiting for specifications or changes to specifications

■ Delays due to metadata getting out of sync

■ ETL tool issues requiring a service request with the vendor

■ Waiting for available environments (either source or target)

- Waiting for initial data loads to complete

- Needing to repeatedly load data during troubleshooting

- The time it takes to create a load execution plan and a sequence of ETL tasks

Many projects stumble because the reusability of components is not considered. Here are some other points to consider:

- How do you provide an easy way to add new fields later on?

- How do you ensure you don't have redundant transformation objects?

- How do you get different ETL developers to coordinate with each other?

- What happens if you have a conflict between end users wanting to test while your developers want to truncate and reload their data at the same time?

Test ETL

During this step, you need to unit test each of the possible ETL mappings (which could be in the hundreds) and then get signoff. You also need to test end-to-end execution of the entire ETL load, both for correctness and to ensure it will run in the required time window.

A number of delays will inevitably occur that are often not planned properly for. These including the following:

- Waiting for end users to validate data on reports

- Waiting for ETL data loads to complete

- The time it takes to trace records through, end to end, to pinpoint errors or validate accuracy

- The time it takes to document various test plans

- The need to constantly revisit tests when the underlying ETL changes

This can all be compounded based on the number of environments you have in place, such as Dev, Test, QA, Prod, and so on.

Work efforts are often badly estimated. You should have at a minimum a 40-to-60-percent contingency plan added to the project plan to allow time for the resolution of issues that are certain to crop up. Another area of testing that's often overlooked but can have far-reaching implications is ETL and query performance. Consider the following:

- How long does an ETL end-to-end load take? How long for incremental loads?

- How long do queries take on average?

- How much hardware and memory are actually required, both short and long term? What's the lead time to repair if the environment is undersized initially?

- How much disk space is required (for example, temp space for the initial load or temp space for index building)? And what's the lead time to request more?

While much can be done around performance and tuning, it's usually done at the end of a project life cycle; in the meantime you may have delays in your development environment with less than performant ETL.

Develop Reports

With a proven low-TCO BI tool such as OBIEE, if you have done the preceding steps well, developing reports is a minor part of the overall project plan. With many other BI tools, you need to consider how much you have to develop at the report layer. Here are some examples:

- Percentage calculations or any formulas requiring division
- Time series measure calculations
- Level-based measure calculations (e.g., Sales by District)
- Any other type of advanced calculations that can't be pushed into the semantic layer

The more you have to develop at the report layer, the harder it is to keep everything synchronized, especially when you need to change how a metric is calculated. You could theoretically have hundreds of reports affected.

To reiterate, the more logic and calculations you put into the report layer, the harder the environment will be to scale and maintain.

We find it more useful to think of the challenge of building reports, dashboards, and so on as developing the following classes of objects that can be linked together and reused as necessary:

- Individual reports with dynamic filters, summary, and detail.

- Dashboard prompts.

- Dashboard layout standards, standard skins, and UI best practices.

- Linking everything together to provide drilldown from summary to detail.

- Various ways of slicing, dicing, and viewing data for interactive experiences.

- Role-based dashboard views for fostering collaboration. For example, the manager sees the team data whereas each direct report views the same dashboard but only their own data.

- Proactive alerts and actions (assuming your BI tool supports them).

In most cases, report and dashboard construction should only be 10 to 15 percent of the overall project plan. However, companies starting out with BI think report construction is 90 percent of the total effort. The classic analogy for this is an iceberg (see Figure 2-12). You need to remind or educate people that much is hidden under the waterline. If you only look at the surface (the tip of the iceberg) and do not perform adequate due diligence (the bulk of the ice underwater), you're likely to purchase something based on price only rather than comparing price to value.

Document the Application

Documenting the application is mind-numbing, lengthy grunt work nobody wants to do; most projects don't have time for this step and therefore it often doesn't get done. However, without it a custom solution is hard to maintain, end users will struggle to understand what they're looking at, and IT will struggle to provide an explanation. The problem will become even more acute when the initial developers eventually leave.

FIGURE 2-12. *BI Applications analogy (most of the effort is under the waterline)*

Documenting the application includes the following types of metadata (that is, data about your data):

- ETL, including each transformation object within a mapping, each mapping, and the end-to-end schedule/coordination of mappings

- Data model (physical)

- BI tool semantic layer (each logical attribute and metric, including definitions and usage)

- BI tool end-user layer, including dashboards and individual reports
- Overall end-user guide
- Overall IT guide for new people working on application down the road

Perform Power-User Training on the BI Platform

Not to be confused with end-user training, power-user training is for a smaller subset of users who design and build the majority of the dashboards. This step requires a special type of end user with the following type of profile:

- Passionate, full of energy, but also patient.
- Business user with an interest in technology. (Note that the primary emphasis is on business, not technology. This is not a closet IT person but rather someone with a "real" business day job.)
- A strong vision of why they need the information (in other words, they need to have skin in the game).
- Willing/able to carve out time to properly validate data.
- A champion within the business who can get other users excited.
- Ideally, the one who delivers the end-user training
- Visually oriented

Perform Rollout to Production

Unfortunately, performing a rollout to production can take many more weeks than initially planned—for the same reasons most projects and technology implementations do. If the testing doesn't go well, the documentation isn't sufficient, or the ability to migrate between environments is not well designed, then often the brakes will be applied to the project.

Keep in mind that you need to factor in time for the initial load and testing of historical data into production. You need to have a healthy time budget for performance and tuning both in QA and production, as described in the next section.

Test Performance and Tuning

It's very difficult to design an aggregation strategy ahead of time. You need real-life production experience, but often a good first guess can be gleaned from some of the use cases developed as part of the requirements gathered. The bulk of this aggregation development, however, typically requires being in production first and monitoring real-life performance and usage.

Much can be done on the ETL and database side for performance and tuning. Although multiple vendors support data warehouse types of databases, the Oracle database provides the largest range of "low-hanging fruit" options, including materialized views for aggregates, data compression, data and index partitioning, and, for the ultimate in performance, Oracle Exadata Database Machine.

OBIEE provides usage tracking, with a single view from all access points (Office plug-in, dashboards, formatted reports, portal usage, and so on). Combined with the aggregation wizard, there's a straightforward way to refine aggregations periodically to reflect changing usage patterns. It's important to understand that most other BI tools require hard-coding of SQL pathways to get aggregate navigation to work, which is not as dynamic as the Oracle BI Server functions. Exalytics goes one step further, recommending the required aggregates with the Summary Advisor and then putting the data into memory using the TimesTen database. Exalytics is covered in more detail later in this book.

Ideally, you will have a QA environment the same size as production with a copy of production data to test the end-to-end ETL load times. Often, this is where weaknesses in ETL architecture, design, and development surface—which results in rework near the end of a project plan when you're probably already over budget and past your deadline. And had neglected to budget for performance and tuning.

Perform End-User Training

Due to the large amount of buffer required in a project plan for a custom-built data warehouse, it can be difficult to determine the right date for end-user training. If users are trained too early, they forget (within days) what they've learned, which hurts user adoption of the application. Users are rarely trained too late because custom data warehouse projects rarely get delivered on time; in many cases, training too late should be the goal to ensure the users work with the environment immediately and therefore retain their training.

If you need to develop a training plan, Oracle provides training on OBIEE; however, you'll need to put together training specific to your implementation.

For example, what attributes have been exposed in what folders to create an ad-hoc query? What are the analytical application workflows baked into the dashboard (for example, what business process does the design assume you'll follow to go from insight to action)?

Users almost never understand all the nuances of their own data. The data warehouse will expose them to more of their data in more depth. Consequently, they will look at parts of data they have never looked at extensively before. Be sure to spend time training users in what their data means. Of course, the meaning of the data needs to be documented so users can reference this after the class is over.

Project management overheads and risk management overheads both need to be taken into consideration. Delays are inevitable on any custom-built data warehouse project: You'll have to perform more test runs of loading historical data than you planned, you'll have more changes than planned, you'll have more downtime than planned, and so on.

Finally, the way to screen out experienced data warehouse resources is simple: They'll openly talk about their failures, not just their successes. They're more likely to brag about their battle wounds than have a large ego.

Bringing It All Together with a Prebuilt Solution

As you can see, the list of things to plan for and manage is overwhelming, even for veteran data warehouse professionals. Any one of the activities described can go off course, either for technical reasons or personnel reasons. All things need to be carefully coordinated to occur in sequence; one delay can start a chain reaction. The first release (set of dimensions and fact tables) might not be too bad, but when it comes to properly setting resource levels and creating an assembly line for your data warehouse factory delivery, it's challenging to ensure no wrenches get thrown into the gears—and then the business changes.

It should be noted that having a prebuilt BI Application doesn't automatically remove all the steps you'd go through to build a custom solution: You will have customizations, users will still want different reports, there will still be data-quality issues, and users will still need training on their data. Oracle's prebuilt BI Applications assume these issues from the beginning. The architecture is designed for them, just as it's designed to support multiple data sources. The key takeaway is that you'll benefit from the following with a well-designed prebuilt BI Application:

- You get a similar sort of project plan, but one that's very much compressed and requires fewer resources.

- You get an app that can deliver many times the quantity and quality you could otherwise provide.

- You don't have to put together the best team of experts from around the world.

- You're far less likely to fail, especially when you defer customizations to a Phase 2 deliverable.

- People are often promoted (or at least advance in their careers) with a successful BI Application deployment, and Oracle's prebuilt BI Applications can help accelerate this.

- Companies can realize benefits months or even years in advance, making for a strong business case on that point alone. In fact, faster realization of business benefits usually trumps reduced implementation and support cost as the biggest benefit to the organization.

- The most challenging parts of an implementation have either been prebuilt or have been well thought out. Some examples are provided in Table 2-2.

The intent of this chapter is not to be overly pessimistic, but rather realistic based on real-world technology-agnostic experiences. There are many reasons for deciding to custom build a data warehouse. For some verticals, for example, no prebuilt or fully prebuilt solution is available. Certain applications are so highly specialized and proprietary that it wouldn't make sense to develop a commercially available prebuilt solution. As mentioned earlier, Oracle has close to 80 different prebuilt BI Applications currently available. This book discusses primarily the core ERP- and CRM-based applications; however, many industry-unit-specific and "edge" applications are available, including the following:

- Oracle Transportation Management—Fusion Transportation Intelligence

- Oracle Advanced Supply Chain—APCC (Advanced Planning Command Center)

- MOC (Manufacturing Operations Center)

- P6/Primavera—P6 Analytics

Where Things Can Go Wrong	How Oracle BI Applications Help
Naming conventions are not properly defined, making maintenance difficult.	You get pre-developed best practices, in the areas of naming conventions, architectural designs, ETL, BI, and physical data model best practices.
The security model is not properly designed and is inflexible and thus a barrier to performance and the end-user experience.	The security model is prebuilt as much as possible, with a detailed security guide provided to show various options, depending on requirements.
The ETL architecture foundation is not properly established, resulting in a data warehouse built on sand instead of a rock.	The ETL architecture is prebuilt, has been proven across thousands of customers with over a decade of R&D, is designed assuming you will connect to data sources with both known and unknown structures.
The semantic layer is poorly designed, resulting in end-user frustrations. It's difficult to learn and adopt, eventually becoming a barrier to growth.	The semantic layer is prebuilt with thousands of objects, well thought out, and proven across thousands of customers.
Testing is not planned out properly or coordinated. Nobody knows what to test (or even do), thus leading to a descent into chaos.	Prebuilt reports/dashboards are provided as a starter set and are often used as a test plan to validate data by power users.

TABLE 2-2. *Benefits of Using Oracle BI Applications*

Where Things Can Go Wrong	How Oracle BI Applications Help
Poor work effort estimations are delaying the project, requiring repeated requests for further funding and delivery extensions.	With a compressed project plan, many customers are able to show data to end users in a matter of weeks rather than months or years.
There's a risk of eventual obsolescence, especially when the source system changes; for example, in some cases, up to 50 percent of ETL needs to be rewritten (ETL is often up to 70 percent of a new data warehouse project).	Oracle BI Applications are an integral part of Fusion Applications, providing a bridge to Fusion. They are on Oracle's long-term roadmap for maintenance and growth. Oracle provides updated BI Application mappings that correspond to incremental Applications Unlimited changes, and to Fusion Changes.
Users are losing confidence and want to move on.	Oracle has done much of the testing ahead of time, which speeds up the testing by end users; if end users find data to be missing or incorrect, often it's only a minor change to correct. Then it's relatively easy to reload the data for the next round of testing.
End users are trained too early.	Project plans tend to be far more accurate, with compressed (agile) delivery cycles. Prebuilt reports provide the best place to start to become comfortable with technology. Power users can get early access to the environment. Joint Application Development (JAD) sessions can then be held with rapid prototyping of dashboards.

TABLE 2-2.   *Benefits of Using Oracle BI Applications* (continued)

Where Things Can Go Wrong	How Oracle BI Applications Help
A series of stovepipes (disconnected data marts) ends up being generated for specific application and reporting requirements. This causes redundancy and limits the ability to perform cross-functional analysis.	Oracle BI Applications start you with an enterprise data model spanning many facts and dimensions that can meet a large range of BI requirements. This has been done in a "sterile" environment that's not constrained by specific user requirements, which gives you the best of both worlds: You can use what you need in the short term and not lose the ability for cross-subject area analyses later on.

TABLE 2-2. *Benefits of Using Oracle BI Applications* (continued)

Common Objections to BI Applications

If you're still not convinced of the benefits of a prebuilt BI Application, let's review the most common objections customers have to Oracle BI Applications, along with our typical response.

I Already Have a Specific Technology Investment

This is a valid concern for the following reasons:

- You need to cross-train your resources.
- You might need new environments.
- You'll need to think about what to do with your legacy environments.

In the end, when you add up all the benefits to end users, the business case often dwarfs existing standards when you compare the buy-versus-build ROI and TCO.

To quote Gregg Mondani at Oracle, "Standards are great; that's why companies have so many of them." Here's another perspective: "Standards were put in place for a reason; they need to continue to make sense and not become a religion." One of our customers hired a BI director. During the first week, his people told him, "We are a BusinessObjects shop." He replied, "No, we are a [company name] shop."

I Have Different Data Sources, Not All Oracle

Oracle's prebuilt BI Applications were specifically engineered to handle different data sources, from day one. This was not an afterthought:

- The staging area is not source specific, nor are the BI Applications.

- Many customers load data from more than one source system.

- The Universal Adaptor concept is in place to allow for custom data feeds.

Not to take away from the BI Applications; however, it is advisable to plan long term for ERP/CRM consolidation rather than to force a data warehouse to integrate data. It's well understood, however, that acquisitions can make this difficult, and it's faster to do at least an initial consolidation of data for data warehouse purposes than it is to rip and replace an acquisition ERP/CRM application.

I Only Need a Handful of Reports

If report requirements are truly analytical in nature, then rarely does a company only need a handful of reports; it is important to look across the organization and across many projects over a period of time.

If you succeed in satisfying your users' initial requirements with this handful of reports, they *will* want more. Building them without a scalable architecture and without the opportunity for users to meet many of their own needs will cause the backlog of requests to increase until users get frustrated by IT's inability to deliver—and you don't want that.

If you build point solutions driven by specific report requirements, you lose the opportunity to build a scalable architecture, and you run the risk of having many stovepipes to maintain over time.

What About My Existing Data Warehouse?

Oracle's prebuilt analytical applications are not an all-or-nothing scenario; they can coexist with other environments. For example, they can add to an existing database but in a different schema, provided there's compatibility with Oracle's DB configuration recommendations (there should be because they follow data warehousing best practices).

Often Oracle's BI Applications can provide net new subject areas, and dimensions can be potentially linked and cross-referenced to tie environments together. Also, when a data source is due to be upgraded, it might make sense to look at phasing out the legacy data warehouse if the upgrade costs approach the reimplementation costs.

I Need to Implement EBS First

Implementing Oracle's BI Applications at the same time as your ERP (or CRM) is of high value for many reasons:

- You can use Oracle BI Applications to identify data-quality issues in migration or implementation.

- You can identify early on the domain values (codes used on transactions) required to support report requirements, which drives quality data entry at the source.

- End users will need data on day one, not weeks or months after your ERP is moved to production.

- You can offload the migration of old data to the new ERP instead of routing historical data to Oracle BI Applications to provide a seamless transition from a reporting perspective.

- BI can be integrated as part of the initial training and use of the ERP, from the business process and technical perspectives.

- Many reports that now run directly against the OLTP can be migrated to run against the BI Application, which removes the load from the OLTP and is less costly to implement and maintain than many of the tools used to query an OLTP directly.

It should be noted there are also challenges to this approach:

- The same end users testing ERP also need to test BI around the same time.

- The implementation team needs to wait for the ERP team to have sufficient data to test.

- Changes to ERP configurations ripple to BI Applications' configurations.

- The quest for a vanilla ERP install occasionally makes the BI Applications a dumping ground for handling data issues and operational report requirements that should otherwise be kept in the ERP; for example, if building new BI Publisher reports to run against an ERP is viewed as a customization, the answer is not to avoid the customization in the ERP by customizing the BI Applications instead.

- Building business rules in the BI Applications to handle incorrect or incomplete data is not better than getting the data right in the ERP in the first place.

How Do I Know This Will Be a Good Fit?

Oracle recommends a fit/gap analysis to assess (at a high level) an out-of-the-box fit. Assuming the fit/gap shows an adequate level of fit, then the next step would be to obtain an implementation estimate from an experienced implementer (recommended by Oracle). Fit/gaps don't always come back positive, and Oracle's BI Applications don't offer 100 percent coverage of all possible subject areas. Here are some points to keep in mind:

- Focus is on the most important areas with the highest value and in biggest demand. To illustrate this, plot a 2×2 matrix, with one axis being time to benefit and the other being business value. Figure 2-13 shows an example.

- Additional coverage is added with each new release.

- Even a 60-percent fit could still be highly valuable, because it gets you much closer than starting from scratch.

- Many customers also combine third-party bolt-ons (such as several partners' Salesforce.com adapters that extend Oracle's prebuilt BI Applications).

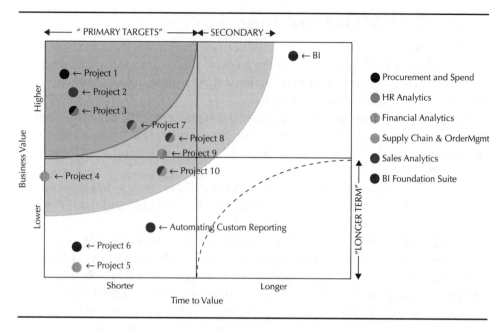

FIGURE 2-13. *How to focus on key wins when evaluating BI Applications.*

I Can Build It Myself

This chapter addresses this assumption head on in order to challenge this notion. It's virtually impossible to stand up a custom data warehouse and a prebuilt ERP at the same time. Do your users want to wait a year after the ERP goes live to get good analytics?

If a team's members think they can do a better job than a well-designed prebuilt BI Application that meets the business needs, then they either don't know what they're signing up for or haven't performed the required due diligence on the BI Applications.

Oracle recommends at least one in-depth workshop to educate potential customers on what's already prebuilt (often numerous meetings are required); this way, a company understands the full spectrum of what it takes to support Business Intelligence.

I Need an MDM Solution First

Users will make decisions as to whether or not the Master Data Management (MDM) effort is undertaken. It is better to have them make those decisions with a good analytic infrastructure. At least they will be able to see where they have duplicate or poor quality data.

MDM is a paradox, you need it, but can't wait for it; MDM projects can take years or more. The better answer in many cases is ERP consolidation or, better yet, looking to Fusion Applications where you can address ERP and CRM consolidation.

Data quality issues should be addressed at the source, not downstream in your data warehouse; otherwise, you lose your data lineage and the ability to test the accuracy of your reports.

Oracle's BI Applications don't handle Master Data Management, and with good reason. Also, they are not dependent on MDM. It's best to look at specific MDM solutions Oracle offers—for example, DRM (Data Relationship Manager) —to augment a BI Application implementation in parallel or after the fact. Don't delay a BI Application implementation because you haven't harmonized all your key dimensions, such as customers, suppliers, products, and so on.

Oracle BI Applications keep the data separate by striping the data in different rows in the same tables. This allows for automatic rollup of data for summary views when an MDM solution is eventually implemented. This gives you the best of all worlds: You can implement without MDM, you have a placeholder for MDM outputs when ready, and you maintain full data lineage of what came from what source.

MDM can be used to provide common display names and/or to provide hierarchies for roll-ups; either way, this can be done after the BI Applications have been implemented. Figure 2-14 illustrates how this works: Although each source system may have a unique name, you can later augment your data set with a display name used for reporting purposes. You can toggle between the display name (which would group/aggregate the data naturally) and the transactional source name.

My Data Is Too Dirty to Report On

If there are plans to analyze the data anyway, and/or clean it up, then the BI Applications can support this effort. BI Applications will help users and IT identify and call attention to the poor quality data more quickly than any

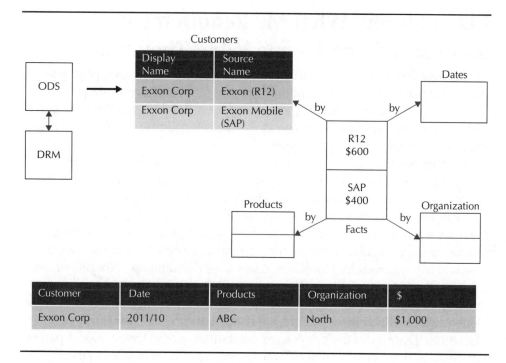

FIGURE 2-14.   *Display name versus source name, in the context of MDM*

other tool we have seen. CRM Sales Analytics provide a usage accelerator with prebuilt data quality reporting for sales rep data entry of opportunities, accounts, and so on.

Most likely, users are doing their own manual cleanup, pulling the data to Access or Excel and then manipulating it in an offline database. If so, several people are likely "cleaning up" the data in an inconsistent manner. This may be worse than not cleaning it up at all. But it is likely going on. This is an opportunity to understand what they're doing and to automate this process or at least provide some level of IT support.

Look at implementing IT controls over the offline data for security reasons and provide MDM and/or data-entry screens along with an ODS (operational data store). There are many better ways of operationalizing data cleanup, such as providing cross-reference tables, hierarchies, and so on. This can also be used as a data source to Oracle prebuilt BI Applications.

I Don't Know What My Requirements Are and Users Can't Define What They Want

All the more reason to start with a prebuilt solution—to quickly populate out-of-the-box reports and dashboards to educate users on what's possible. As one of our customers said, "I am giving users paint-by-numbers instead of a blank canvas." You can use these as the basis for further requirements, and to allow yourself to build prototypes.

Even before that, you can show end users the Oracle BI Application product guides, which contain screenshots of all the out-of-the-box reports, which you can use for a quick pulse check on applicability.

Best-practice metrics help users understand how best-in-class organizations measure a given process. Industry-standard or best-practice formulas help ensure they are calculating the metric correctly. At one of our clients, we found they had five methods for calculating "days sales outstanding." Not one of these followed the GAAP definition. They were calculating it based on a rolling three months sales. In one definition, they assumed three months had 91 days. Depending on which three months are chosen, they could have anywhere from 89 to 92 days. So their days sales outstanding could have varied 3 percent just because they were putting different numbers of days of sales in the calculation, not because they were changing the aggressiveness with which they were collecting their bills.

BI Applications Are Too Expensive

BI Applications are too expensive compared to what? Do you have a detailed work effort estimation tool, as described earlier in this chapter, to fully understand how to calculate your prebuilt implementation approach? Keep in mind that it's important to conduct an apples-to-apples five-year TCO comparison with alternatives. You find that the greater the due diligence, the more likely the "cheap" alternatives become less appealing.

Several Oracle partners have documented that implementing a BI Application cuts 75 percent of the implementation costs. It also cuts about half the ongoing support costs. These costs typically dwarf the cost of the BI Applications. Moreover, the cost of not having the functionality in place by another 6 to 18 months typically also greatly exceeds the cost of BI Applications.

What Happened to Discoverer and Daily Business Intelligence (DBI)?

This can be a touchy subject, depending on your experience and history with these technologies. DBI was a great product, but at times it was over-promoted as a replacement for a data warehouse; in reality, it provided a quick hit of operational reporting with little effort to implement. It was not meant to be extended, even in small ways.

Discoverer was provided to allow for ad-hoc reporting directly on EBS, for operational report purposes. It did not provide the benefits of a data warehouse.

I Don't Want to Hire an Implementer

Although many customers have implemented Oracle BI Applications successfully without outside help, it's most effective when you have an experienced data warehouse team on staff already that's familiar with the underlying technology. In most cases, however, it's recommended that you hire contractors, especially the first time you are implementing something like this. Here are some points to keep in mind:

■ Even a single consultant can help coordinate and direct as well as provide training and best practices; most importantly, the consultant can make sure unnecessary customizations aren't applied.

■ In many cases, an implementation team butchers Oracle BI Applications because they don't know what's already prebuilt; this includes contractors who don't have the right experience. In addition to hiring an implementer, you should ensure the team that's provided has implemented BI Applications before.

■ This is a short-term situation to provide a knowledge transfer. There's only so much you can teach through formal training; you need hands-on experience. By all means, when you do hire an implementer, ensure that both parties understand that knowledge transfer is one of the deliverables. Get it in writing.

Implementing using resources who are learning on the job erodes the "time to value" benefit of a prebuilt BI Application. Although this may seem counterintuitive, it plays out in real life. In one example, a customer hired a very low-cost implementer who kept fumbling over the basic product installation and configuration documentation, and lost weeks on the project plan when compared to using a team that had already learned to "ride that bicycle." Also, the documentation isn't always perfect, so you can't completely rely on it as the only source of experience.

What's the Point of Implementing a Prebuilt Application If I Have to Customize?

There are two major types of scenarios to consider: Are you customizing something that's prebuilt, or are you adding new content? The latter means you're going to have to custom build anyways, but get a head start with the out-of-the-box content. The former needs to be drilled into to understand what can happen:

- Are you adding fields to existing facts/dimensions via descriptive flex fields in EBS, extension columns in Siebel, and so on? If so, then this is normal and expected in any BI Application implementation; descriptive flex fields in EBS, for example, could end up anywhere in Oracle BI Applications, depending on what the data means.

- Are you changing the granularity of a fact or dimension table? This is not common and could require a significant change to Oracle BI Applications. Fortunately, all fact tables are implemented at the lowest possible grain to avoid this scenario. Before you do change the granularity of a fact table, ensure you understand the rationale. As we have said before, users will find a need to analyze data at the lowest level at which it is stored in the OLTP.

- Are you adding dimension or fact tables? This is normal; you should reuse existing dimensions when adding facts, and you can add new dimensions for your new facts.

- Are you adding new data sources? In this case, you need to build your own ETL to populate the staging tables or flat files that can be loaded to the staging tables (CSV file specifications with prebuilt ETL is the Universal Adaptor concept). The staging area is mostly source agnostic (a handful of source-specific temp tables exist), and then the prebuilt ETL and BI tool semantic layer handles the rest.

- Best practices are documented for making changes to protect you for upgrades down the road.

I Already Have OBIEE, So Why Do I Need a BI Application?

OBIEE is a tool—a front end to a data warehouse. BI Applications, on the other hand, comprise a prebuilt data warehouse that can be extended with custom content, and they use OBIEE as the front-end tool.

NOTE
BI Publisher (BIP) is part of OBIEE, and can also be used standalone for transactional reporting, making it a highly versatile formatted reporting tool.

Figure 2-15 doesn't do justice to the amount of prebuilt content available in each of the four boxes; however, it does attempt to clarify the mix of technology

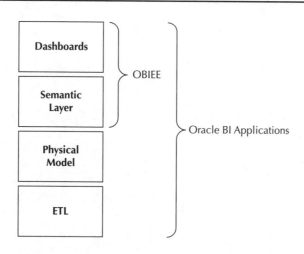

FIGURE 2-15. *OBIEE Versus BI Applications*

and content provided out of the box with the BI Applications. For example, the ETL box is Informatica with prebuilt ETL mappings; the physical model could be an Oracle database with predesigned physical tables. The OBIEE layer also contains prebuilt metrics and dashboards, not just a blank slate.

Conclusion

Why Oracle BI Applications? This may be obvious, but it still needs to be said: Oracle knows Oracle better than anyone else. Oracle engineers work together to ensure the best possible architecture is in place to extract from Oracle Applications, to leverage the Oracle Database, and to maximize the use of Oracle-engineered systems such as Exalytics and Exadata. Oracle has made significant investments into the BI Applications over the years, taking them way beyond the initial versions.

Consider the importance of the BI Applications, with the role they now play in Oracle's Fusion Applications. Business Intelligence was a consideration for every business process built into Fusion Applications. It's now part of the DNA. Currently, thousands of customers are in production, which shows the value for customers and the commitment by Oracle to continuously invest. This book doesn't assume BI Applications are a fit for you, but rather provides the tools you need to decide for yourself.

CHAPTER
3

Oracle BI Applications
Architecture

Whenever we're asked to explain the Oracle BI Applications architecture in detail, it can take three hours or longer to walk through the layers and pieces. Typically, there's an interactive show-and-tell session to keep the audience engaged. The more comfortable one becomes with the various components, the easier it becomes to lay things out in a reasonable manner. Whenever a customer asks for a proof of concept (POC), very often it's (at least initially) because they don't know the technical details of Oracle BI Applications. Oracle encourages this half-day technical walkthrough prior to any POC discussions.

This chapter walks you through the end-to-end stack, starting with the dashboard available to end users and ending at the back-end data source. We'll cover the key tools you'll need to manage your environment, including the following:

- Your web browser for OBIEE

- The OBIEE Admin Tool

- The DAC (a Java-based application built in the Siebel days)

- Informatica PowerCenter Designer

If you're an IT resource, then understanding this chapter is mandatory to properly evaluate this solution. If you're more of a functional resource, feel free to skim through this chapter and focus more on the following chapters.

If you're already a seasoned data warehouse practitioner, this chapter should feel very comfortable and familiar to you. In fact, you may experience an "I wish I had time to design and build that" moment when thinking about past projects. If you're new to data warehousing, this may be a bit disorienting to you. Please keep in mind that if you compare Oracle BI Applications to industry best practices (influenced by Ralph Kimball), you'll find that Oracle is simply delivering what has proven to be successful over a matter of decades by countless companies around the world. It's not that the development is special or proprietary; it's that you have an opportunity to leverage the hard work of hundreds of developers before you.

Oracle BI Applications can be thought of as a "clear box" and not a "black box." Once you've made your purchase of one or more BI Applications, you can modify any or all components and have full access to everything Oracle has built from a metadata perspective. Of course, you'll want to follow best practices for modifications, which we describe in Chapter 14, to allow for smoother upgrades in the future.

OBIEE Dashboard

Let's start with what an end user sees: an Oracle Business Intelligence
Enterprise Edition (OBIEE) dashboard (see Figure 3-1), which is part of the
Oracle BI Foundation Suite license. Whether a dashboard is built by an
end user or an IT resource, the functionality is the same for both types of

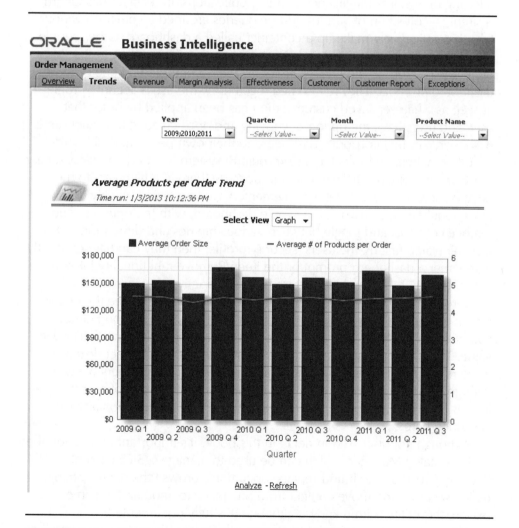

FIGURE 3-1.   *Top-left corner of an OBIEE dashboard*

users. Although many dashboards are provided out of the box, you can expect to quickly build your own as appropriate for the various roles within your organization. Ideally, power users would design and build an initial shared corporate dashboard, and then IT would operationalize it to make it more dynamic, ensure it follows standards and best practices, and validate performance.

Although it's normal to constantly use the dirty word "reports" when referring to Business Intelligence and BI Applications, in reality a dashboard is simply a collection of various ad-hoc queries grouped together on various tabs that collectively make up a container called a dashboard. Other people refer to these queries, graphs, or reports as "portlets," a term we prefer. Most often one or more of the queries are collectively controlled by one or more dashboard prompts. They're also tied together by the user's security profile as well as whatever saved customization has been applied by or for that user. End users have the option of copying and/or re-creating the exact same dashboards from a corporate dashboard to their own personal dashboards.

Often, when we look at a custom-built BI system, we find countless similar reports. Someone has to maintain and upgrade them at a high cost to the organization. We (and systems implementers we know) will quickly distill those requirements down into a simple dashboard, with the option to add/ remove columns, and toggle between various metrics and dimensions. Data is manipulated first by the users' security profile; then they can filter on the fly with either a dashboard prompt or the Keep/Remove functionality introduced with OBIEE 11.1.1.6. Dashboards are highly interactive; for example, with Master/Detail linking, you can click slices of a pie graph and see the details for each slice in a table beside the graph. With the OBIEE Action Framework, you have full control over what happens when a user clicks a particular data value. Thus, a single tab of a dashboard could theoretically meet dozens or more report requirements. In fact, when implementation partners we work with go into a client, they typically can condense the volume of reports by at least 80 percent, and often over 90 percent by using the functionality we have described here.

Although not discussed in detail in this book, it's important to mention the OBIEE Catalog Manager, which can be used to manage OBIEE content by IT. You can perform search-and-replace operations, browse the entire catalog, define security, and move content from one place to another. For some reason, this utility is little known although it is fully documented.

Ideally, as your organization matures with Oracle BI Applications, you'll go far beyond simple disconnected dashboard tabs. A good design, for example, will start with a summarized overview tab, with careful consideration to the various drill and navigation paths to more detailed content. Thought should be put into why you're presenting the data to which users. For example, the Kaplan Norton Score Scorecard methodology uses the concept of not showing data to users unless they can effect change. The same can apply here.

One approach worth considering is to design a dashboard first on a whiteboard, mapping out a flow chart of the user experience. This can help link the overall company objectives to the specific metrics the end user is responsible for managing to the specific root causes driving those metrics to the specific actions they can take. Revenue is down? Is it due to an increase in backlogs? Where the backlogs are, what's causing them, and what actions can you take can all drive the overall purpose, scope, and design of the dashboard. This is better than the common approach of "give me as many attributes as you can, so I can download to Excel." An example is provided in Figure 3-2 for how you can apply this to Project Analytics. The use of

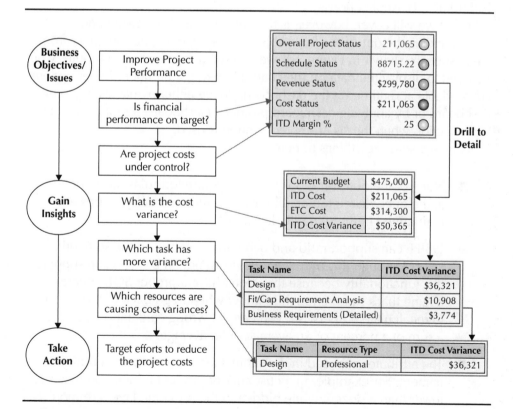

FIGURE 3-2. *Analytic workflows: a better way to design dashboards*

dashboards linked in this manner, rather than using Excel, helps standardize the paths users employ to analyze problems, thus leading to more predictable results. Their use can also help avoid the many problems we have described when Excel is used as a data analysis tool, problems such as the lack of consistency of calculations and lack of auditability of the data in the analysis.

OBIEE Ad-hoc Queries

From the dashboard, you can open each of the underlying queries to look at how they've been set up and designed. We're not going to drill into the specific steps for how to create charts, pivot tables, and other types of views. That's well covered in Rittman Mead's book on OBIEE 11g and through Oracle University Training. When presenting this content to a customer, we might have a side breakout session that covers the basics of OBIEE. We try not to confuse how OBIEE works with the prebuilt OBIEE content delivered with Oracle BI Applications.

What we will cover, however, is the importance of reviewing and understanding the out-of-the-box subject areas. Opening up the query from the dashboard shown in Figure 3-1, we can see that only three attributes were required to display the data on the chart. However, a number of filter options are available at runtime on the dashboard, driven either by navigating to the dashboard or by applying dashboard prompts. Dashboard prompts talk to the filters section when the "is prompted" option is used.

Here are some key things to note:

- None of the out-of-the-box queries require formulas hard-coded at the query level; rather, all business rules and calculations are maintained in the semantic layer.

- OBIEE can support ratio and percentage metrics in the semantic layer. Although this may seem obvious, not all BI tools can support this functionality because they don't have a proper SQL generation engine that's smart enough to know when to go back to the database to recalculate. Otherwise, you can get wrong calculations, such as a sum of a percent or an average of an average.

- The attributes exposed in the subject areas are only the tip of the iceberg. For example, in a customer or product folder, you may see fewer than a dozen, while hidden in the semantic layer are more than a hundred. It's a drag-and-drop exercise to expose for end users as required.

■ Most likely you'll end up creating your own subject areas or customizing the out-of-the-box ones. Make sure, however, you don't mix measures with incompatible dimensions, or you'll set up your end users for frustration and confusion.

■ You can also have reusable shared filters that are dynamic (for example, "current month" or "rolling three quarters") and allow you to refresh your content without having to manually specify new filters each month. This is especially useful when using the BI Office plug-in (prior to OBIEE 11.1.1.7, where Smartview is replacing the BI Office plug-in). If you do hard-code filters, this would likely be a personal version of a corporate report that you can save in your own folder.

Keep in mind that when people historically think about creating a report, it reinvents some sort of wheel, with embedded programming and a multimonth project required to define, test, and deploy. This is often due to developers trying to do too much in one report, getting data directly from the source without storing and transforming the data into physical structures along the way. The better way is to leverage a data warehouse with raw data, some transformations, aggregations, and so on, and then leverage a semantic layer that translates the physical structures, table joins, business rules and calculations, and so on, into a format end users can understand. This way, when it comes time to develop a new "report," all that's really left to do is to drag and drop the attributes that need to be viewed, assuming those attributes have been exposed for you, of course.

You can see from Figure 3-3 that creating an ad-hoc query doesn't require an end user to know where the data is coming from, how to calculate the metric, or even how to combine both order-line and invoice-line transactions into a single query. If you want to extend or modify the out-of-the-box queries, all you have to do is to edit the query and add the columns from the subject area you require. This doesn't need to be an IT function, unless you want IT to approve your change before sharing with the rest of your company on a corporate dashboard. Alternatively, you can make the change and save it to your local folder or to a shared team folder (for example, a department or small project team).

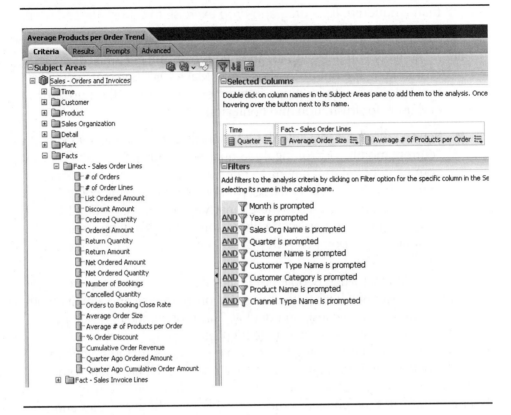

FIGURE 3-3. *Example of a typical report (ad-hoc) query*

OBIEE and the Semantic Layer

Both the OBIEE server and the supporting semantic layer (often referred to as the "RPD" file) are large parts of why OBIEE has a relatively low total cost of ownership (TCO) and high performance. The semantic layer is much "thicker" than with other BI tools and has layers: the Presentation layer, the Business Model and Mapping layer, and the Physical layer. Each has a series of configurations required to allow OBIEE to dynamically generate the SQL (or other) code to acquire the data requested by the end user in the most efficient manner. Figure 3-4 shows the three layers in the context of the same dashboard, query, and subject area as earlier.

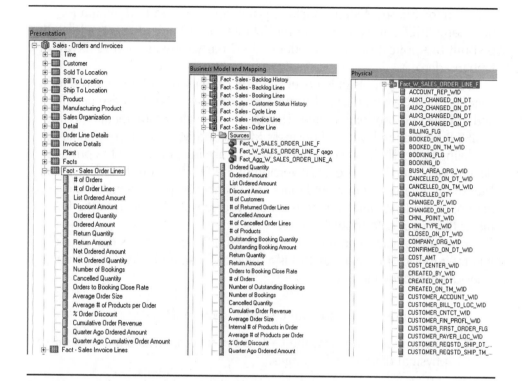

FIGURE 3-4.   *The OBIEE Admin Tool—mapping logical to physical*

Let's walk through each of the three layers in detail. Although it's beyond the scope of this book to discuss everything in detail, we'll highlight the key areas relevant to Oracle BI Applications. Figure 3-4 highlights a difference between OBIEE and the BI Applications. With the BI Applications you get prebuilt content. With OBIEE, you start with a blank slate. It's worthwhile spending time either on your own or with an Oracle pre-sales representative walking through various areas of the prebuilt content to develop a level of familiarity with both the logical and physical models.

Physical Layer

The Physical layer is where you can import tables and views, create aliases, and specify joins. The standard design for the prebuilt BI Application content is to create an alias for each physical table and to specify the joins between the aliases. Often a sticking point comes up around integration between OBIEE and various data-modeling tools. Oracle doesn't publish the prebuilt BI Applications data model in third-party formats such as ERwin or Embarcadero.

Data-modeling tools only cover a subset of what would be required to generate a full semantic layer because they represent the database perspective and not the end-user experience. There's no equivalent functionality to the OBIEE Presentation layer and Business Model and Mapping layer in data-modeling tools. The best you could hope for are integrations at the physical data model layer. With the latest version of the DAC (covered in more detail later in this chapter), you would make the changes to your prebuilt table designs in the DAC and forward engineer your physical DDL from the DAC rather than your data-modeling tool.

Some customers try to reverse engineer the BI Applications data model into their BI tool, but in a way this is a futile exercise and adds little value. Consider the following points:

- The content is already built, so why rebuild it?

- As mentioned already, the DAC is the recommended place to make physical data model changes.

- OBIEE allows you to isolate specific physical and logical star schemas (facts and conformed dimensions). If you need to print off the data model, OBIEE now supports this functionality. Figure 3-5 shows how you can browse the physical data model in the Physical layer of the Oracle BI Administration tool, selecting specific tables to view.

- Finally, the physical data model is so large and comprehensive, you'll quickly find yourself drowning if you try to reverse engineer it. That being said, you can export your OBIEE semantic layer to XML if you choose to go down this path.

    Also, if you do reverse engineer the data model, you will probably have to upgrade it if users want functionality Oracle provides in a future release. One buys an application to take advantage of the vendor's knowledge.

There aren't any specific BI Applications best practices you need to follow when working with the Physical layer—it's the same as any other

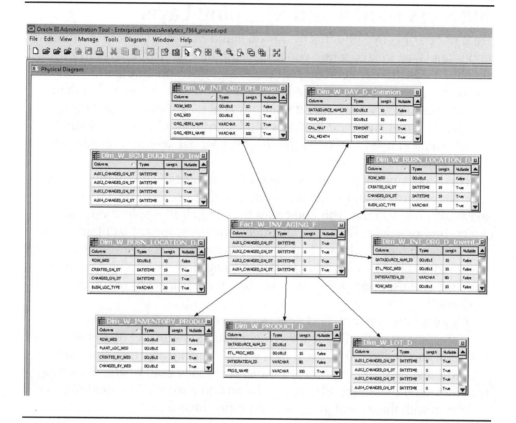

FIGURE 3-5.   *Viewing the BI Applications data model in the OBIEE Admin Tool*

BI Application, whether built from scratch or prebuilt. You use a separate connection pool for initialization blocks, for example, and manage your connection pool the same as you would with any data warehouse content and access. Note that due to the tenure of the BI Applications, some of the tables are deprecated and many of the tables you may never use. Past customers have been supported over the years as the data model has matured and evolved—Oracle historically doesn't usually remove RPD and physical content but rather modifies and adds content. This way, during your upgrade you can migrate from the old to the new more easily.

Business Model and Mapping Layer

From our perspective, the Business Model and Mapping layer is the most important layer. In fact, when you're developing a semantic layer from scratch, it's recommended you start development in the middle to ensure you're designing a user interface based on user requirements rather than the way your data is designed. If your physical data model is well designed, then the Physical layer and Business Model layer should look very similar. Otherwise, you need to rely on the Business Model layer to compensate for a poor physical data model.

The important thing to stress is that this is a logical view of the data, in a format end users can review and understand. It needs to be a pure (non-snowflake) star schema. The content of the prebuilt BI Applications follows design best practices, with logical dimension tables, logical fact tables, and logical hierarchies. Each fact and dimension has the grain (or dimensionality) identified to allow for dynamic aggregate navigation. Hierarchies are used to define end-user drill paths and level-based measures (for example, sales by district).

All joins between facts and dimensions are logical because the physical joins are defined in the Physical layer. No outer joins are set up because this has been handled in the physical data model. Specifically, there's a dummy seeded "unknown" record on each dimension that would be the default key on a fact table should the ETL lookup fail to find a match. The cardinality is defined with the logical joins, and this differentiates for OBIEE which table is a dimension and which is a fact. Each logical table has one or more logical table sources, mapped to one or more physical tables. Snowflakes are represented by a single logical table source, unless one of the tables in the snowflakes is connected directly to an aggregate, in which case you would see the same table referenced on its own in another logical table source. Priority levels can be assigned to logical tables, to nudge aggregate navigation one way or another where row counts are similar between fact tables.

The change from physical to business names occurs in the Business Model and Mapping layer. Security filters from a row-level data perspective are also applied here. The logical keys for each dimension are identified. Aggregation rules for each metric are defined, as are any calculations and business rules. In some cases, you may have layers of calculations either at the logical level or physical level. For example, if you need to generate a formula applied at run time to the database, such as a case statement in your physical SQL, you would apply this formula in your logical table source. If this is an OLAP-style calculation, such as dividing sales for a sales rep by sales for the district, you would define this in the metric definition. You may need a combination of both and layers of derived metrics, depending on your requirements.

Time series metrics need a special discussion for you to understand how they're handled out of the box and what your various options are. There's an "old-school" method and a simple method. Oracle BI Applications use the old-school method, partly for legacy reasons, but mostly for better SQL generation and performance. The simple method is to use the built-in time series functions for calculating "today" and "ago" type of metrics (month ago, month to date, month to date at the same time last month, and so on). This is easy to set up; however, the SQL generated needs to be verbose against the database, meaning you might see pages and pages of physical SQL that could otherwise be eliminated with a minor data model enhancement used to support the old-school method.

The old-school method ensures you have special columns added to your date dimension table and aggregates, specifically MAGO (month ago), QAGO (quarter ago), and so on. You can then alias your fact table and join it to the "ago" columns rather than the columns for the current day, month, quarter, and so on. The metrics from the aliased fact table can then be labeled according to the type of "ago" column it's joined to. This is well covered in OBIEE Data Warehouse Developer (Admin Tool) Training offered by Oracle University.

Presentation Layer

The Presentation layer is simply a logical representation of how you want to present slices of your data model to end users. As mentioned earlier, you don't want to mix metrics with incompatible dimensions into one subject area. Instead, you can deploy detailed presentation layers specific to a fact table representing a transaction type (order lines, invoice lines, purchase orders, and so on), alongside dimensions unique to that fact table.

You can then have a separate subject area that spans across multiple fact tables (transaction types) with a subset of dimensions common to each of the facts. Don't create an "everything-by-everything" subject area for IT for dashboard development and ad-hoc subject areas for end users. This erodes your ability to have collaboration between IT and business users. As mentioned earlier, you'll most likely end up creating your own subject areas, which is an intuitive drag-and-drop exercise.

Here's a list of some of the less obvious functionality available but important-to-be-aware-of configurations (some prebuilt, some optional):

- **Security setup**   You can define a data-driven business rule to determine whether the subject area is hidden (dynamically), and you can define security rules for access based on application roles.

- **Sort columns**   When you need a specific sort not based on the alphabet (for example, months or days of a week), you can point an object to an ID column to define the sort; however, you must make sure the sort column is the same or higher grain as your display column.

- **Descriptor columns**   These help eliminate the need for indexes on description fields and allow end users to filter on descriptions rather than codes in an ad-hoc manner. They also allow descriptions to be changed without filters breaking.

- **Implicit fact column**   When querying the relationship or association between two dimensions without specifying a fact table, you can force OBIEE to choose which logical fact table to go through to find that association.

- **Child presentation tables (new in OBIEE 11.1.1.6.2)**   Originally you could specify a naming convention such as "- Customer" in the Admin Tool to tell OBIEE to treat a folder as a subfolder. However, if you wanted to move folders around and change levels, your reports would break. Then the option to put "->" in the attribute description became available. Aside from other limitations, you couldn't have more than one level of folder nesting. With OBIEE 11.1.1.6.2, you can now define multiple nested subfolders formally, thus insulating yourself from changes and maintenance tasks down the road.

- **Aliases**   Every time you make a name change, an alias is automatically created to provide a level of insulation against breaking reports. Ideally, you should update your OBIEE catalog to stay in sync when you rename objects as well as remove aliases as soon as you can, to keep things clean. Although there are advantages to having file-based metadata (such as performance), this isn't one of them. It's best to finalize a subject area design before doing much dashboard development.

■ **Language translation**   If you require a multilanguage deployment, you can follow best practices to link your Presentation layer objects to a translation table, where the language displayed is linked to a user's profile. You can do similar translations at the dashboard level as well.

■ **Presentation hierarchies**   Each hierarchy can be displayed either as individual columns in your subject area and as a single presentation hierarchy column. For example, if you want to drill from year to quarter to month to day in a single column, you can expose a presentation hierarchy. This was adopted and prebuilt starting with BI Applications 7.9.6.3.

Whenever we're asked the question, "Can I use my existing (non-OBIEE) BI tool," the technical answer is "yes." However, in reality (license issues aside), an estimated 60 percent or more of the metrics provided out of the box are derived in the Business Modeling and Mapping layer. They are not stored in the data warehouse. Don't underestimate the amount of prebuilt content in the semantic layer. It would be a daunting task to re-create this from scratch using another BI tool.

OBIEE is exposed as an ODBC data source, essentially as a virtual data warehouse, and most BI tools can query the OBIEE server and the semantic layer directly. Although this sounds good in theory, you still need to maintain two semantic layers and pay for multiple BI tool licenses. The cost justification doesn't work out. It's easier and cheaper to train users on OBIEE in most cases.

When initially reviewing the out-of-the-box subject areas, don't be discouraged if you're initially underwhelmed. Not to worry: Many more attributes are available out of the box in the Business Model and Mapping layer. Adding more fields from the Business Model to the Presentation layer is part of any implementation.

DAC: Execution Plan and Dependencies

DAC stands for Data (Warehouse) Administration Console. It's not pretty, but it is valuable and a critical component of Oracle BI Applications. It can take a bit of time to understand the purpose of the DAC, for those with experience scheduling ETL jobs manually. We'll cover enough information to make you comfortable with what it is and why you might need it.

Informatica is data aware, but not application aware. For example, if you want to dynamically create an execution plan for a specific slice of the BI Applications (for example, inventory transactions), the DAC will automatically know all the steps and the sequence required for an end-to-end load that includes aggregate and index management. With a few mouse clicks, you can generate the entire plan and execute it.

Figures 3-6 and 3-7 give you a flavor of what the interface looks like. The three main sections are Design (of the data warehouse), Setup (of the DAC and integration points), and Execution (of the ETL).

The DAC's role is essentially to manage the life cycle of a data warehouse. With it, you can create and upgrade your BI Applications schemas, define your high-level ETL logic via a semantic layer, and run and monitor the ETL process. Whereas Informatica is configured, designed, and set up to populate individual tables, the DAC defines how to load one or more star schemas. When running and monitoring ETL jobs, the DAC coordinates what gets run, and when, using the pmcmd and pmrep APIs from Informatica. The restartability functionality allows you to fix a problem and restart where you

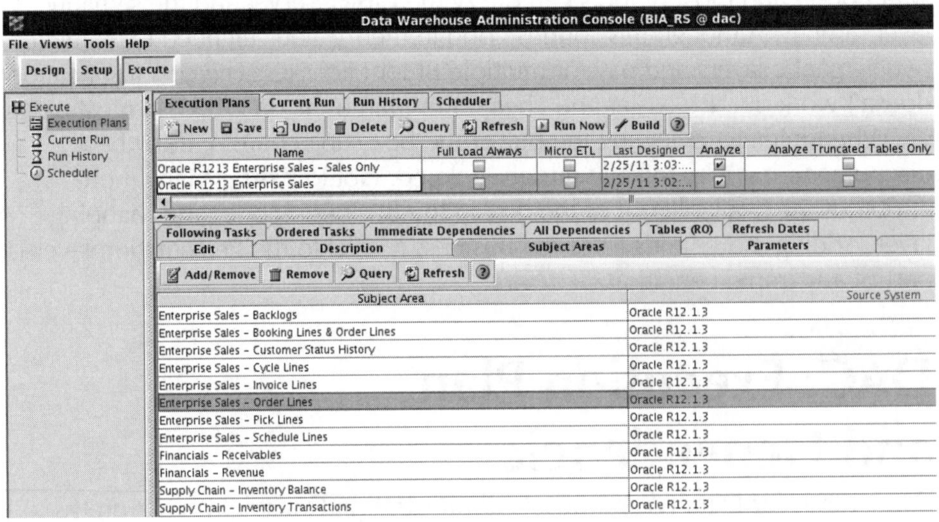

FIGURE 3-6. *DAC execution plans by subject areas*

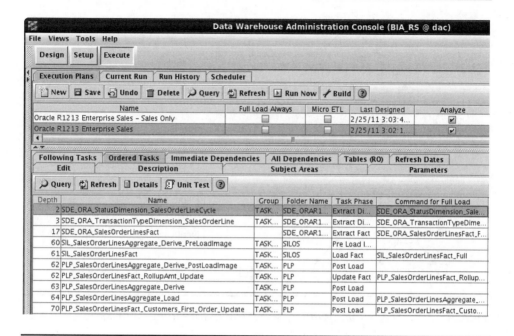

FIGURE 3-7. *DAC ordered tasks within an execution plan*

left off. It also manages indexes and analyzes tables. The DAC also generates session logs used to support Informatica logs. Figure 3-8 illustrates how the DAC can dynamically queue multiple tasks based on dependencies defined in the metadata.

The DAC provides an application-aware metadata (semantic) layer over and above what's provided with Informatica. The specifics are illustrated in Figure 3-9, and described below:

- **Containers/adaptors** Partitions specific to each version of each supported data source.

- **Tables** Schema details, relationships, and ETL indexes versus end-user query indexes.

- **Tasks** Source versus target tables, full versus incremental commands and parameters, and phases of an end-to-end ETL load.

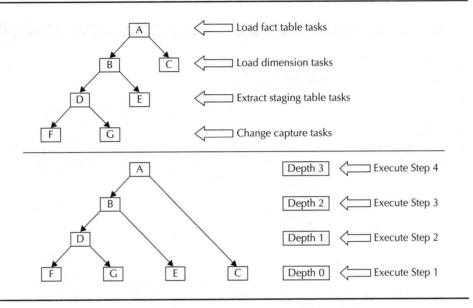

FIGURE 3-8. *Dynamic queuing and parallel threading of tasks*

- **Schedules** You may want to load payroll every two weeks, for example, but load everything else on a daily basis.

- **Subject areas** Defined by one or more star schemas, driven by fact tables. An understanding of the tasks required to populate a group of tables that make up a specific application and what the dependencies are between those tasks.

- **Execution plans** Combines one or more subject areas from one or more containers; assembles a collection of ordered tasks based on application requirements and hardware constraints.

The DAC has well-defined incremental extract and load strategies, by maintaining refresh dates of all the tables touched by the ETL process. The same execution plan is used for both the initial and incremental runs, and the

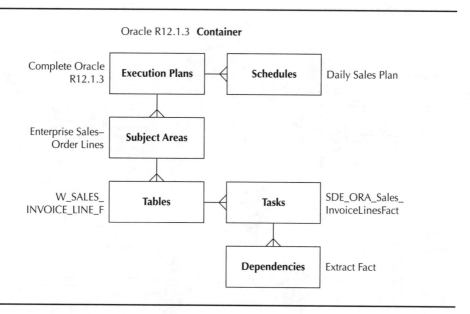

FIGURE 3-9. *DAC metadata and sample values*

table refresh dates (or lack thereof) are used to issue a full load or incremental load command. The first time the ETL is run, all tasks are run in full mode, because there are no refresh dates. At the end of the load, the refresh dates for the source and target are updated by the DAC, within the DAC metadata repository. Should the ETL fail, even fail multiple times, the timestamp of the first attempt is maintained as the last refresh timestamp. Timestamps are adjusted to the local timestamp of the data source. Also, an override command forces a full load where required.

The logical DAC architecture is shown in Figure 3-10, showing the interactions between the DAC client and server, along with Informatica and the various database schemas.

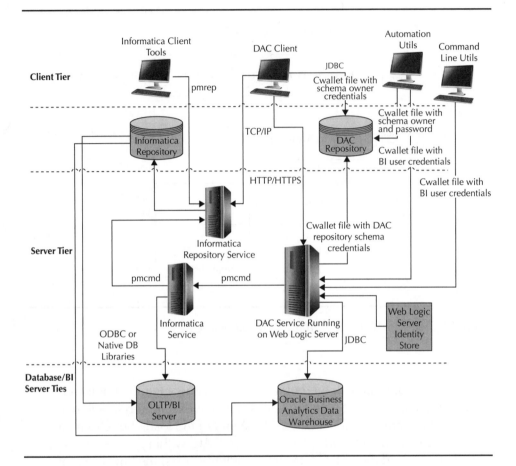

FIGURE 3-10. *DAC architecture in relation to the BI Applications*

Informatica: Mapping Walkthrough

Oracle is actively working on releasing an Oracle Data Integrator version of the Oracle BI Applications (other than version 7.9.7, meant only for SAP customers) while still supporting Informatica as an ETL tool delivered with prebuilt content. This is for customers who wish to deploy an all-Oracle solution. If you prefer Informatica, either because you already own this technology or because you feel you can better staff your project with Informatica resources, you can rest assured Informatica will continue to be supported for a very long time.

Depending on when you make your purchase, you may or may not have a choice of ETL tools. Because the ODI version is not yet available, and because the over 4,000 Oracle BI Applications customers today are using Informatica, this book only discusses how Informatica is used to prebuild content. Informatica provides an industry-leading ETL technology, and Oracle provides an OEM version through a reseller agreement with Informatica. This is for the core ERP and CRM BI Applications, and not the Edge BI Applications (for example, P6 Analytics, APCC, MOC, FTI, and so on).

Some customers chose to upgrade to full-use Informatica, called the Advanced Edition, to take advantage of all the added features; however, most do not. These "extras" include dynamic partitioning, full grid processing for HA (highly available) support, metadata management and services, and many others. The OEM version does include the team-based development option. In many ways, these additional options make sense if you're doing a significant amount of development, which is not likely to be the case with a Oracle BI Applications implementation. The Informatica OEM license combined with the DAC functionality is probably all you're going to require when fully deploying Oracle BI Applications.

The screenshots in this section walk you through some of the highlights you'd expect to see when digging into the prebuilt ETL. As an aside, customers and implementation partners can download a fully configured and installed Oracle virtual machine (VM) using Oracle Virtual Box that includes all the software components installed, along with source and target databases. This is for training and demonstration purposes only, and is the same environment used by Oracle pre-sales consultants for showing customers prebuilt content. This image can be downloaded from the Oracle Technology Network (OTN), or you can contact your Oracle BI representative for help in obtaining a copy of this image. Technically, it was released for partners, but customers are entitled to it as well.

Using the Informatica PowerCenter Designer client, you can scroll through the prebuilt content. What you'll notice are three main types of mappings: SDE (source-specific dependent extracts, one folder for each supported data source and one for the Universal Adapter), SIL (source-independent loads, agnostic to data source), and PLP (post-load processing, also source agnostic). Oracle BI Applications support both an initial full load and incremental loads run on demand when required. Some customers run the incremental load daily, some three times a day (follow the sun between North America, Europe, and Asia—at the end of each business day), and some more often (for example, at month end on an hourly basis). Generally speaking, the same mapping is used for both the initial and incremental load; the difference is in the parameters passed by the DAC.

Universal Adaptors

One of the SDE type of mappings is for what's called the *universal adaptors*—a fancy term for loading predefined flat files into the staging area. You would use these mappings if you have a mainframe data source, for example, and you would populate CSV files predefined by Oracle and provided as part of the software install. Generally speaking, these files map one to one to the staging area, and there's little or no transformation of the data because the goal is to simply load the data as quickly as possible into the target database. Most customers instead create their own custom SDE mappings for sources not covered by the BI Applications out of the box. For example, if you're loading something like Great Plains into Financial Analytics, it would make more sense to migrate data from one database to another without incurring the risk and maintenance of converting to and from flat files.

SDE Mappings

Oracle has invested time in understanding the best way to identify change capture detection within the supported source systems. Every source has a completely different strategy, whether JD Edwards, Siebel, PeopleSoft, or Oracle. On the roadmap is a plan to include Oracle Golden Gate for real-time replication for trickle feeding data into the BI Applications out of the box. This is an available option today, with some relatively minor customization described in the Oracle BI Applications Performance and Tuning Guide available at My Oracle Support. In the case of Siebel, change-capture tables and triggers on the Siebel side are used to capture changes. In the case of ERP, a SQL source qualifier is used, with parameters passed from the DAC during run time. In Figure 3-11, using an Oracle EBS R12.1.3 instance as an example, you can see the $$LAST_EXTRACT_DATE variable used to filter on the EBS LAST_UPDATE_DATE field.

Every EBS and JD Edwards (JDE) table should enforce a last update date column, to keep track of when data has been touched. In the case of PeopleSoft, most implementations have less than 10 percent of their tables with some sort of clear indicator. Therefore, business logic needs to be applied to the source qualifier and designed by Oracle on a case-by-case

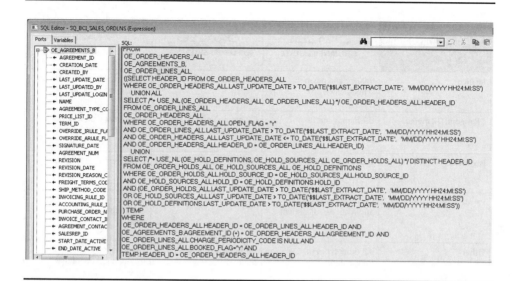

FIGURE 3-11. *SDE source qualifier, with parameters passed by DAC*

basis for each mapping. Siebel can handle source system triggers being applied, mainly due to CRM being smaller and simpler than ERP applications.

Figuring out how to detect changes in each source system is just the start. The next challenge the Oracle BI Applications handle is what to do when you're rationalizing transactions that are stored in different physical ways and use different naming conventions. Oracle BI Applications keep track of the source system codes for display as well as testing and data lineage, and also store the universal data warehouse version for display and aggregation purposes. Figure 3-12 provides a number of examples that the Oracle BI Applications handle and the resulting display code provided.

Questions often arise on the EBS side, such as "Should I index my last update field?" The answer is to look to the product documentation and check with Oracle support before doing so. Oracle has classified EBS tables into categories to define where you don't need to apply indexes, where you do need to apply indexes without affecting EBS negatively, and where you shouldn't apply indexes. You would only have this conversation during performance tuning activities, where you've identified a bottleneck. This is not part of the standard implementation, and only applies to customers with larger EBS implementations. Occasionally Oracle Engineering and Support

Standard Warehouse Code	ORACLE E-BUSINESS SUITE	ORACLE PEOPLESOFT ENTERPRISE	ORACLE JD EDWARDS ENTERPRISEONE
Invoice	Invoice and payment schedules	Invoice items	Document type RI, other user-defined document types
CR memo/DR memo	CR memo and DR memo	CR memo and DR memo items	Document type RM, other user-defined document types
Payments	Cash receipts and so on	Payments/deposits	Document type RC, RU
Payment applications	Cash/CR memo applications/adjustments	Payment item activities	Document type RB, other user-defined document types
Other	All other types of transactions	BI/AR: all other types of items	Document type R1, other user-defined document types

FIGURE 3-12. *How Oracle BI Applications map different source system transactions into a common format*

will rewrite the source SQL qualifier for your organization (via the Service Request process), to help you improve the performance of specific mappings, rather than applying an index on the source side.

The Informatica mappings are highly parameterized, to help you use as many as possible out of the box. When you make changes, hopefully it's only to add descriptive flex fields. This parameterization makes upgrades simpler. If you do have to open an Informatica mapping and make a change, for example, you'll need to save to a custom folder. You then need to register this new mapping in the DAC. When it's time for an upgrade, you'll need to review the changes you've made in this customized mapping. This is why you'll see parameters in the source qualifier (identified with $$) as well as the use of domain values via flat files for lookups and cross references. During the implementation, you'll be presented with a number of domain value files that need to be fully populated. This not only helps dynamically drive the Informatica mappings, but also allows for harmonization of values when viewing content in OBIEE. Figure 3-13 shows an example of this, in the context of extracting and displaying AR transactions.

ORACLE PEOPLESOFT ENTERPRISE			ORACLE E-BUSINESS SUITE		
TYPE CODE	TYPE_DESC	WAREHOUSE CODE	TYPE CODE	TYPE_DESC	WAREHOUSE CODE
REG, PPAY, IN	Invoice items	Invoice	Invoice	Invoice	Invoice
CR	CR memo items	Credit memo	Contra	Contra	Invoice
DR	DR memo items	Debit memo	Credit memo	Credit memo	Credit memo
PY, AO, AU	Payment item activities	Payment applications	On-account credit	On-account credit	Credit memo
Other	Other miscellaneous invoice types	Other	Debit memo	Debit memo	Debit memo
			Debit note	Debit note	Debit memo

FIGURE 3-13.   *Oracle PeopleSoft versus Oracle EBS domain values*

For the most part, the staging area is source agnostic, and all staging tables are truncated at the beginning of each ETL load. There are exceptions to the persistence of data (with some HR Analytics tables, for example). There are also some source-specific temporary tables used prior to loading the final source-agnostic staging tables. Each row contains important metadata to maintain lineage back to the source, including the natural keys (source system keys) concatenated by a tilde (~) symbol, source system IDs, ETL run identifiers, and others. This is important to understand, to fully realize how Oracle BI Applications support multiple data sources out of the box.

The staging area was designed to handle a wide range of data types and lengths, for example. Custom BI Applications often break when you add a second or third data source, when developers realize how source specific the first design was. In the custom scenario, there could be lots of data model changes—in one source a customer identifier could be numeric but in the second source it could be alphanumeric. An example of a benefit is how the data lineage and joins work with the Integration ID column. This universally used alphanumeric single column keeps track of the keys from the source system and is used for joins in the staging area before the formal data warehouse keys are generated, irrespective of the source. This also helps in debugging the final data warehouse. If a value is suspect, this can help determine exactly where it came from in the source system.

A key piece of architectural design to be aware of is the X_CUSTOM field on every Oracle BI Applications table. It provides a pathway you can follow when adding fields to existing prebuilt tables. The beauty of this design is the separation of extension fields used as a "passthrough" and not involved in transformation logic. Figure 3-14 shows an example of a transformation object that isolates extensions, for ease of implementation and insulation from upgrades down the road. The other reusable transformations can be overwritten in this example, and you would preserve your extensions.

Something custom BI Application implementations tend to miss out on is the time to properly design and implement reusable and shareable Informatica transformations and mapplets within the ETL. Oracle BI Applications make extensive use of mapplets and reusable transformations such as dimensional lookups. In Figure 3-15, a mapplet is used to capture and stamp the currency conversion rates (to allow for the toggling between global, document, and local amounts). This is shared extensively across multiple mappings, thus minimizing maintenance and upgrade effort.

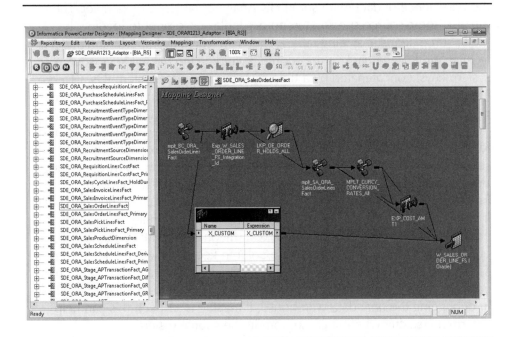

FIGURE 3-14. *Source-dependent extract (SDE) example*

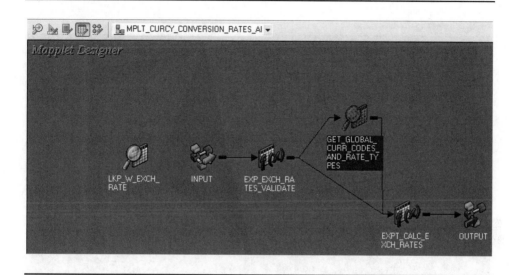

FIGURE 3-15. *A shared and reusable mapplet within SDE mapping*

SIL Mappings

Once the staging table is loaded using the SDE mappings, then the SIL mappings are run to populate the BI Applications data warehouse. Dimensions are loaded first, then fact tables, then aggregates. This is to establish and maintain referential integrity. Slowly changing dimensions are supported via configuration. Keys are generated and used to link fact and dimension tables, rather than the original source system keys. "Upsert" strategies are applied, so logic is in place to tell Informatica to either update existing records or insert new records.

Figure 3-16 shows an example of a Sales Order Line fact table being populated. A large number of dimension tables are linked to the fact staging table. The records that have already been processed from the staging table are tracked in case the ETL needs to restart. Currency conversions are stamped. If a matching record isn't found in a dimension table, a default "unknown" value is stamped on the key, so records aren't orphaned and OBIEE won't be required to generate outer joins anywhere. This practice also ensures that if control totals are used to verify that all records from the source were loaded into the data warehouse, the control totals will match.

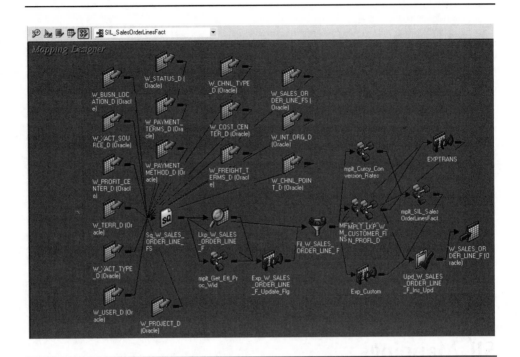

FIGURE 3-16. *Source-independent load (SIL) mapping*

Restartability of SIL mappings is a very important piece of architecture, for both obvious and not-so-obvious reasons. Aside from the obvious of an operator not having to restart an ETL load from scratch if you run out of temp space (for example, in a production environment), even more time is saved in the actual implementation. It's common for ETL jobs to fail or have to be rerun for repeated full/initial loads during an implementation as domain files are being populated, parameters are being set for filters, source system cleanups occur, source system updates to hierarchies are made, and so on.

If each load takes five hours, for example (remember, this is the initial load of all history), and you experience three failures during a load, you could lose two to three days of project time. This can quickly add up. It's the paper cuts that can kill you on custom BI implementations; this is a good example of where you'll benefit from prebuilt architecture. You wouldn't have the time, budget, or scope to enforce restartability in a custom-built environment.

In a production environment, if you have a failure in the middle of a fact table being loaded, it can get messy if you don't have restartability. Either you would need to figure out how to surgically back out the records you've already loaded or more likely you would need to restore a backup and then restart the complete load. This is why there's no restartability on SDE tables—they're always truncated and reloaded anyways, so the impact of a load failure is minimized.

As data is loaded into the target tables at each step along the way, bulk loaders are used for the initial load because indexes can be dropped anyways. You can configure the DAC to determine where and when indexes are either maintained or dropped. If, for example, you're increasing a table by more than 15 percent each time, it might make sense to drop and rebuild indexes. Best practices are covered in detail in both the documentation found on the OTN and in the "BI Applications Performance Recommendations" document available via your My Oracle Support website (Doc ID 870314.1).

PLP Mappings

PLP mappings are used for the final round of preparing the data for reporting, including the generation of aggregates, and any other type of cleanup jobs required. Aggregates include not only summary tables, but snapshots such as AR/AP balances as well as cycle line facts such as sales order line (time) cycles.

Oracle SQL Developer: Physical Data Model

When reviewing the physical data model, you need to look at both the forest and the trees. At a granular level, you'll see a consistent approach to the table design with certain fields you can count on being present. At a higher level, you can see how those tables are interrelated into an enterprise data warehouse. In some ways, the data model is the most important piece of intellectual property within all the BI Application components.

When Simon Miller attended the original partner implementation training in April 2002, long before Siebel and then Oracle acquired the product, the entire data model was printed out on a wall and framed. It must have covered 35 square feet—and that was just the first-generation version. After the various implementation partners were witnessed furiously taking notes from this wall tapestry, it was quickly and quietly taken down and hidden from view. Today, the model is much larger; however, it's fully open for anyone with access to Oracle Support to review, either on their own or with Oracle. This book certainly can't cover the entire model, so we'll provide an introduction to get you started.

A commonly used tool during implementations is Oracle SQL Developer. Not only is it free, it has developed into a very mature technology over the years. You can use it to view the table structures and data, to issue SQL queries during testing, to apply indexes, and so on when your target is an Oracle database. If you're using other databases such as Teradata as your target, you would use what you already have (for example, Teradata SQL Assistant) for the same sort of purpose. Whereas the DAC can directly create and modify Oracle, DB2, and Microsoft SQL structures, you would generate a DDL script for Teradata and run it manually to create your tables. Figure 3-17 is a screenshot from Oracle SQL Developer.

The best way to review the physical data model is to use the OBIEE Admin Tool, remembering the joins are defined on the aliases of the physical tables. You can print off sections of the data model as required. In Figure 3-18, the

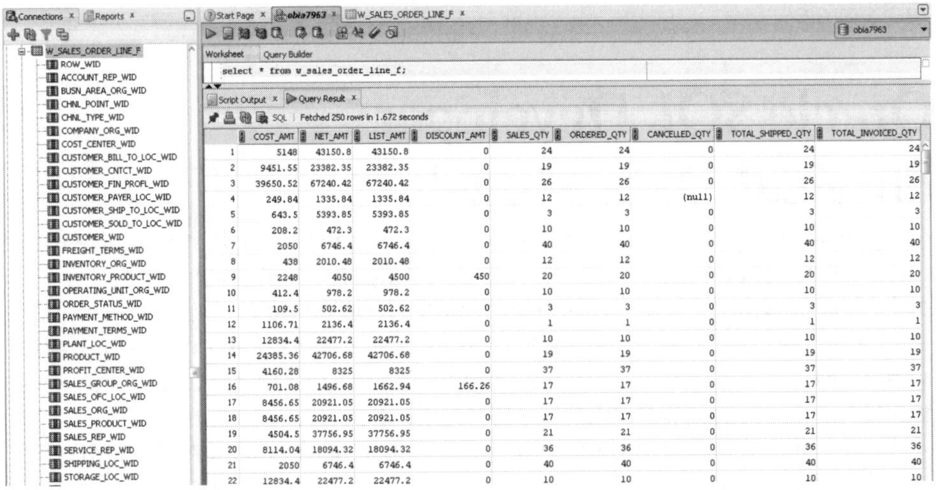

FIGURE 3-17. *Viewing a table and data (a tree) within Oracle SQL Developer*

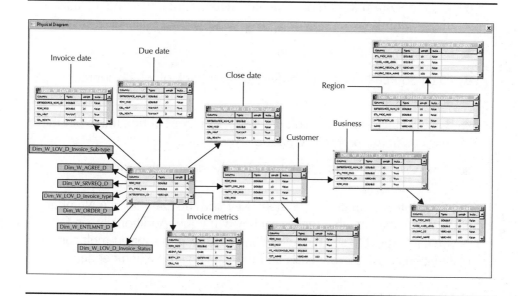

FIGURE 3-18. *Viewing part of the data model (the forest) using the OBIEE Admin Tool*

call-out labels highlight the key information provided in the tables and how they are related.

The BI Applications data model is for the most part a traditional Ralph Kimball–style star schema with some Inmon influences around the party/person model. There's minimal snowflaking. When snowflaking is used in the data model, it's to support multiple hierarchies with dimension helper tables. Some of the key fields you can expect to see on all tables include the following (logical names):

- Insert Date.

- Update Date.

- ETL Run Identifier, to keep track of which DAC execution plan last touched the record.

- Tenant Identifier, to support multitenant deployments.

- Source System Keys (concatenated with a tilde), forming a Data Integration Key.

- X Custom field for extensions.

- Data Source Number Identifier, to keep track of which source provided the data.

- Delete Flag, to identify soft deletes. (OBIEE out of box filters out these records in the prebuilt semantic layer.)

- Row WID (warehouse ID), to uniquely identify that row.

The Data Integration (Source System) Key and the Data Source Number Identifier are ultimately what makes each row unique. Additionally, on fact tables you can expect to see the following fields used to support multicurrency calculations on a row-by-row basis and then aggregated when needed:

- Document/Transaction Currency Code

- Local/Regional Reporting Currency Code

- Local Exchange Rate

- Global Exchange Rate (three of them, actually)

Although all metrics are stored in the document amount, the prebuilt OBIEE semantic layer multiplies the amount on the physical table by the Global 1 Exchange Rate and displays this in the out-of-the-box semantic layer. Project Analytics has an executive dashboard where a toggle is fully built out and delivered to show how end users can view their dashboards by various currencies on the fly. You can use this as a frame of reference for how to extend to other metrics. A detailed explanation is provided in Chapter 14.

Although other software vendors may claim to have a prebuilt BI Application comparable to what Oracle provides, all it takes is a couple of hours comparing both the data models and prebuilt semantic layers to see there's really no comparison in the depth and breadth of coverage. For example, one of the strengths of Oracle BI Applications is the types of fact tables provided:

- **Transactional facts** Standard type of fact tables (for example, invoice lines, purchase order lines, sales opportunities, employee events, and so on)

- **Snapshot facts**   For capturing a state from a point in time for trending purposes (for example, AR/AP balances and aging balances, inventory balances, employee daily snapshot, and so on)

- **Cycle lines facts**   For capturing the time it takes to go from one stage to another, usually across multiple fact tables (for example, from requisition to purchase order to receipt to supplier payment times and so on)

- **Aggregate facts**   Used primarily for performance (for example, order revenue per month instead of per day, where you would have one row per month rather than one row per day)

Multiple fiscal calendars across multiple source systems, ledgers, and operating units are all supported in the data model. BI Applications also support multiple adjustment periods in each fiscal calendar as well as support a project calendar as one of the calendars. Furthermore, you have the option of using generated calendars such as Gregorian, 4-4-5, 13 period, and 52 week. This has also been designed using snowflaking to support aggregations at various levels (for example, a fact table at a fiscal day level and a fact at a fiscal quarter level).

Improved party/person model support was introduced with BI Applications 7.9.6.x, to allow for both a customer and a supplier 360-degree view. Previously, suppliers and customers were in separate dimensions, and it was challenging to identify which customers were also suppliers, and vice versa. W_PARTY_D is a master dimension table used to store customer org/contact, customer person (B2C), prospects, suppliers, and competitors. This is linked to a table called W_PARTY_ORG_D for organizations and a table called W_PARTY_PER_D for persons. Customer accounts, however, are maintained as separate dimensions to track your financial relationships with your customers.

Review the subset of the data model shown in Figure 3-19 to see how you can perform cross-functional analysis between sales opportunities and orders with invoices using conformed (shared) dimensions. The larger data model set allows for many other fact tables to be linked via these common master dimensions.

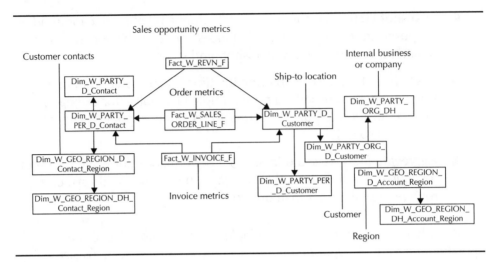

FIGURE 3-19. *Oracle BI Applications logical party model*

NOTE
In a traditional Inmon-influenced party model, you would have all parties regardless of whether or not you have any transactional history with them. With Oracle BI Applications, you'll only see the parties for which you have historical data, in the context of the transactions you're looking at. In other words, with the BI Applications, you select the transactions you want to see first and get the corresponding dimensions for those transactions.

What's New with DAC 11g

For those who are not familiar with the DAC and are starting with a fresh BI Applications 7.9.6.4 implementation, you can skip this section and refer to the earlier section that explains what the DAC is. If you are already familiar with the DAC and/or are planning an upgrade, this section will be important to you. Numerous significant improvements were made to the DAC between 10.x and 11*g*. These include the following (note that this is not the full list):

- Support for Fusion Middleware Security (optional).

- Enhanced index creation and management, including the following features:

    - Query indexes are created in parallel immediately following the creation of ETL-related indexes.

    - DAC notifies the successor tasks as soon as the ETL indexes have been created, allowing query indexes and additional unique indexes to be created sooner.

    - You can specify for one table or all tables within a DB connection how many indexes can be created in parallel.

- The ability to test an individual workflow.

- The ability to run execution plans concurrently (for example, from different sources at the same time). This is probably the most significant improvement, especially for customers pulling in data from more than one source system into the BI Applications.

- Support for running multiple instances of an execution plan concurrently.

- Time difference awareness between the source system database and the DAC server instance.

- New metadata patching support.

- The looping of workflows, which supports logical partitioning of the mappings for parallel execution (not limited to one reader and one writer thread).

- The ability to set up event-based delays (for example, from source systems indicating readiness for extraction).

- New heuristics to manage tasks, tables, and indexes. To optimize performance, you can use this intelligence to decide whether a task will run, whether tables are analyzed, and whether indexes are dropped and created.

- Integration of the DAC with ETL tools other than Informatica.

- DDL management, including the ability to modify individual tables and even upgrade the entire data warehouse.

- TimesTen database support, which is important in the context of an Exalytics deployment.

- EM Beans implementation, for providing an API for monitoring DAC activity and jobs (for example, running, failed, executed, and so on).

- The ability to migrate your DAC environment using Oracle Fusion Middleware movement scripts between Dev, Test, QA, Prod, and so on.

- The ability to hotfix failed tasks and then restart, without having to wait until all other tasks are finished running.

- The ability to export the logical model into CSV format.

- More granular event notifications.

Larger customers with multiple systems and complex environments will benefit significantly with the upgraded DAC. End-to-end ETL times should be much faster, along with development and implementation times. Early indications show customers can expect a 20-percent to 30-percent increase in performance for the initial load.

Security

The purpose of this book is not to outline how to set up security for your source system because this is well defined in the product documentation. What needs to be reviewed is the importance of properly scheduling security design and testing into your architecture and why. In a perfect world, you wouldn't need a separate security model for your data warehouse and your transactional systems; in reality, you do.

Every customer and implementation is different; it's nearly impossible to prebuild a "one size fits all" model. Therefore, don't get caught off guard with your project plan; you'll need a sizeable chunk of time (depending on your requirements and resource availability) to define requirements and design your approach. It's not the implementation time. It's figuring out what you need to design.

Security can be broken down into the following categories:

- Authentication. Ideally this is done via an existing single-sign-on mechanism.

- Authorization. Ideally OBIEE should be able to inherit groups and application role information so you don't require dual maintenance.

- What content users can see.

- Row-wise security (what filters are applied).

Security should never be put on a report or query level, but rather managed centrally at a semantic layer so when new reports and queries are created the security is automatically inherited. OBIEE uses a technique called initialization blocks that fires off a query when a user logs in and populates a session variable (for example, what application roles the user is assigned to in the source system). Application roles (formerly called groups) are used not only to drive the content of a filter or "where" clause on a SQL query, but also to determine if the user can see an object or content in the first place.

There are some wrinkles to be aware of. The three we'll discuss are legacy EBS Security, OBIEE login performance considerations, and BI Office limitations. EBS Security, even with R12.1.3, doesn't fully adopt Fusion Middleware Security and instead relies on a legacy security design for authentication and authorization. For those who know EBS, the specific reasons are twofold:

- You're not able to obtain from EBS the ICX session cookie after authenticating an SSO technology.

- You can't pass the ICX session cookie back to your SSO technology.

What you can do, however, is leverage Oracle Security Products such as Oracle Access Manager and Oracle Identity Manager, to eliminate the need for the ICX session cookie from EBS to be used by OBIEE.

NOTE
This is a limitation of EBS, not of OBIEE or the BI Applications. Please refer to "Overview of Single Sign-On Integration Options for Oracle E-Business Suite (Doc ID 1388152.1)" found on the My Oracle Support website.

The BI Office plug-in doesn't support a single-sign-on model, and even if it did you wouldn't be able to use it with EBS Native Authentication. Fortunately the BI Office Plug-in was replaced with Smartview, as of the OBIEE 11.1.1.7 release. Smartview supports SSO authentication. It's probably better to not use EBS Native Authentication Security; however, if you do, the setup is the same as for OBIEE 10g. Keep in mind you can still use initialization blocks to access the EBS FND_USERS table for authorization purposes. Plenty of online blogs discuss this in detail, for example, using an LDAP to store application roles rather than the EBS FND_USERS table. This is applicable for any OBIEE content, not just with the BI Applications.

OBIEE 11g supports deferred initialization blocks, meaning they'll only fire off when required (for example, when a user accesses a specific dashboard). This is a good thing; otherwise, you could have login performance issues waiting for a number of SQL queries to run. The wrinkle is that if you need something called a "row-wise" variable (meaning more than one value for a session variable), you can't defer this execution. Therefore, you need to be very strict and judicious in this design. Your options are as follows:

- You can obtain application roles via LDAP rather than initialization blocks.

- You'll most likely always need initialization blocks to determine row-level security (for example, what org, region, business, and such a user can see); therefore, you can restrict all row-wise session variables to a single generic model that all developers leverage.

Again, the detailed specifications of these various implementations are beyond the scope of this book; however, you can refer to Oracle product documentation, various blogs, and the Rittman Mead book on OBIEE 11g. You can also contact Oracle or your implementation provider for assistance in this area.

Upgrade Considerations

Every upgrade of Oracle BI Applications is unique, depending on what changes are required. For a sense of what to expect in the future, you can always review Oracle product documentation for past BI Application upgrades. Application upgrades are separate from technology upgrades. For example, you can upgrade OBIEE at any time and still be supported. You can upgrade to a certified version of Informatica, but keep in mind you need to perform the corresponding DAC upgrade at the same time because they're so tightly connected.

In some application upgrade cases, you'll be provided new DDL to modify tables (directly via the DAC, starting with DAC 11g and BI Applications 7.9.6.4). In other cases, there will be new or modified Informatica mappings.

There will always be a new OBIEE semantic layer with each release, along with an Informatica technology upgrade requirement. For a more detailed idea of what to expect during an Oracle BI Applications upgrade, you can always review the current "Upgrade Guide for Informatica PowerCenter Users" documentation; not every upgrade is the same, but you'll get the picture from what customers have had to do in the past. Generally speaking, an application (content) upgrade would follow the steps shown in Figure 3-20.

Migrating the OBIEE content follows the standard three-way merge functionality used by OBIEE for any development. Informatica content migrations can be trickier because no tools are available for comparing changes.

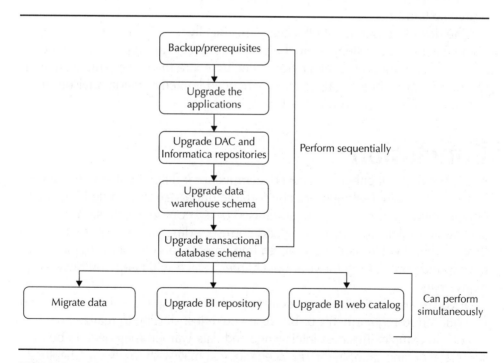

FIGURE 3-20. *General application upgrade content process*

Oracle has documented best practices in great depth on how to modify and customize your BI Applications. Make sure you follow them to make the upgrade as easy as possible. Some upgrades will be smooth; some won't be as smooth. You can be confident, however, that Oracle has put significant thought, engineering, and documentation into how you're going to migrate (we all fail if customers are left behind on old application versions).

Another scenario is when you upgrade your source system. The high-level consideration is turning off one source system adaptor and turning on the new adaptor. In reality, there's more to it than that because you need to think about what to do with your source system ID. In many cases, you would want to keep the same ID for your old and new source system; otherwise, Informatica will load all your master dimensional data again.

This won't result in wrong results on the dashboard but may create unnecessary overhead in performance and in the long term make it hard to seamlessly group transactions between your old and new ERP. If, for example, you change a supplier name in your new source system and want to see that name restated across all your reports, it would help if you have the same suppliers in the BI Applications shared between your old and new source system.

The downside is that data lineage—specifically which dimension came from which source system—could be tricky. This also assumes your source system keys, found in the integration ID column, are the same. This is an area where it's worthwhile engaging an experienced implementation advisor for formal recommendations on your best options.

Conclusion

At this point, you'll either be relieved, alarmed, or indifferent. If you're relieved, it's because you're feeling more comfortable understanding something your organization has either already purchased or is about to purchase. You may also better understand the pricing and corresponding value from your Oracle BI sales rep. If you're coming from an implementation perspective, you may have found your calling for your next career, which will keep you busy for many years.

If you're alarmed, it's either because you're thinking this is too complicated for your report requirements or because you're just starting to realize how broad and complex Business Intelligence and data warehousing need to be for a successful organization. In the first scenario, you may wish to review Chapter 2, which provides a primer on data warehousing. In the latter scenario, you may have learned the hard way there's no such thing as "I just need a handful of reports." Also, if your initial project is successful, users will want you to add more content. The data warehouse will become more strategic to your organization. At that point, you will need many of the features built into this architecture. It is much easier to have them built in from the outset than to try to retrofit them later.

If you're indifferent or underwhelmed, you should set this book aside and refer to it when you have a compelling need for and are responsible for delivering better analytics within your organization. Ironically, Oracle BI Applications sell better in a down economy, when management is starving and looking to cut expenses, maximize every purchase, hold on to every customer, and maximize the value of every sale. When data needs to be scrutinized, you don't have months to stand something up or the time to fall flat on your face with a custom implementation. BI Applications can therefore support both proactive (long-term, enterprise, strategic) and reactive (short-term, urgent, tactical) needs.

CHAPTER
4

Exalytics:
Go Fast, Not Slow

Oracle Exalytics In-Memory Machine (referred to as Exalytics for the remainder of the chapter) is a fairly new engineered system from Oracle, used as a Business Intelligence–engineered solution that's based on both hardware and software. The value of Exalytics can be summed up in one word: *performance*. Not only is it designed to maximize the use of hardware and networking specific to BI needs, it comes with software that has features only available to Exalytics hardware. It's not a black box, however; it's just good engineering. It's not hard to understand what makes it work, and the following section will lay out things simply and plainly for you.

Why would you care about Exalytics? Because it can provide significant benefit to your users, including the following:

- Less time to identify root causes

- Faster decision making

- Less turnaround time for tuning

- Higher user adoption rates

Primer on Data Warehouse Tuning

Before digging into the value of Exalytics, you need to first understand the value and importance of aggregate or summary tables in the context of Business Intelligence. The more you understand basic data warehouse theory and specifically how aggregate navigation works, the more you'll understand what's going on under the surface. The first step is to review what aggregate or summary tables are and how to design them, create them, and maintain them. The next step is to compare the manual process used without Exalytics and how Exalytics automates the life cycle of performance for end users.

The diagram in Figure 4-1 illustrates what an aggregate table looks like.

Both tables contain the same sales information: The difference is that one can be viewed by month and the other by day. If you only need your sales information broken down by month, it would only make sense to pull data from the smaller (monthly) table. If you need to drill into a specific day, you would need to be pointed to the larger table. A typical use case for a properly designed dashboard would be to show a trend of a number of months from the smaller table, with the ability to drill into the more detailed

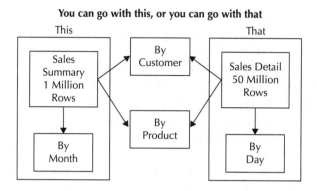

FIGURE 4-1. *Importance of dynamic aggregate navigation*

table that would filter on a specific month. The key thing is that you're not starting with the largest table as a data dump; you're first isolating a month or two of summarized data and then bringing back just a slice of data from the big table.

Why aren't aggregate tables often used properly? They sound simple enough to implement and use, so what's the downside or challenge? Companies go through a number of internal barriers when trying to take this approach, so be prepared for objections.

Who's in Control of the Data Design?

Many companies don't follow best practices with the design of their data model. If you don't have a well-designed star schema, it's hard to generate aggregates. The data modeler needs to understand the various types of aggregates:

- **Plain vanilla summary tables**   Each metric has an aggregation rule such as sum, count, average, and so on.

- **Cycle times**   Times from lead to quote, to order to shipment, to invoice to payment, for example.

- **Snapshots**   For example, inventory balances, AR balances, AP balances, and headcount over time.

NOTE
The first type of aggregate is the topic of discussion for this chapter because it specifically relates to performance and tuning once you're in production. The second two types of aggregates can also be summarized the same way the first type is created, just with very different ETL (for example, the monthly inventory balance as a summary view of the daily inventory balance).

Although Oracle BI Applications come with a set of aggregate tables out of the box, it's common practice to add more as required. Unfortunately, you need a few months of any data warehouse (BI Applications or custom) to monitor the usage of key reports and dashboards. Ultimately, you want to have a report that tells you the top ten most used queries that take the longest to run. You can build aggregates on a case-by-case basis, as you find bottlenecks. Every customer has a different amount of data, concentrated in different areas. This is one area where one size does not fit all. If one size does not fit all, you might ask, why does Oracle supply any aggregates at all? Because, although one size does not fit all, it is fairly easy to come up with a set of aggregates that almost everyone will need. Also, if Oracle supplied no aggregates, customers would almost invariably find performance to not be acceptable, which would decrease customer satisfaction and inhibit Oracle from selling more analytic applications to its customers.

DBA Objections

Depending on the type of database, you might encounter resistance from the DBA team, who, for dogmatic and possibly technical reasons, think the underlying database can provide functionality equivalent to aggregates. In some cases, such as with the Oracle Database with plain vanilla summary tables, you can use something called materialized views. In this case, they're right, and you're talking about the same thing using different words or terms. In other cases, such as with Teradata, there's a concept called an aggregate join index (AJI), which tends to give you mixed results. There have been many times a Teradata DBA has had to cave in and admit the need for a physical aggregate, despite the admission they'll be replicating data.

It should be noted that Oracle BI Applications are fully supported on Teradata, and they have been since the beginning. As a side note, Oracle has had on contract at least one Teradata resource for many years (the same person, actually), and her role has been to ensure the BI Applications are fully certified, supported, and optimized for Teradata. The BI Applications don't use the approach preferred by Teradata, but they perform just as well (or better) regardless. There were many discussions between Siebel and Teradata (and now Oracle and Teradata) around creating a Teradata-specific data model. In the end, it was decided there would be no benefit to end users and therefore no business case to pursue this. With regard to aggregates, if a Teradata DBA doesn't want to use them, it would further make sense to look at using Exalytics on top of Teradata.

Picking the Right Aggregates

This is hard to figure out if you don't already have OBIEE with the Aggregate Persistence Wizard, usage tracking, and Summary Advisor for Exalytics. Many BI tools have fragmented products superficially joined together and have a hybrid of web and desktop client access. Security models and semantic layers (business translation of underlying technical tables/cubes and so on) make it difficult to distill a common set of business requests that need to be optimized and used for various display formats. This means there's no way to centrally monitor who is doing what and the resulting performance.

In the case of OBIEE at least, you have the BI Server as the central gateway to all business requests for data, regardless of how you're going to format the data (for example, SmartView, BI Publisher, dashboards, alerts, scorecards, portal integrations, and so on). Usage tracking is out of the box functionality that allows you to pinpoint your top offenders, either specific reports or dashboards, or common data requests across various dashboards. Behind the scenes, there's a logging of user activity, whether the BI Server cache was hit, and the time it took to run. You can quickly put together a dashboard and reports on this data to garner some insight.

The end result is that you can identify which part of your logical business model is commonly accessed but not performing properly. Figure 4-2 shows an example.

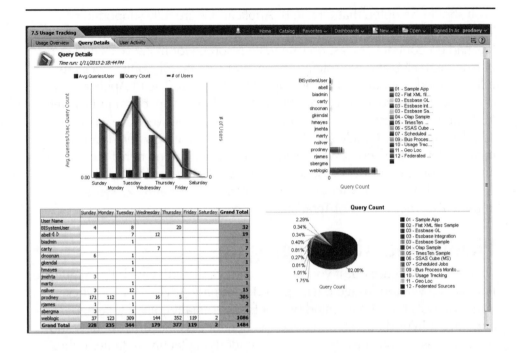

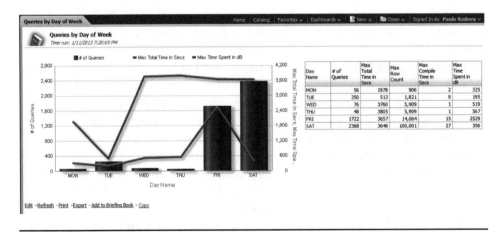

FIGURE 4-2. *Example of a usage-tracking dashboard*

Webcat Path	Cache Hit Ratio	# of Queries	Avg Total Time In Secs	Avg Row Count	Avg Compile Time In Secs	Avg Time Spent in dB	Avg Num dB Queries
/shared/Airlines/Demo/A/Heatmap	14.00%	7	8.00	14	0.0	19.0	1
/shared/Airlines/Demo/A/Counter Table	13.00%	15	58.00	2	0.2	41.6	1
Unspecified	1.00%	3465	99.57	11	0.8	13.8	14
/shared/2. Functional Examples/Descriptive Stats/Distribution/Comp Dist/Distribution Comparative	0.00%	3	5.00	8,919	0.0	1.0	3
/shared/2. Functional Examples/Descriptive Stats/Distribution/Distr/Distribution Report	0.00%	4	2.00	4,000	1.0	0.0	4
/shared/2. Functional Examples/Descriptive Stats/Distribution/Distr/Metrics Distribution by Customers	0.00%	3	2.00	10,234	0.0	0.7	3
/shared/2. Functional Examples/Descriptive Stats/Distribution/Distr/Metrics Distribution by Orders	0.00%	3	170.00	100,001	0.0	7.3	3
/shared/2. Functional Examples/Descriptive Stats/Distribution/Distr/Selected Dimension	0.00%	1	2.00	6	0.0	0.0	1
/shared/2. Functional Examples/Examples/Benchmark/Benchmark To Individual	0.00%	2	0.00	22	0.0	0.0	2
/shared/2. Functional Examples/Examples/Index to Avg/Index To Avg	0.00%	2	0.00	40	0.0	0.0	2
/shared/2. Functional Examples/Examples/Indexing/Indexing	0.00%	1	1.00	36	0.0	1.0	1

FIGURE 4-2. *Example of a usage-tracking dashboard* (continued)

How to Implement

Determining what aggregates to build and actually implementing them is a manual process, but at least you can do this with the most primitive of tools. There are three parts to this, aside from the obvious testing required:

- Generate the physical DDL (the database language that creates the physical tables or materialized views).
- Import into the semantic layer of the BI tool.
- Populate it via ETL or database scripts, setting up initial loads and incremental updates.

Each of these steps can be labor intensive with other BI tools, but at least with OBIEE you can use a utility called the Aggregate Persistence Wizard for plain vanilla aggregates. To use it, you need access to the Administration Tool, which is meant for the technical BI team to manage. The Aggregate

Persistence Wizard allows administrators to select the facts and dimensions they need to optimize, and the wizard completes the preceding three steps for them. At that point, either they can continue to use the BI Server to populate the new aggregates (initial load only; incremental loads not supported) or the BI Team can turn them over to the data warehouse team to populate via other tools (a better option for production).

How to Maintain, Monitor, and Refine

Once this is implemented, you need to continue to monitor the performance of your environment. Not only do you need to ensure your tuning is working, but you also need to look out for changing user needs. At this point you're essentially repeating the process just described. The key thing to understand, however, is how your underlying BI tool is responding to the new aggregates. Most BI tools are "dumb," meaning they don't have an engine that optimizes the SQL query and dynamically pushes as much work to the underlying database as possible (function shipping). OBIEE does have this intelligence via the BI Server, and the semantic layer doesn't require hard coding of database-specific syntax (although this is an option).

Note, however, the BI Server caching mechanism is not the same as an aggregate/summary strategy. The BI Server caching is a first line of defense against performance problems. It's a file-based cache of data temporarily stored on the server and can be purged and refreshed as required. It can be designed to go against specific tables and shared across common requests for data. If required, in the case of Oracle VPD (Virtual Private Database), it can be restricted to the specific end user. The BI Server can pull subsets and derivations from the cache. There are limitations, though, as there is with any technology. For example, at some point the reading and writing (I/O) to the file system would be slower than direct access to an aggregate in a database. Most BI tools don't provide dynamic aggregate navigation and advanced caching the way that OBIEE does.

Shifting Priorities Within a Month, Quarter, or Year

Understanding your top ten long-running queries with the highest usage is hard enough for reasons already explained. In reality, you need a three-dimensional view (what queries, for what users, during what part of a business process) that includes looking at various time windows. For example, one group may be the most active during a fiscal month end, whereas another group may be most active during a specific event or season. Being able to sample specific window ranges is key. Furthermore, implementing a strategy that allows for a dynamically changing aggregation strategy can be very difficult because IT will always be trying to catch up. Knowing what data needs to be "hot" at any given period is one thing, but making it available when needed is another.

Enter Exalytics

Exalytics X2-4 Release 1 is made up of the following six parts:

- The hardware, which includes 40 Intel cores and 1TB of DRAM (see Figure 4-3)

- Oracle Business Intelligence Foundation Suite (BIFS)

- TimesTen in memory database

- Summary Advisor software

- Other EPM (Enterprise Performance Management) software and applications not covered in this chapter, including Endeca

- Other internal software, for example Oracle Enterprise Linux, Oracle Virtual Machine (optional), and other monitoring and patching software

The software installed on Exalytics is a special version that allows for the use of the Summary Advisor, with an optimized hardware flag flipped to on. Oracle Virtual Machine (OVM) can be used to support multiple BIFS installs on the same machine. Figure 4-4 illustrates the Summary Advisor Wizard.

FIGURE 4-3. *Exalytics hardware*

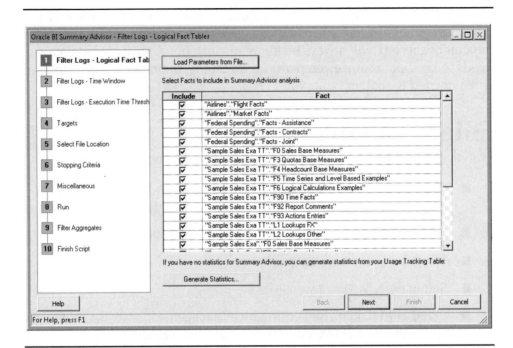

FIGURE 4-4. *Summary Advisor—only with Exalytics*

How You Can Improve Your End-User Experience

OBIEE now allows for the removal of the "Go" button otherwise associated with prompts. This means users can select from lists of values and see the data immediately change on their screen. Unlike other BI tools on the market that require smaller data sets and/or large amounts of data to be downloaded to your desktop, OBIEE gives you the best of both worlds—advanced visualizations on any size data set without degradation of performance. Oracle calls this "Speed of Thought" because, in theory, you shouldn't have to press a button and wait for the data to come back.

It should be noted that "Go"-less prompts are available for any hardware platform; however, in reality this functionality wouldn't work as well with a non-Exalytics environment, unless you have a really big server and highly tuned database. Ideally, you can use both Exalytics and Exadata together. Exalytics would be your BI machine, and Exadata your database machine, connected together by twin Infiniband cables (40 GBps each). Note that both OVM and Infiniband (together) are not currently a supported combination.

Figure 4-5 illustrates some examples of dense visualizations and "Go"-less prompts.

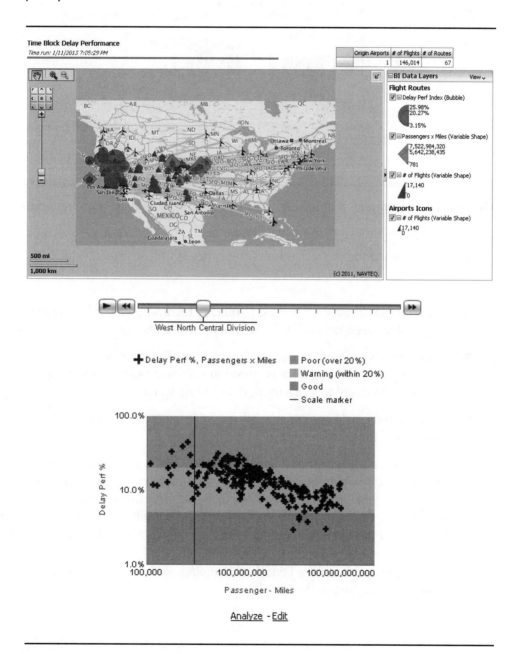

FIGURE 4-5.   *Examples of advanced visualizations with dense data*

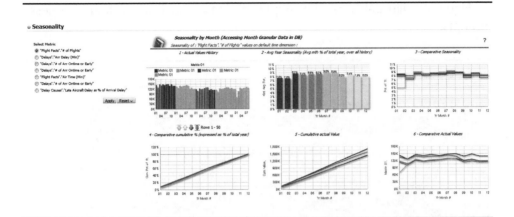

FIGURE 4-5. *Examples of advanced visualizations with dense data* (continued)

In case you're wondering what the secret sauce is behind Exalytics, it's really simple:

- OBIEE Summary Advisor is used to quickly recommend and implement aggregates based on available memory constraints.

- Aggregates are stored in memory using TimesTen via columnar compression (meaning data is stored in columns rather than rows, and is compressed to store more data in less space).

- Finely tuned hardware ensures all software components are maximized for performance.

- The secret sauce within the secret sauce is OBIEE, specifically the BI Server, which is intelligent enough to seamlessly transition between multiple data sources, such as TimesTen and your underlying data warehouse. End users won't know what data source they're hitting because it's the same interface all through a navigation (drill) path.

Exalytics is also optimized for Hyperion Planning, Endeca, and Essbase; however, that's a topic for another book.

How Does It Work?

All queries go through the BI Server, regardless of format (mobile, portal, Microsoft Office, dashboards, and so on). Figure 4-6 illustrates the overall life cycle of the process used to load Oracle TimesTen. Here are the stages:

■ Summary and query statistics are collected and stored in a database table (a system table is created when OBIEE is installed).

■ The Summary Advisor is run.

■ Recommendations are made.

■ The administrator accepts or rejects the recommendations.

■ A script is created.

■ When the script is run, the BI Server loads the data into TimesTen while also updating the metadata (semantic layer), called the "RPD" file.

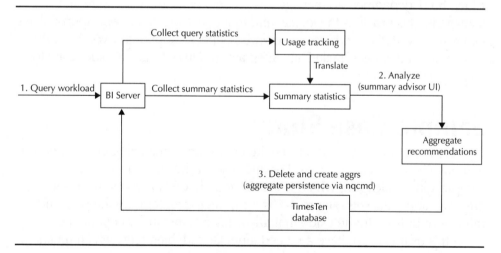

FIGURE 4-6. *Life cycle process to create aggregates in TimesTen*

NOTE
*The RPD file is called such because it has an
.rpd extension. Don't ask what the RPD acronym
stands for—nobody knows. OBIEE uses this
semantic layer file to translate what the end user
has asked for into the language required to retrieve
the data from the underlying source.*

When it's time to update the TimesTen database, it's simply a matter of running the script again. The script performs the following actions:

■ It removes the logically and physically defined aggregate tables in the RPD file.

■ It then purges the TimesTen database.

■ It runs the script used to restart the load process.

Different scripts can be kept on hand for different users and/or different times in the month, quarter, and year. Organizations can choose either to allow the IT department to manage this process or to allow the BI team to manage it. This provides the logical and functional separation of responsibilities into respective teams and breaks down bottlenecks. Optionally you have the choice of using either Oracle Data Integrator (ODI) or Oracle GoldenGate to load Oracle TimesTen.

Sample Case Study

One area of OBIEE where you'll see the largest performance gains is wherever you have hierarchical columns. For this case study, we can use Oracle's SampleApp application, which is distributed via OTN along with scripts for creating large data sets. Figure 4-7 is a simple example; note the plus and minus symbols on the left side that allow for expansion and contraction.

In this example, we have a ragged (unbalanced) hierarchy, which means there are no fixed number of levels in the structure. An example of an unbalanced or ragged hierarchy is an org chart. You'll notice five levels of data—from "Total Products" down to the actual product. Behind the scenes, OBIEE issues multiple different requests for data, navigating down the hierarchy.

Product Line Analysis
Time run: 1/11/2013 8:38:19 PM

Products Hierarchy	1- Revenue		
	2008	2009	2010
⊟ BizTech	$6,990,740.76	$6,302,087.48	$7,707,171.76
⊞ Communication	$3,533,490.25	$3,278,612.52	$4,073,313.61
⊟ Electronics	$3,457,250.51	$3,023,474.96	$3,633,858.15
⊞ Accessories	$896,151.90	$819,282.47	$983,280.69
⊟ Audio	$2,561,098.61	$2,204,192.49	$2,650,577.46
MicroPod 60Gb	$1,733,901.78	$1,469,915.73	$1,735,066.22
SoundX Nano 4Gb	$827,196.83	$734,276.76	$915,511.24
⊟ FunPod	$5,723,187.40	$5,160,339.85	$6,616,472.75
⊞ Digital	$2,586,776.75	$2,227,308.67	$2,921,019.15
⊞ Games	$3,136,410.65	$2,933,031.18	$3,695,453.60
⊟ HomeView	$3,786,071.84	$3,537,572.67	$4,176,355.49
⊞ Services	$298,446.86	$330,837.32	$376,560.72
⊞ TV	$3,487,624.98	$3,206,735.35	$3,799,794.77
Grand Total	**$16,500,000.00**	**$15,000,000.00**	**$18,500,000.00**

FIGURE 4-7. *Example of a resource-intense analysis against a relational database*

For example, one query would bring back BizTech in one row. Another query would bring back Communication and Electronics in another row. When you click on Electronics, the BI server brings back Accessories and Audio. When you click on Audio, you get MicroPod 60Gb and SoundX Nano 4Gb. OBIEE will then stitch all this together with the plus and minus symbols to allow you to drill within a single column. This is arguably the only and best way to pull data from a relational database (unnatural process) and make it look like it came from a cube (for example, Essbase that does this naturally).

If you look at the underlying OBIEE server log files after expanding the hierarchy in Figure 4-7, you would see that the cumulative time will be a number of seconds (for example, 20 seconds after seven to ten mouse clicks on Oracle's SampleApp). After switching to Exalytics, and going through the same process, you can reasonably expect to see the cumulative time indicate 0 seconds in your log file. This is only a simple example of a massive performance gain.

Exalytics and BI Applications

Exalytics allows you to accelerate the performance and tuning process as well as to ramp up to more users, faster. BI Applications are not cheap and are rich in content. It's important to realize your ROI as quickly as possible, and to ensure a high level of satisfaction for end users. We often hear about the "Google experience," where users are accustomed to accessing information in their web browser lightning fast. This puts a high level of expectations on the BI team to provide the same sort of performance. The good news: With the BI Applications, the more data you have, the more insight you can gather. The bad news: The more data you have, the more you need to pay attention to performance and tuning.

Exalytics provides 1TB of memory that's available for the software, TimesTen data storage, and TimesTen temp storage. For some organizations, this means their entire data warehouse can be stored in memory, which allows for lightning fast data retrieval. In the case of Oracle's prebuilt BI Applications, this is a great way to accelerate user adoption, to buy time for the IT staff to create permanent aggregates in the data warehouse, and to dramatically accelerate development time of a dashboard. As pre-sales consultants, we often wish we were assigned a personal Exalytics system to develop demos; we could avoid more all-nighters preparing for a last-minute demo request.

With a typical custom-built data warehouse, you have all the time in the world to build an aggregation strategy because you're going to have a small number of users to start, slow adoption over time, and a slow rollout of new functionality, assuming your users will wait that long and not fire you. You're also going to have a large team of developers with lots of time on their hands waiting for someone else to do something—until management cuts your budget. For example, the ETL developer is waiting for the data modeler to finish, who's waiting for the business analyst, who's waiting for the.... Things change when you instead implement Oracle's prebuilt BI Applications. You don't need to hire a large team for a project, you have far fewer bottlenecks, and you can stand up a large amount of content to a large end-user base very quickly. This means you need a high level of performance the day you go into production.

Now to be fair, you may not see as drastic a performance increase using Exalytics on the BI Applications compared to a custom-built data warehouse. This is because much work has already been done to tune the physical data model, and high-value aggregates are already available out of the box.

Therefore, with a custom data warehouse, you'll typically jump from no aggregates to aggregates in the TimesTen in-memory database; with the BI Applications, you'll shift from aggregates in the database to aggregates in TimesTen.

The ideal combination is actually the Oracle Exadata Database Machine X-3 (or later if available) and Exalytics. Exadata would store the BI Applications facts, dimensions, and aggregates. Exalytics would load some or all of your aggregates into TimesTen. You would be able to take advantage of the Infiniband (40 GBps) connection between the two. Exadata would be responsible for the database performance in returning the raw data, whereas Exalytics would be responsible for OLAP-style calculations that can't be function-shipped to the underlying database.

As a final point, Exalytics hardware allows for a higher level of concurrency than traditional architectures because there is less network traffic to access aggregates. Exalytics helps maintain a consistent response time for dashboards as user concurrency increases. This is especially important when you're mandated to meet an SLA and/or are supporting an external customer-facing application. This becomes even more critical with Fusion Applications, due to the amount of embedded analytics (that is, all OLTP users load analytic data, even if they do not intend to use it, because it is part of their screen).

Conclusion

While Oracle BI Applications are optimized ahead of time, Exalytics only helps to improve their performance. For example, at one large biotech company end users experienced a 5X to 10X improvement in the time it took to load their BI Application Dashboards. They also reported performance of 4 seconds with Exalytics vs. 22 seconds with same hardware without in-memory analytics. Another energy company reported 8X improvement in their BI Application dashboards and reports. Other companies have taken advantage of leveraging both Oracle Exadata and Exalytics to take advantage of the 40 GB/s Infiniband connection.

There is also a performance and tuning guide available for Exalytics to help you plan your deployment. You can find the most current version on the My Oracle Support website. Also please keep in mind Exalytics comes with full Premium Support, which is mandatory. The support covers all hardware and software issues on a 24x7 coverage model. In general, a hardware failure would be addressed in the same manner as any other hardware failure in one of Oracle's engineered systems. You would log a service request ticket with Oracle, the issue would be diagnosed, and Oracle would send out an engineer if hardware repair was required.

Premier Support includes the following for Exalytics from a hardware perspective:

- Exalytics system hardware, integrated software (such as firmware), and Oracle Linux operating system

- 24x7 Oracle Exalytics Support team and Customer Incident Manager (remote)

- 24x7 Access to My Oracle Support and powerful proactive support tools and resources

- Product enhancements, fixes, upgrades and Lifetime Support policy

- Time-based escalation alerts and escalation hotline

While it would make sense to start with Exalytics with a BI Applications implementation if you need to purchase net new hardware anyways, the good news is that you can always migrate to Exalytics at a later date without having a negative impact on any of your BI Applications.

CHAPTER
5

Financial Analytics

Financial Analytics, contrary to its name, is not necessarily just for finance people. It's highly useful outside of the Finance department (for example, for line managers with budget responsibilities). It's one of the most popular BI Applications and also the one with a high level of confusion and even controversy. The goal of this chapter is to get to the bottom of all the noise you might hear, to properly explain what you need to know when evaluating and implementing this module.

Description of the Business Process

Most commonly, we find people can justify Financial Analytics by providing non-finance profit and cost center managers access to income statement information. This lets them see how to monitor revenue and, in particular, expenses to hit profitability or expense targets. We find that by monitoring expenses in detail, they are often able to cut expenses by several percent, just by monitoring what gets spent, by whom, and for what. The procurement people call this "demand suppression." Examples include

- Better monitoring of travel expenses.

- Better monitoring of real estate, data, telecoms, and other recurring expenses to ensure they are still needed every month.

- Better matching of assets to their intended use. For instance, is the PC allocated to a given employee overpowered, underpowered, or appropriate for their needs?

Compared to this justification, the justification of saving a few financial analysts a day or so each month to help speed up the close is minor.

Comparing BI Applications to Other Reporting Options

Customers get confused when they evaluate Financial Analytics, especially when they're also evaluating Oracle Hyperion Financial Management. Questions arise regarding whether you can use Financial Analytics for financial statements, and whether you can get full reconciliation to source systems. Other questions often come up around how to handle multiple General Ledgers, and how quickly the data can be refreshed in Financial Analytics. To start, we need to consider all the various financial reporting options from Oracle.

Financial Reporting Options

Here is a list of Oracle provided technology and application options that may be of interest to you. Some of these are source system dependent, others are not.

- **FSG—Financial Statement Generator (EBS)**   This utility has been around for many years, and is useful when financials are closed in a single EBS instance. A wizard will allow for the mapping of accounts to group accounts and for the layout of the financial statements. The key benefit is that reports are generated in real time, directly against EBS.

- **PeopleSoft nVision**   This Excel-based utility knows how to navigate complex leaf structures, setIDs, and other PeopleSoft-specific application requirements. Reports are also generated in real time and layouts can be set up ahead of time. It has the same limitation as FSG: It is limited to a single GL and not a consolidated set of books from multiple source systems.

- **JD Edwards Financial Reporting**   This is similar to the EBS FSG described previously, with same benefits and limitations. The Financials module provides some integration with Hyperion. The most recent addition to the JD Edwards toolbox is JD Edwards EnterpriseOne One View Reporting, which is based on Oracle BI Publisher.

- **Hyperion Financial Management (HFM)**   HFM is the recommended financial reporting platform for post-close, after consolidations and eliminations are complete. Not many customers are able to close their financials in a single GL, and even those that do find the Hyperion application and technology suite to be more flexible and easier to maintain. Using an OBIEE-based application called OFMA (Oracle Financial Management Analytics), OBIEE can report directly off HFM with prebuilt dashboards.

- **Essbase**   This is cube technology from Hyperion that can be loaded directly from the GL for a single ledger view, or from HFM to provide a consolidated view. Historically, Hyperion licensed an OEM version of Informatica and special integrations (called DIM Adaptors) to provide a tool for data loading, but now Oracle provides Oracle Data Integrator (ODI), formerly known as Sunopsis before the 2006 acquisition. This is not prebuilt, but rather a relatively straightforward and common approach. You'll experience latency in reporting, however, because the data needs to be migrated into Essbase. Front-end reporting options include Hyperion Financial Reporting (FR), dashboards, and SmartView.

- **Hyperion Production Reporting (SQR) and BI Publisher** This requires a brute-force approach and is therefore not recommended as a standalone approach. You'll find many tools out there that are better. Standard banded reporting tools require much hard-coding, pivoting, and translations to structure useful financial statements.

- **OTBI: Oracle Transactional Business Intelligence** Specific only to Fusion Applications, this is a real-time Business Intelligence solution that uses OBIEE. Although normally you would have performance issues with ad-hoc queries on a transactional application, Fusion was designed to allow for this functionality.

- **Financial Analytics (the BI Application)** This is appropriate for a near-real-time, pre-close view (no eliminations or consolidations) of financial data. Multiple data sources can be fed into this, but from a data perspective the ledgers and thus the charts of accounts are kept separate. In addition to viewing GL balances, you can drill through to the sub-ledgers.

Business Benefits
Financial Analytics should not be used for statutory reporting. In fact, you should *never* use a data warehouse for statutory reporting for the following reasons:

- The data warehouse is not your system of record.
- It is read-only.
- It is not the place to manage the mappings of your financial accounts to group accounts.
- It is not where you handle eliminations and consolidations, or where you submit manual journal entries.

Using a data warehouse for statutory reporting would simply be reinventing the wheels called Hyperion Financial Management (HFM) and Hyperion Data Relationship Management (DRM). Data warehouses need to have the flexibility to meet current reporting needs and not be limited by past reporting structures. Data warehouses, excluding Operational Data Stores (ODS), should always be the end point of data and rarely used as a data source for another application. Simply put, you don't want a conflict between what end users need for analytical purposes and the design requirements of a data feed to an application.

What's more, the GL portion of Financial Analytics is meant to be used as a proactive analytics mechanism to understand where you'll land at the end of your fiscal month from the cash flow, expense, balance sheet, and income perspectives. This is in comparison to Hyperion HFM, where a typical implementation only allows for viewing financial data post-close. Financial Analytics provides intra-period (unconsolidated and non-eliminated) data. Hyperion HFM provides formal financial reporting, whereas a balance sheet, a cash flow statement, and a P&L within Financial Analytics would never be used for statutory reporting.

Trial balances for a single ledger can be viewed on a daily basis, and period-over-period comparisons are available out of the box. Post-close, it's still appropriate to view one ledger at a time when looking at historical data. Keep in mind, however, you won't be able to view consolidated data. A good example of value outside of finance is allowing managers with cost center responsibilities to see how much budget they have left at any given time before making spending decisions.

Financial Analytics can be fed by multiple source systems and can therefore contain multiple ledgers and charts of accounts. You need to be careful, however, when aggregating across more than one ledger at a time on a dashboard. Without consolidations and eliminations, you could get unexpected results.

Key Stakeholders

As mentioned earlier, what might be surprising is that Financial Analytics is not necessarily just for finance users. Anyone with budget responsibilities can potentially benefit to understand their actual spend versus their budget. In fact, in many respects, because the Hyperion applications handle the needs of finance users so well, they often find very little additional value in Financial Analytics at the GL level. Financial Analytics does offer improved insight into the sub-ledgers, however, such as AR and AP. Hyperion provides the ability to drill directly back to the source, whereas Financial Analytics provides drill-down to the journal details stored in the BI Applications data warehouse.

Users outside of finance, however, often find Hyperion applications do not cater to their needs nearly as well. They find Financial Analytics adds plenty of value to their ability to understand the financial ramifications of their decisions. Ensure you include a sampling of influential budget holders outside of finance in your list of stakeholders. For one client, for instance, IT managers acted as the beta testers for the Cost Center Manager dashboard. Yes, they were IT people, but in this role they were acting as budget holders.

Sales teams may also use the Financial Analytics portion exposed in Order Management and Supply Chain Analytics (Accounts Receivables) to understand the current state and historical trends of their customer receivables, depending on how that affects their compensation, negotiations, and customer communications. Procurement teams may use the Financial Analytics portion exposed in Procurement and Spend Analytics (Accounts Payables) to better understand supplier behavior (for example, have we paid our suppliers, and when?).

Cross-Functional Analysis

Cross-functional integration is set up out of the box via common facts and dimensions. Although at first glance AR and AP transactions seem to overlap with Order Management and Supply Chain Analytics as well as Procurement and Spend Analytics, Financial Analytics provides a much lower grain of detail (all possible dimensions). Order Management and Supply Chain Analytics leverage AR Balances from Financial Analytics, whereas Procurement and Spend Analytics leverage AP Transactions from Financial Analytics. HR Analytics (out of the box) uses a company-wide revenue metric from Financial Analytics to calculate some HR metrics. You may find yourself limited from a license perspective if you don't implement Financial Analytics because of the linkage between the different BI Applications and the ability to drill from your GL back to your underlying source transactions. Finally, the AR and AP subject areas that contain the Project Dimension allow you to link Financial Analytics to Project Analytics. Specific details on how to expose hidden dashboards to show this type of out of the box functionality are described in the Project Analytics chapter. For example, you can view open purchase orders by project to help understand the impact of any delays.

Subject Areas

Financial Analytics includes the following modules: GL, Profitability, AR, and AP. AR and AP are essentially mirror images of each other. One is based on customers; the other on suppliers. Although it may sound obvious, keep this in mind when reviewing the content: Once you know one side, you'll automatically know the other side. GL is made up of GL Balances and GL Transactions. Profitability provides a P&L view of the data. Fixed Assets will be available with the 11*g* version of the Oracle BI Applications and is not covered in this book.

Because AR and AP are essentially mirror images of each other, there's little need to describe them separately. The three main areas involve raw transactions, current balances, and aging balances. For example, you can easily analyze a comparison of payments due to payments overdue or look at aging trending over time. Other examples are payment performance, effectiveness of invoice processing, and "Top 10" type of reports to detect exceptions. As with all BI Applications, the product guides will give you a great sense of the type of metrics available.

AR and AP Balances

AR and AP Balances are derived from the underlying transactions, forming daily and monthly snapshots (see Figures 5-1 and 5-2). These underlying fact tables are populated near the end of the ETL process (PLP mappings).

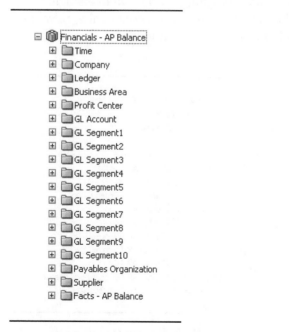

FIGURE 5-1. *Financials – AP Balance*

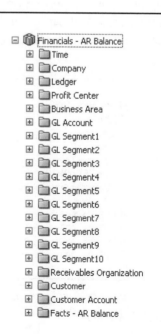

FIGURE 5-2. *Financials – AR Balance*

These two subject areas allow you to analyze the credit amounts as well as opening balances and closing balances for suppliers (AP) or customers (AR). This can be further broken down by your financial structure (GL segments). Typically, these subject areas are used to detect trends over time as you're able to compare snapshots over time.

NOTE
The labels "GL Segment1, GL Segment2" etc. are expected to be relabeled during your implementation based on the setup of your Financials ERP. These labels would therefore reflect the proper business names that map to your GL Segments organization.

AR and AP Overview

These subject areas shown in Figures 5-3 and 5-4 provide a summary view, blending the other subject areas together. This view allows you to compare balances, aging, balance aging, payments due aging, payments overdue aging, payment performance, and underlying transactions, all in a single ad-hoc query. It can be broken down by business area, profit center, payables or receivables organization, supplier or customer, and ledger.

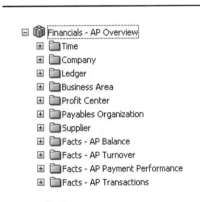

FIGURE 5-3. *Financials – AP Overview*

FIGURE 5-4. *Financials – AR Overview*

AR, AP, and GL Transactions

The subject areas shown in Figures 5-5 though 5-8 provide details around the underlying transactions, including the full financial structure. These are very detailed subject areas with a large number of textual (descriptive) attributes. Ideally, you'd use one of these subject areas to look up a specific transaction or as the final landing spot for an Analytical workflow (starting from summary view, drilling to transactional view, with filters and context applied). It's obvious from the name that there's a subject area (GL Detail Transactions) specifically designed for the U.S. public sector.

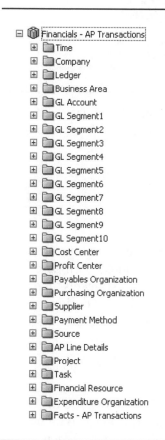

FIGURE 5-5. *Financials – AP Transactions*

FIGURE 5-6. *Financials – AR Transactions*

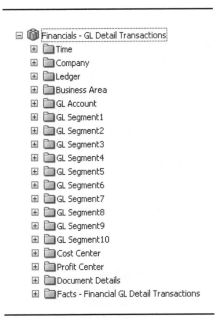

FIGURE 5-7. *Financials – GL Detail Transactions*

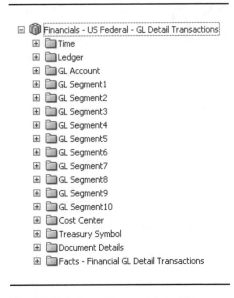

FIGURE 5-8. *Financials – US Federal – GL Detail Transactions*

AR and AP Invoice Aging

The subject areas shown in Figure 5-9 and Figure 5-10 are also mirror images to each other, providing an aging perspective. You can compare the total AR amount with the remaining AR amount, aging buckets, and amount due and amount overdue. Buckets can be configured during implementation; the out-of-the-box buckets are 1–30 days, 31–60 days, 61–90 days, and over 90 days.

GL Budget and Expenses

The subject areas shown in Figure 5-11 and Figure 5-12 allow you to compare your actuals to budgets on a daily basis. Ideally, this can be used by Cost Center owners to pro-actively track what's left in their budgets

```
⊟ 📦 Financials - AR Invoice Aging
  ⊞ 📁 Time
  ⊞ 📁 Company
  ⊞ 📁 Ledger
  ⊞ 📁 Business Area
  ⊞ 📁 Sales Organization
  ⊞ 📁 Profit Center
  ⊞ 📁 Receivables Organization
  ⊞ 📁 Customer
  ⊞ 📁 Customer Account
  ⊞ 📁 AR Line Details
  ⊞ 📁 Project
  ⊞ 📁 Project Agreement
  ⊞ 📁 Project Organization
  ⊞ 📁 Facts - AR Balance Aging
  ⊞ 📁 Facts - AR Payments Due Aging
  ⊞ 📁 Facts - AR Payments Overdue Aging
  ⊞ 📁 Facts - AR Invoice Amount
```

FIGURE 5-9.   *Financials – AR Invoice Aging*

```
⊟ 📦 Financials - AP Invoice Aging
  ⊞ 📁 Time
  ⊞ 📁 Company
  ⊞ 📁 Ledger
  ⊞ 📁 Business Area
  ⊞ 📁 Cost Center
  ⊞ 📁 Profit Center
  ⊞ 📁 Payables Organization
  ⊞ 📁 Purchasing Organization
  ⊞ 📁 Supplier
  ⊞ 📁 AP Line Details
  ⊞ 📁 Payment Method
  ⊞ 📁 Source
  ⊞ 📁 Project
  ⊞ 📁 Expenditure Organization
  ⊟ 📁 Facts
    ⊞ 📁 Facts - AP Balance Aging
    ⊞ 📁 Facts - AP Payments Due Aging
    ⊞ 📁 Facts - AP Payments Overdue Aging
    ⊞ 📁 Facts - AP Invoice Amount
```

FIGURE 5-10.   *Financials – AP Invoice Aging*

```
⊟ 📦 Financials - Budget and Expenses (PeopleSoft
  ⊞ 📁 Time
  ⊞ 📁 Company
  ⊞ 📁 Ledger
  ⊞ 📁 Budget Ledger
  ⊞ 📁 Business Area
  ⊞ 📁 GL Account
  ⊞ 📁 GL Segment1
  ⊞ 📁 GL Segment2
  ⊞ 📁 GL Segment3
  ⊞ 📁 GL Segment4
  ⊞ 📁 GL Segment5
  ⊞ 📁 GL Segment6
  ⊞ 📁 GL Segment7
  ⊞ 📁 GL Segment8
  ⊞ 📁 GL Segment9
  ⊞ 📁 GL Segment10
  ⊞ 📁 Cost Center
  ⊞ 📁 Profit Center
  ⊞ 📁 Budget
  ⊞ 📁 Facts - Actuals
  ⊞ 📁 Facts - Budget (PeopleSoft Standard)
```

FIGURE 5-11.   *Financials – Budget and Expenses (PeopleSoft Standard)*

```
⊟ 📦 Financials - GL Budget and Expenses
  ⊞ 📁 Time
  ⊞ 📁 Company
  ⊞ 📁 Ledger
  ⊞ 📁 Budget Ledger
  ⊞ 📁 Business Area
  ⊞ 📁 GL Account
  ⊞ 📁 GL Segment1
  ⊞ 📁 GL Segment2
  ⊞ 📁 GL Segment3
  ⊞ 📁 GL Segment4
  ⊞ 📁 GL Segment5
  ⊞ 📁 GL Segment6
  ⊞ 📁 GL Segment7
  ⊞ 📁 GL Segment8
  ⊞ 📁 GL Segment9
  ⊞ 📁 GL Segment10
  ⊞ 📁 Cost Center
  ⊞ 📁 Profit Center
  ⊞ 📁 Budget
  ⊞ 📁 Facts - Budget
  ⊞ 📁 Facts - Actuals
```

FIGURE 5-12.   *Financials – GL Budget and Expenses*

during their fiscal year. As you can tell from the name, one subject area is specific to PeopleSoft customers. The difference is under the hood with the Budget table.

GL Balance Sheet

The subject areas shown in Figure 5-13 and Figure 5-14 allow you to review changes to GL balances (debits and credits), asset turnover ratios, balance sheet ratios, and of course balance sheet statement items. Whereas Essbase provides an Account dimension to organize the balance sheet statement items, Financial Analytics provides a flattened view where you use a pivot table to stack each metric on top of the other to simulate a traditional balance sheet view. As you can see, there's a subject area specifically designed for the U.S. public sector.

FIGURE 5-13. *Financials – GL Balance Sheet*

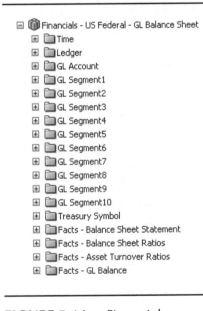

FIGURE 5-14. *Financials – US Federal - GL Balance Sheet*

GL Cash Flow

The subject area shown in Figure 5-15 allows you to build a cash flow statement. Whereas Essbase provides an Account dimension to organize the cash flow statement items, Financial Analytics provides a flattened view where you use a pivot table to stack each metric on top of the other to simulate a traditional cash flow statement view.

Profitability

The profitability subject area shown in Figure 5-16 though Figure 5-18 is essentially the generation of a P&L, either at the grain provided by the GL or at a lower grain if you've done activity-based costing allocations elsewhere (for example, with Hyperion Profitability and Cost Management). Typically, you would use the Universal Adaptors to load allocated data into the customer and/or product profitability fact tables.

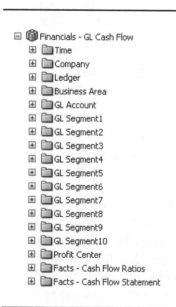

FIGURE 5-15. *Financials – GL Cash Flow*

FIGURE 5-16. *Financials – Profitability – Company*

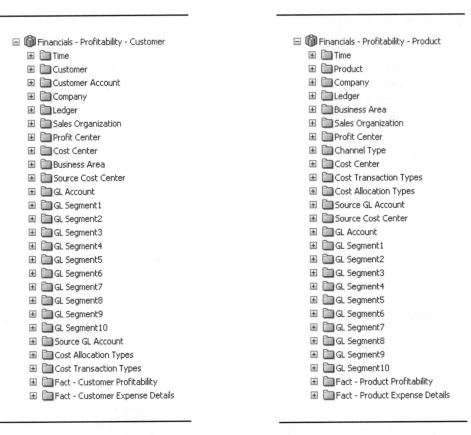

FIGURE 5-17. *Financials – Profitability – Customer*

FIGURE 5-18. *Financials – Profitability – Product*

A common use of this area is to look at profitability by customer, by product, or by company, or to look at an unconsolidated P&L trended over time. Much can be done with margin analysis by comparing one or more costs with revenue. The value of these subject areas is directly related to the depth of allocations and the number of expenses configured during the ETL load. Whereas Essbase provides an Account dimension to organize the P&L items, Financial Analytics provides a flattened view where you use a pivot table to stack each metric on top of the other to simulate a traditional P&L view.

Revenue Analysis

The subject area shown in Figure 5-19 allows you to analyze GL posted revenue, broken down by customer, product, sales organization, and financial structure. You can link the accounting document number to the GL journal ID to the invoice number.

EBS R12 SLA Transactions

Oracle has made available to Financial Analytics customers a patch that allows you to analyze SLA transactions. This is only applicable if you have EBS R12 as a data source. This patch allows you to link and drill from your ledger to sub-ledger details when requiring linkages from EBS SLA tables as a reference. This patch can be downloaded from My Oracle Support and includes metadata that needs to be added to be able to use the additional star schema. You can search on "(Patch 13697336: PROVISION FOR LOADING

FIGURE 5-19. *Financials – Revenue Analysis*

SUB-LEDGER SLA ENTRIES FOR EXCHANGE GAIN/LOSS.)" The metadata includes a readme file, OBIEE content, Database DDL to create the new table, and content for both Informatica ETL and the DAC. Specific to OBIEE, the RPD (OBIEE Semantic Layer) file has the following modeled:

- A physical table named "W_SLA_XACT_F", which is aliased as "Fact_W_SLA_XACT_F"

- Two logical tables and a logical dimension (mapped to the same fact table)

    - Logical Table "Core"."Fact - Fins - SLA Transaction", as seen in Figure 5-20

    - Logical Table "Core"." Dim - Subledger Journal Details", as seen in Figure 5-21

- A dimension called "Subledger Journal Details", as seen in Figure 5-22

- A new subject area called "Financials - SLA Transactions", which is what end users would actually see, as seen in Figure 5-23.

FIGURE 5-20. *SLA Logical Dimension Table*

FIGURE 5-21. *SLA Logical Fact Table*

FIGURE 5-22. *SLA Logical Dimensional Hierarchy*

NOTE
The OBIEE content for the SLA patch is still in OBIEE 10g format, you'll need to upgrade the RPD prior to using, or create from scratch based on the screenshots provided in this book. The complete logical star schema model can be seen in Figure 5-24.

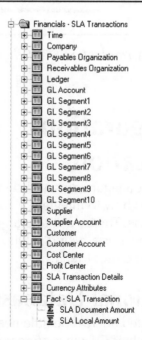

FIGURE 5-23. *SLA Transaction Presentation Layer*

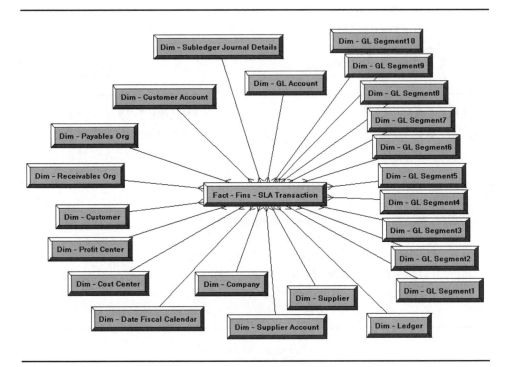

FIGURE 5-24. *Logical SLA Transaction Star Schema*

Typical Configurations and Customizations

When looking at common configurations and customizations, the most important one to consider is how to integrate to Oracle Hyperion products such as Planning and Essbase. There's a strong argument to be made for the use of Essbase for GL Balances as a hybrid solution, extending Financial Analytics in a way that's more user friendly.

Essbase vs. Relational Database Storage

If Essbase were never invented, there'd be little need to think about why you wouldn't use a database such as Oracle to store your general ledger. After all, most financials are stored in a relational database, right? There's a missing link, though, in your ERP, and that's the mapping of your accounts to your group accounts. For example, what are the accounts that make up "Revenue" or "Cash"? When you're building a financial statement, where is the layout defined and what are the relationships between the group accounts? This needs to be mapped out before you can do meaningful reporting.

First, let's review what Essbase provides over the Oracle Database. Forget about the technical back-end stuff. End users don't care if pages and pages of SQL (database language) gets written instead of MDX (cube language), and theoretically neither should the BI team if OBIEE is generating it automatically. Forget about the performance comparison because you could argue either way. So what's left?

- Essbase can calculate some functions that OBIEE and Oracle Database can't.

- Essbase provides an Account dimension for the financial view of data, and it's designed to have different aggregation rules for each account.

- Write-back is available with Essbase, using the Excel-based SmartView plug-in.

- Essbase handles ragged/unbalanced hierarchies better, especially from a performance perspective.

- Essbase was designed for spreadsheet consolidation.

- Essbase allows for data management without IT interference.

- Essbase allows for easier maintenance and design of hierarchies than a relational database.

How does this apply to Financial Analytics? The "magic" is with the Account dimension provided by Essbase that you can't easily replicate in a relational database. Financial Analytics doesn't use Essbase out of the box, so we'll compare the two approaches. Some companies will be happy with the out-of-the-box approach; others will prefer the customized Essbase approach. Keep in mind that what Financial Analytics provides out of the box is the best possible design when you're using relational tables.

NOTE
The Oracle OLAP option is the next best thing, even though it was not explicitly designed for financial reporting. A full comparison of Oracle OLAP to Essbase is beyond the scope of this book.

Out-of-the-Box (OOTB) Approach

Figure 5-25 shows an out-of-the-box balance sheet in OBIEE, and how it maps to the OBIEE semantic layer behind the scenes. The semantic layer is how OBIEE translates what an end user asks for to the request required from the underlying data source. What's not immediately obvious is that the creation of this report isn't trivial, because each metric on the left side had to be added to the ad-hoc query. A pivot table was then created, and each attribute had to be pulled into the pivot table and ordered properly. It's difficult to format each line and show the hierarchy of the measures. Again, this is a relational database limitation rather than a limitation of OBIEE, as will be explained.

Out of the box Balance Sheet report   Metadata repository (rpd file)

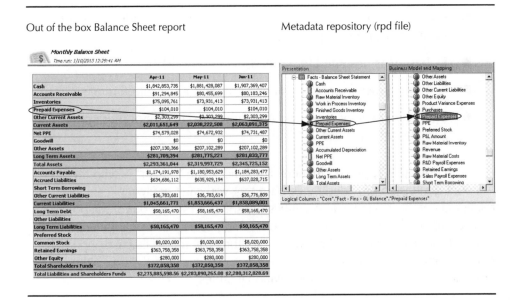

FIGURE 5-25. *Out-of-the-box balance sheet, with one metric used as an example to map to a centrally defined formula managed by IT*

Figures 5-26 though 5-28 show the next layer down of mapping or the lineage of where the metrics are defined. Every metric requires a case statement, which is part of the implementation because this is specific to your financial structure.

NOTE
The file_group_acct_codes_ora.csv file is manually populated prior to the first data load and then maintained when there's a change in the source financial system.

Metadata repository (rpd file)

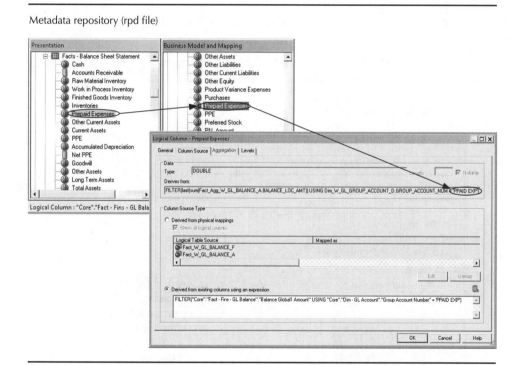

FIGURE 5-26. *Mapping from what the end user sees to the centralized logical data model containing formula*

Metadata repository (rpd file)

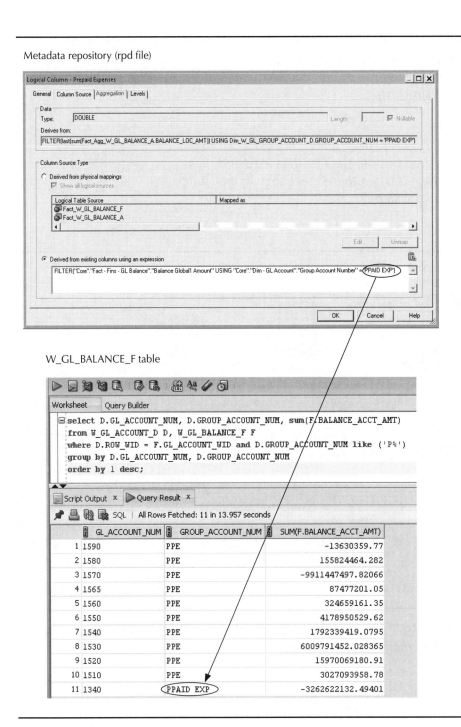

FIGURE 5-27. *How the metric maps back to the underlying database table*

W_GL_BALANCE_F table

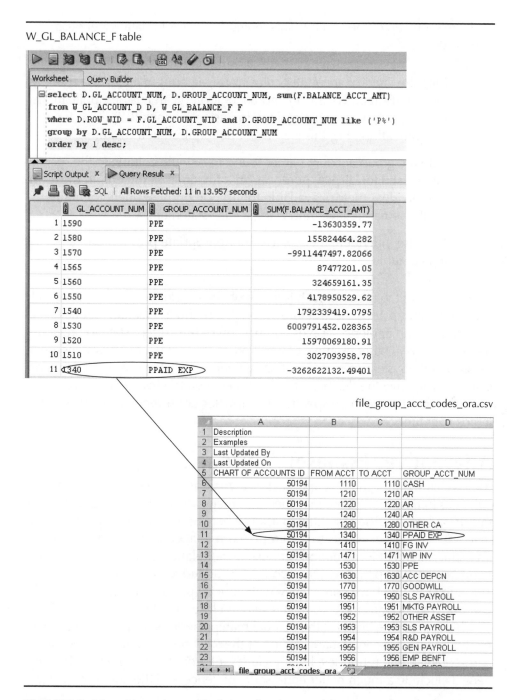

FIGURE 5-28. *How the underlying database table is populated partially from a spreadsheet*

Here's a recap of the touch points (going from ERP to data warehouse to report):

1. Map the chart of accounts to the group account in a CSV file used by the ETL (Extract, Transform and Load) tool. (With Fusion Applications, this mapping is now maintained in Fusion Financials itself, so with BI Applications 11*g* this step won't be required in the future.)

2. Map the group account names found in a single column to the specific name used for display purposes on a financial statement, in the form of individual metrics available for ad-hoc purposes defined in the OBIEE semantic layer and using a case statement.

3. Map the individual metrics to their appropriate position on a pivot table.

A key benefit to this approach is the flexibility to add, remove, or completely change the group account structure (through a prebuilt "cleanup" process) and allow for an apples-to-apples comparison of the current state to previous periods. This is another example of why you don't want your data warehouse to be used as the system of record for financial reporting. When your organization changes, you have the flexibility to switch between the historical perspective and the current restated perspective, to allow for consistency in viewing data trends over time.

Alternative (Essbase) Approach

Although the out-of-the-box approach is a good and proven way to map GL balances to financial statements, there's perhaps an easier way to accomplish this using Essbase. The first thing to ask is where and how you're going to map your chart of accounts to the group (parent) account you see on your financial statement. One option is to use Data Relationship Manager (DRM) to update your mappings when accounts are added to your source system. This allows you to have consistency with your Hyperion environment, should you use Hyperion, as most companies do to close their books.

This approach eliminates the manual manipulation of an Excel spreadsheet on the Informatica server, hard-coding of the RPD on the semantic layer, and hard-coding at the report level that includes a lot of formatting effort. The key benefits include a much better end-user experience and the ability to navigate seamlessly to the AR/AP part of Financial Analytics. For example, to create the pivot table displayed in Figure 5-29, all that is required is to pull in three items into the ad-hoc environment (the Time Hierarchical column, the Group Account Hierarchical column, and the Amount).

NOTE
This requires OBIEE 11g and the simultaneous loading of Essbase and Financial Analytics.

In this figure, you have the ability to expand and collapse the Account dimension hierarchy, rather than simply view metrics stacked on top of each other with labels to the left. You have control over your formatting on a row-by-row basis and can set up action links to have completely different navigation paths from each line item (which can also be conditional). The assumption here is your Essbase cube has been loaded directly from your source, at the same time as your Financial Analytics data load, so you can reconcile your balances and transactions.

Figure 5-30 shows the ability to expand the hierarchical column, which is a way of drilling within the same column. For demonstration purposes, the Accounts Receivable – Billed item has been highlighted in gray. An action link has been set up to drill into the underlying transactions from Financial Analytics.

ORACLE **Business Intelligence** — Search All · Advanced · Administration · Help · Sign Out

General Ledger — Home · Catalog · Favorites · Dashboards · New · Open · Signed In As ebs

Overview · Balance Sheet · Cash Flow · Budget vs. Actual · Asset Usage · Liquidity · Financial Structure · GL Balance · Trial Balance · **Demo: Essbase**

Balance Sheet for Vision Corporation
Date run: 12/5/2012

Year: ● Yr 2009   ○ Yr 2010
Scenario: ● Actual   ○ Budget   ○ Forecast
Company: Operations

Apply   Reset

Organization: Operations

	⊟ Yr 2009	⊞ 2009 Q 1	⊞ 2009 Q 2	⊞ 2009 Q 3	⊞ 2009 Q 4
⊟ Balance Sheet	100,922,270	83,487,676	100,922,270	100,922,270	100,922,270
⊟ Total Assets ◁ ▷	1,757,701,474	1,724,595,828	1,757,701,474	1,757,701,474	1,757,701,474
⊟ Current Assets	1,461,943,944	1,427,614,106	1,461,943,944	1,461,943,944	1,461,943,944
⊞ Cash and Short Term Equivalents	1,242,039,641	1,098,274,665	1,242,039,641	1,242,039,641	1,242,039,641
⊞ Accounts Receivable Total	22,717,909	120,365,092	22,717,909	22,717,909	22,717,909
⊞ Other Current Assets Total	2,430,277	2,430,277	2,430,277	2,430,277	2,430,277
⊞ Inventory	194,756,117	206,544,072	194,756,117	194,756,117	194,756,117
⊞ Fixed Assets	87,827,649	89,057,941	87,827,649	87,827,649	87,827,649
⊞ Other Assets Total	207,929,882	207,923,781	207,929,882	207,929,882	207,929,882
⊟ Total Liabilities and Owners Equity	1,656,779,204	1,641,108,152	1,656,779,204	1,656,779,204	1,656,779,204
⊞ Total Liabilities	1,339,371,072	1,323,700,020	1,339,371,072	1,339,371,072	1,339,371,072
⊞ Other Accounts	37,756,865	37,756,865	37,756,865	37,756,865	37,756,865
⊞ Total Owners Equity	279,651,266	279,651,266	279,651,266	279,651,266	279,651,266

Gen2,Scenario is equal to **Actual**
and Year is equal to **Yr 2009**
and Gen3,Company is equal to **Operations**
and Gen3,Account is equal to / is in **Balance Sheet**

Analyze -Edit -Refresh -Export

FIGURE 5-29. *OBIEE Balance Sheet sourcing from Essbase*

Balance Sheet for Vision Corporation
Date run: 12/5/2012

Organization Operations ▾

	⊟ Yr 2009	⊞ 2009 Q 1	⊞ 2009 Q 2	⊞ 2009 Q 3	⊞ 2009 Q 4
⊟ Balance Sheet	**100,922,270**	**83,487,676**	**100,922,270**	**100,922,270**	**100,922,270**
⊟ Total Assets	1,757,701,474	1,724,595,828	1,757,701,474	1,757,701,474	1,757,701,474
⊟ Current Assets	1,461,943,944	1,427,614,106	1,461,943,944	1,461,943,944	1,461,943,944
⊞ Cash and Short Term Equivalents	1,242,039,641	1,098,274,665	1,242,039,641	1,242,039,641	1,242,039,641
⊟ Accounts Receivable Total	22,717,909	120,365,092	22,717,909	22,717,909	22,717,909
Accounts Receivable - Billed	62,501,347	79,088,771	62,501,347	62,501,347	62,501,347
Notes Receivable	11,000	11,000	11,000	11,000	11,000
Investor Receivable	7,183	7,183	7,183	7,183	7,183
Loan Principal Receivable	1,316,193	1,316,193	1,316,193	1,316,193	1,316,193
Other Receivables	-21,977	-21,977	-21,977	-21,977	-21,977
Autoaccounting Clearing	1,401,556	1,401,556	1,401,556	1,401,556	1,401,556
Deferred Receivables	-1,000	-1,000	-1,000	-1,000	-1,000
Unbilled Receivables	11,579,426	11,602,378	11,579,426	11,579,426	11,579,426
Unapplied Cash	-81,146,763	-401,218	-81,146,763	-81,146,763	-81,146,763
Receivable Factoring/Remittance	48,524,482	48,524,482	48,524,482	48,524,482	48,524,482
Proceeds of Sale Clearing	177,710	177,710	177,710	177,710	177,710
Cash Clearing	-20,196,706	-19,905,445	-20,196,706	-20,196,706	-20,196,706
Allowance for Bad Debt	-1,434,542	-1,434,542	-1,434,542	-1,434,542	-1,434,542
⊞ Other Current Assets Total	2,430,277	2,430,277	2,430,277	2,430,277	2,430,277
⊞ Inventory	194,756,117	206,544,072	194,756,117	194,756,117	194,756,117

FIGURE 5-30. *Drilling into Balance Sheet (still Essbase source)*

Once you've drilled from the link in the previous figure, you can then view the filtered target report as displayed in Figure 5-31. At this point, you've seamlessly drilled from your Essbase cube into Financial Analytics, maintaining your context of your GL segments, ledger, and time. Now you can drill down to the underlying sub-ledger (AR Transactions), shown in Figure 5-32.

From here you can drill in two different directions—either directly back to your source system to look at the original invoice (as one of many possible examples) or to Order Management and Supply Chain Analytics. Although this is all custom, it's a common sort of setup we'd hope you try. Customers are actively encouraged to build their own analytical workflows such as this shown in Figure 5-33. This example was built by using out-of-the-box reports, adding and removing fields, changing filters, and linking those reports together via action links.

GL Account Name	Segment Name	GL Journal ID	Accounting Document Name	Accounting Document Number	Fiscal Date	Transaction Amount
1210	Operations	5931072~3	Feb-09 Receipts USD	Receivables A 2716488 6410416	02/28/2009	($17,257,714)
1210	Operations	5931051~3	Jan-09 Receipts USD	Receivables A 2716472 6410363	01/31/2009	($14,854,194)
1210	Operations	5931094~3	Mar-09 Receipts USD	Receivables A 2716504 6410463	03/31/2009	($14,031,883)
1210	Operations	5931084~3	Feb-09 Receipts USD	Receivables A 2716496 6410442	02/28/2009	($13,667,089)
1210	Operations	5931104~3	Mar-09 Receipts USD	Receivables A 2716512 6410494	03/31/2009	($12,687,187)
1210	Operations	5931063~3	Jan-09 Receipts USD	Receivables A 2716480 6410387	01/31/2009	($10,552,916)
1210	Operations	5931064~2	Jan-09 Receipts CAD	Receivables A 2716480 6410387	01/31/2009	($355,729)
1210	Operations	5931086~2	Feb-09 Receipts CAD	Receivables A 2716496 6410442	02/28/2009	($353,573)
1210	Operations	5931095~2	Mar-09 Receipts CAD	Receivables A 2716504 6410463	03/31/2009	($351,922)
1210	Operations	5931054~2	Jan-09 Receipts CAD	Receivables A 2716472 6410363	01/31/2009	($303,118)
1210	Operations	5931074~2	Feb-09 Receipts CAD	Receivables A 2716488 6410416	02/28/2009	($216,429)
1210	Operations	5931073~2	Feb-09 Receipts EUR	Receivables A 2716488 6410416	02/28/2009	($165,630)
1210	Operations	5931106~2	Mar-09 Receipts CAD	Receivables A 2716512 6410494	03/31/2009	($128,808)
1210	Operations	5931103~2	Mar-09 Receipts EUR	Receivables A 2716512 6410494	03/31/2009	($101,093)
1210	Operations	5931085~2	Feb-09 Receipts EUR	Receivables A 2716496 6410442	02/28/2009	($87,264)

Rows 1 - 15

Segment Name is equal to **Operations**
and Ledger Name is equal to **Vision Operations (USA)**
and Fiscal Quarter is equal to **2009 Q 1**
and Segment Name is equal to **Accounts Receivable - Billed**

Edit -Refresh -Print -Export - Add to Briefing Book - Copy

FIGURE 5-31. *GL transactions from Financial Analytics*

EBS AR Invoice	Fiscal Date	Accounting Document Number	Sales Invoice Number	Sales Order Number	Customer Name	AR Transaction Status	AR Transaction Sub Type	AR Debit Amount	AR Credit Amount	AR Total Payment Amount
	02/28/2009	Feb-09 Receipts USD	10039508	66933	Imaging Innovations, Inc.	POSTED	CASH APPLICATION	$582,816	$1,117,294	$534,478
	02/28/2009	Feb-09 Receipts USD	10039405	66899	EquipCo Inc.	POSTED	CASH APPLICATION	$426,298	$879,239	$452,941
	02/28/2009	Feb-09 Receipts USD	10039333	66860	SmartBuy	POSTED	CASH APPLICATION	$465,948	$918,184	$452,236
	02/28/2009	Feb-09 Receipts USD	10039509	66934	Imaging Innovations, Inc.	POSTED	CASH APPLICATION	$480,876	$921,870	$440,993
	02/28/2009	Feb-09 Receipts USD	10039518	66925	Discount SuperStore	POSTED	CASH APPLICATION	$413,698	$853,252	$439,554
	02/28/2009	Feb-09 Receipts USD	10039428	66904	Imaging Innovations, Inc.	POSTED	CASH APPLICATION	$477,677	$915,736	$438,059
	02/28/2009	Feb-09 Receipts USD	10039539	66954	Imaging Innovations, Inc.	POSTED	CASH APPLICATION	$455,888	$873,965	$418,078
	02/28/2009	Feb-09 Receipts USD	10039416	66902	Imaging Innovations, Inc.	POSTED	CASH APPLICATION	$454,261	$870,846	$416,585
	02/28/2009	Feb-09 Receipts USD	10039543	66967	Imaging Innovations, Inc.	POSTED	CASH APPLICATION	$444,111	$851,388	$407,277
	02/28/2009	Feb-09 Receipts USD	10039532	66952	SmartBuy	POSTED	CASH APPLICATION	$419,598	$826,847	$407,249

FIGURE 5-32. *AR Transactions*

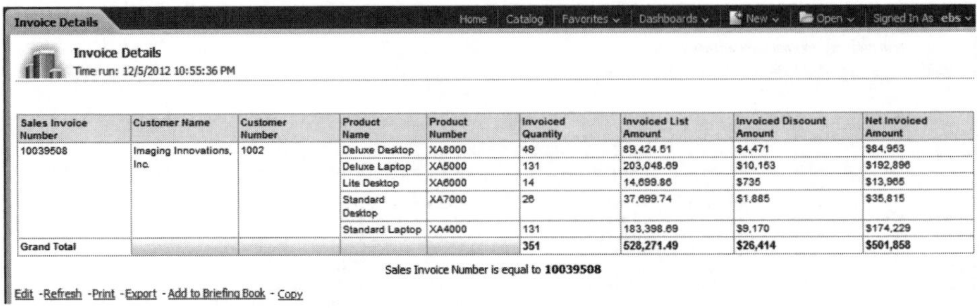

FIGURE 5-33. *Invoice Details example*

By drilling down from the AR Transactions, you can see the original invoice for which a payment was applied (see Figure 5-34).

You can also drill down from the AR Transactions to see the original invoice in the source system (custom action link).

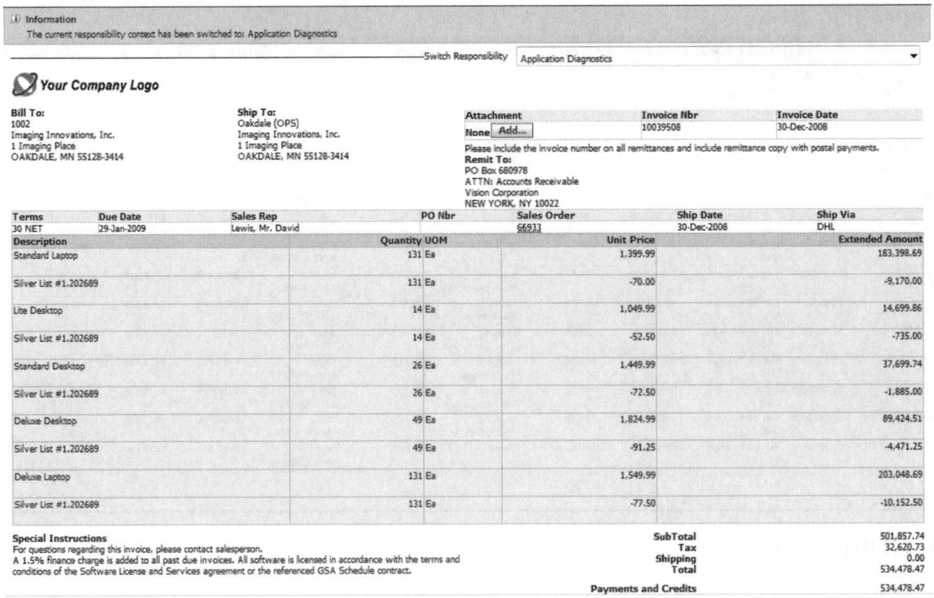

FIGURE 5-34. *EBS Screen, showing the invoice directly from the source*

Other Recommended Enhancements

Depending on your environment and the Oracle product mix you're using, it's important to think about how you're going to connect the dots between Hyperion Planning, Financial Analytics, Essbase, and DRM. You should work with a trusted implementer and Oracle to put together a plan specific to your needs and your organization.

Best practices have been developed by partners around how to best integrate both BI and EPM components. For example, options include using Essbase for GL Balances instead of the Financial Analytics relational star schema, setting up a ragged hierarchy (setting up a relational hierarchy table) that conforms and synchronizes to the Essbase outline used with Hyperion Planning, integrating Essbase and relational metadata in the OBIEE RPD file (semantic layer) and setting up OBIEE analytical workflows. These OBIEE analytical workflows allow you to transform your implementation from a number of disconnected reports into a true analytical application. Finally, Oracle has developed best practices to implement multi-currency, as out of the box all you get are the "stubs." Multi-currency best practices are covered in Chapter 14.

Instead of creating a pivot table where you need to manually stack each metric (the out-of-the-box approach), with Oracle Essbase you can instead utilize a hierarchy to lay out your metrics with a predefined format. This includes the ability to expand and collapse within the hierarchy. There's a trade-off, though: Essbase can potentially provide a better level of performance and flexibility of different aggregation rules within your financial statement, whereas an all-relational solution is more out of the box and requires less customization.

One implementation partner that has been actively researching various integration points with other Oracle applications and technologies is P3 Solutions (www.p3si.net). For example, they're experimenting with Oracle Essbase for Balances while maintaining Financial Analytics for Transactions, blending the metadata into common business models in OBIEE to allow for seamless drill-down. They're comparing this with an all-relational database approach where an existing hierarchy table is repurposed to simulate an Account dimension used in Essbase. They're also looking at integrations with Hyperion Planning for budget-versus-actual views, because out-of-the-box Financial Analytics assumes your budgets are extracted from your source ERP(s). Other partners are either implementing or researching similar approaches, for example, The Hackett Group and TEKsystems (formerly known as FCS – Frontline Consulting Services).

What to Watch Out For

It's important to understand the way end users want to interact with the data. If there's a need for interactive, ad-hoc analysis of GL budgets, then the previous section on Essbase will be of interest. If the majority of users simply want to view formatted reports and apply filters on demand, the out-of-the-box dashboards will be a good start. As another consideration, it's important to monitor changes to the underlying chart of accounts in the source systems. Should there be a change in how your accounts roll up to a group account, IT will need to have the domain file (input to the ETL process described earlier) updated accordingly as a regular maintenance activity.

Most implementations struggle to carefully follow the product documentation and fill out each and every domain value (CSV) file required. Take your time and don't miss any steps, or you'll lose time having to go back and redo your initial load. These files are critical to the ETL process, to allow the prebuilt ETL to work "as is" and have the parameters (domain mappings to be precise) required to map from your source system setups to how you want to organize, summarize, and visualize your financial data.

Although it was mentioned earlier that part of the process is removed with BI Applications 11g, this book covers BI Applications 7.9.6.4, which is the recommended version for most customers at the time this book was published. Even with the removal of the domain value files, there's a drawback to having a flattened financial structure because it doesn't reflect how most customers choose to visualize their financial statements (P&L, cash flow, and balance sheets).

Conclusion

Financial Analytics is a broadly used BI Application, applicable in virtually every industry. There is often confusion, however, as to whom the end users should be and how this is different from other Hyperion products. The best way to compare Hyperion Financial Management (HFM) is to know that Financial Analytics provides financial information without eliminations and consolidations on a daily basis that can be used operationally and not for statutory reporting. Financial Analytics also provides full transactional details and drill-down, plus historical AR and AP balance snapshots not maintained in your source ERP system.

To fully leverage Financial Analytics, you should look carefully at the recommended enhancements laid out in this chapter, especially concerning the management of GL Balance Analysis.

CHAPTER
6

Order Management and
Supply Chain Analytics

For manufacturing or distribution companies, Oracle Order Management and Supply Chain Analytics are the "bread and butter" of the prebuilt BI Applications. Any company creating and managing orders and invoices can benefit, especially if inventory is involved. Even in custom data warehouse builds, this is where manufacturing and distribution companies tend to start. Among the ERP BI Applications, this is where you'll find the most maturity, depth, and time to value when compared to other BI Applications. Furthermore, this application won't necessarily differentiate you from your peers, but it can help you catch up as well as free up time to focus on differentiation.

Order Management and Supply Chain Analytics help customers in the following ways:

- To understand billings, bookings and backlog, both current and over time

- To understand where bottlenecks occur that will affect/delay revenue recognition

- To provide access to inventory levels and "finished goods bill of materials" structures

- To understand cycles times throughout the order-to-cash process, as managed through the ERP

NOTE
ERP doesn't store historical snapshots, but Order Management and Supply Chain Analytics do.

Description of the Business Process

Order Management and Supply Chain Analytics covers two main areas: ERP Orders and Inventory Management (part of Supply Chain process). We'll cover both in detail, to help you understand what coverage is available.

Order Management Process

Table 6-1 describes a typical order cycle in an ERP and provides some examples where delays can occur. We focus on the delays because they represent waste and expense to be eliminated as well as also postpone the recognition of revenues.

Order-to-Cash Process	Things to Watch For
An order is received and entered either manually or through an EDI process.	Orders not yet invoiced make up a funnel of potential revenue for any given time period, which could add to delivery pressures.
The order is verified for accuracy.	Is the order accurate? If not, this can cause delays and customer satisfaction issues. If inaccuracies are caught, manufacturing and shipment could be delayed. Also, the customer could reject the order.
Finance accepts or declines the order.	Does the customer have a credit history of concern? It's important to monitor current and past AR history, prior to approving orders. This may affect the terms offered.
The order is scheduled.	Is there a current finished goods inventory? Or do the goods need to be acquired or manufactured? What facilities have the capacity to handle the order? What are the expected shipment dates for the order?
The order is built.	Are there any backlogs? Can the plant produce and/or ship the order?
The order is picked.	Did the right thing get picked, and/or is there inventory? Did the order get picked or packed correctly? Was any kitting done promptly and properly?
The order is shipped.	The order might get cancelled, and inventory may need to be returned to the original location. Was the order shipped promptly? How did the shipment date compare to the customer's requested ship date?

TABLE 6-1. *The ERP Order Cycle*

Order-to-Cash Process	Things to Watch For
The customer accepts or declines the order.	The shipment does not meet the customer's expectations: ■ It arrives early or late. ■ It fails incoming quality testing. ■ It gets lost in shipping. Did some or all of the order get returned? This affects revenue recognition, inventory, backlogs, and so on, especially if a reshipment is required.
The order is invoiced.	Is the invoice correct? Are adjustments required? Are manual journal entries required?
The invoice is paid (or not).	Payment is incorrect: ■ Customer does not pay. ■ Customer pays incorrect amount. ■ Customer pays late. ■ Customer issues one payment for multiple orders that need to be resolved.

TABLE 6-1. *The ERP Order Cycle* (continued)

Of course, the process isn't always linear. In real life, changes occur and an order can move back and forth through a process in a messy way, as illustrated in Figure 6-1.

Although Order Management and Supply Chain Analytics can't provide detailed insight into all exceptions and reasons for delays, the following types of transactions are made available, either directly from the ERP or derived:

■ Order Lines

■ Invoice Lines

■ Booking Lines

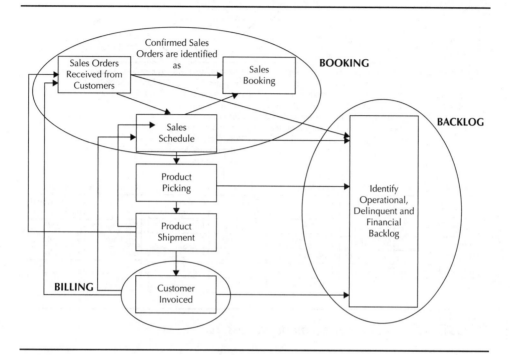

FIGURE 6-1. *Many changes can occur during the life cycle of an order.*

- Backlog Lines
- Inventory Lines
- Scheduled Lines
- Pick Lines
- Receivables
- Inventory Balances
- Inventory Transactions

Figures 6-2 and 6-3 go into further detail concerning the process that occurs in the ERP and is monitored by Order Management and Supply Chain Analytics. Note that leads and opportunities are usually captured in a CRM system. This is reflected in Sales Analytics. Order Management, of course,

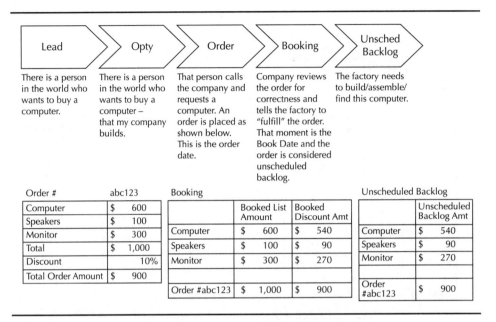

FIGURE 6-2. *Order management process, part 1*

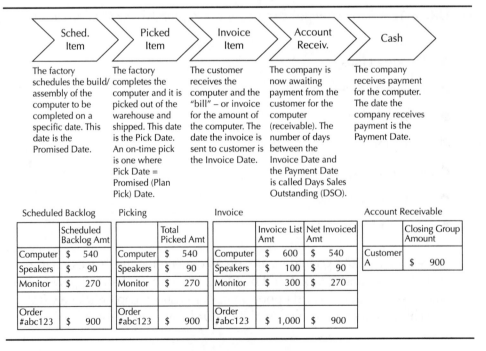

FIGURE 6-3. *Order management process, part 2*

then starts with the order in the ERP (not CRM). At the end of the process, there's a transition to Financial Analytics where you can see detailed AR Transactions and Payments.

Therefore, if the information you're looking for is related to one of the transaction types listed, from Order to Invoice (and perhaps AR Balances), then it's fair to expect it to be stood up relatively quickly and provide immediate value. Some areas are not covered by this BI Application but are available with other Oracle products (using OBIEE), such as Fusion Transportation Intelligence (FTI), that pull data from Oracle Transportation Management. Planning data is generally covered with Advanced Planning Command Center (APCC), and Work in Progress (WIP) is covered with Manufacturing Analytics.

At the heart of this application are bookings, billings and backlogs. Just to provide some context on definitions:

Billings

- Let you see everything you have invoiced to date.

- Synonymous with invoices; they are an exit point from the sales order process.

- Represent net value of the sales invoices for a given time period.

Bookings

- Generated from sales order lines.

- Entry point for the sales order process.

- Need to be derived through an ETL process or derived from other fact tables because this is a point-in-time view and ERPs don't track history.

- Represent a net change in sales order data:

  - Booking lines provide a history of transactional changes.

  - Sales order lines and/or schedule lines drive bookings.

  - Changes in quantities or monetary amounts also generate booking lines.

  - Any alteration to an existing sales order thus results in a new booking.

■ Bookings are handled differently by various transaction systems, but are consistently measured with Order Management and Supply Chain Analytics. This feature lets you combine data from different ERPs, even from different vendors, and lets users see a consistent view of the order-to-cash process spanning all ERPs, without having to understand which ERP a particular piece of data came from. Figure 6-4 shows an example of a quantitative change that can occur. Bookings are driven by sales orders, therefore if the order is reduced before the product is shipped, then you have a debooking, reflecting the decreased quantity.

Figure 6-5 shows an example of a qualitative change that can occur (note that Shipping Location can also be called Shipped To Location).

Backlogs

■ Understanding the different types of backlogs helps your supply chain people understand what bottlenecks are keeping them from shipping product and keeping the organization from recognizing revenue.

■ You can see what has been ordered but still resides in a backlog (not shipped).

■ Once a backlog is created it remains in this state until invoiced.

	Sales Order			Booking	
Day	Line#	Content	Customer Action	Line#	Content
Day 1	1001	100	Customer orders 100	#5010	100
Day 2	1001	120	Customer changes order to add 20	#5034	20
Day 3	1001	70	Customer changes order to subtract 50	#7541	−50

These bookings are driven by sales orders. On Day 3, we have a de-booking, because the quantity has decreased.

FIGURE 6-4. De-bookings example

Day	Sales Order Lines			Booking Lines		
	Line#	Qty	Ship LOC	Line#	Qty	Ship LOC
1	1001	200	NY	2520	200	NY
2	1001	200	SF	2600	–200	NY
2				2601	200	SF

FIGURE 6-5. *Booking line change example*

- Need to be derived through an ETL process, derived from other fact tables.

- The two main categories of backlogs are financial and operational. Financial occurs between the time the order is created and the time it is invoiced. Operational occurs between the time the order is created and the time it is shipped.

- There are also four additional types:

  - Scheduled: Ship date has been set.

  - Unscheduled: Ship date has not been scheduled.

  - Delinquent: Order is delinquent in relation to customer's requested ship date.

  - Blocked: Some detail in the order process prevents the order from being shipped.

Multiple backlog lines can originate from a single order line. Backlog quantities must accurately match the entire "flag set" per backlog line. For example, in Figure 6-6, 70 percent of the order was shipped, but only 50 percent was invoiced. Therefore, out of a quantity of 100, there's an operational backlog of 30 and a financial backlog of 50 (only 50 percent was invoiced).

Order Lines

Order#	Line#	Qty	Picked Qty	Invoiced Qty
255	1	100	70	50

Backlog Lines

Order#	Line#	Backlog Qty	Scheduled Flag	Operational Flag	Financial Flag
255	1	30	Y	Y	Y
255	1	20	Y	N	Y

FIGURE 6-6. *Backlog lines example*

Figure 6-7 illustrates at a high level the ETL process—the relationships and derivations provided out of the box as they pertain to bookings, billings, and backlog. The extracted tables are loaded first from the source ERP(s) and then derived afterward in the ETL process. The booking lines fact table, for example, is populated from the sales order fact table and the schedule lines fact table. Figure 6-7 covers both the ETL process and the available subject areas when building a report and/or dashboard.

NOTE
This is a logical view. In real life you would never physically join multiple fact tables together, but instead OBIEE would use conformed dimensions and multipass SQL to combine the data via the dimensions.

On-time picking is calculated in the following manner:

■ Metrics for on-time scheduling performance are derived by comparing the promised dates and quantities with actual pick dates and quantities. At implementation time, you can specify a tolerance for an order to be considered "on time." For instance, an order could be one day early or two days late and still be considered "on time." The term "promised

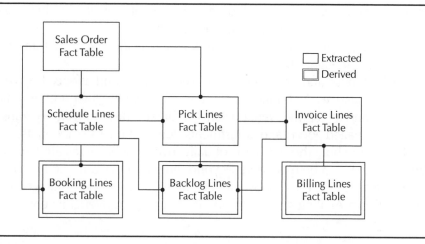

FIGURE 6-7. *Raw versus derived fact tables*

dates" refers to the schedule dates in schedule lines, and the term "actual dates" refers to the pick dates in the pick lines.

■ Deliveries are matched to order schedules systematically based on a FIFO (first in, first out) process. Open order schedules with the earliest promise dates are assumed to be processed first.

Supply Chain (Inventory Management) Process

As a little bit of context, inventory has been and will continue to be shared between BI Applications at different levels of details. The notion of a "supply chain" really belongs to Procurement and Spend Analytics, and this is where Inventory Analytics used to reside. It could also be argued that supply chain includes both procure-to-pay and order-to-cash. Some organizations call procure-to-pay "upstream supply chain" and order-to-cash "downstream supply chain." There's no need, however, to confuse Oracle licensing with how you name things and what terms you use with your end users.

With the recent addition of Manufacturing Analytics to the product family, there is some overlap between subject areas. For example, Order Management Analytics is useful for sales and order management teams, especially when viewing inventory balances in the context of backlogs. Manufacturing Analytics has more detailed information, including lot-level information for inventory transactions. Finished goods bill of materials are also available, showing the BOM breakdown and configuration/relationships.

Back to inventory, the process starts with specific inventory transactions, as illustrated in Figure 6-8.

Each of these transactions has a movement type and affects the overall inventory balances. Naturally, each transaction would either add or remove inventory and affect the overall balances. Other types of inventory transactions include damaged goods and adjustments due to annual stock counts.

Out of the box, three months of daily inventory balances are captured; however, that can be extended. Beyond three months, a monthly snapshot is maintained. Figure 6-9 shows an example of how Order Management and Supply Chain Analytics can help you to reduce your overall inventory.

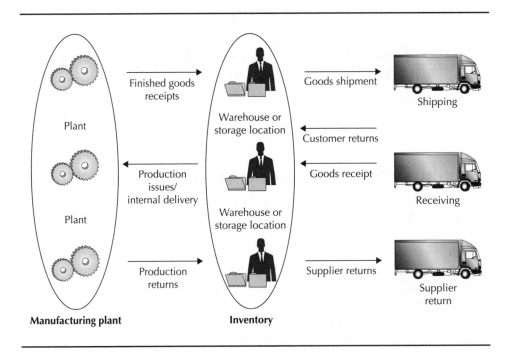

FIGURE 6-8. *Inventory transactions examples*

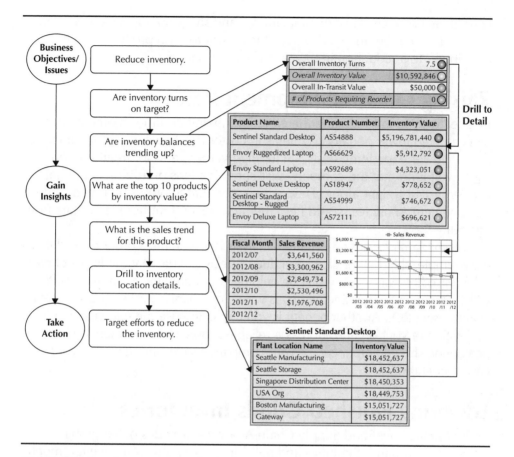

FIGURE 6-9.   *Inventory analytical workflow example*

Business Benefits

There's a number of quantifiable business benefits associated with Order Management and Supply Chain Analytics. We'll focus on the four key themes.

Faster Receipt of Cash (Via Shorter Cycle Times)

By looking at the various cycle time metrics, you can gain an understanding of at what stage the order-to-cash process breaks down. Is it from order to invoice, order to ship, ship to payment collection, or somewhere else? Depending on where optimizations need to occur, this can help you to better coordinate between sales, manufacturing, and shipping. Organizations can potentially cut more than a day from their order-to-cash process, which contributes to a reduction in the cash-to-cash cycle.

Raising On-Time Shipment Rates

By effectively monitoring and therefore optimizing on-time shipment rates, you can help lower penalty payments to customers. You can perform analyses to help lower expediting costs, including overtime and air freight. In one case, we found that the company was spending tens of millions of dollars per year in air freight alone. They anticipated that Supply Chain and Order Management Analytics would help them cut several millions of dollars from this bill.

Another area for action-oriented analysis is to minimize order cancellations (for example, ship before cancelled due to delays). Note that the impact here is increased revenue. You won't be helping your company cut any costs. You will be growing the top line, which is where companies find the bulk of data warehousing ROI. Another benefit is you can help raise the end customer's perception of your organization as a reliable supply chain partner. This perception should help increase your company's sales and minimize your customer churn.

Lowering Finished Goods Inventories

Order Management and Supply Chain Analytics provides better global visibility of on-hand quantities and helps identify where you have too much, allowing you to stop buying raw materials and change shipping patterns to source finished goods from locations with too much inventory. We have also seen cases where sales teams "hide" products for their favored customers because they do not trust Operations to ship product promptly. If, though, someone else needs the product, it cannot be used to fulfill those orders, causing added costs or, even worse, the company to turn down the order because they feel they cannot fulfill it promptly.

Another potential benefit is your ability to produce less waste shipping products unnecessarily. Another potential benefit is to better understand and therefore manage obsolete inventory that should be written down or scrapped. This is of particular value to companies that sell products with short shelf lives, such as fashion retailers, perishable food processors, and high-tech manufacturing companies.

Better Visibility into What Orders to Ship at Month or Quarter End

Order Management and Supply Chain Analytics can help you map factory capacities and raw materials against orders to optimize sales and earnings numbers. This helps you to monitor and prioritize the highest value orders at the most critical times.

Figure 6-10 is an example of one of many analytical workflow processes that can be used with Order Management and Supply Chain Analytics, as it corresponds to the overall ERP process.

This type of analytical workflow is only made possible with how the data is physically stored in the underlying BI Applications database. You simply can't do this type of reporting directly off of EBS. Figure 6-11 is a logical view of how data is organized for high-performance analytics and navigation.

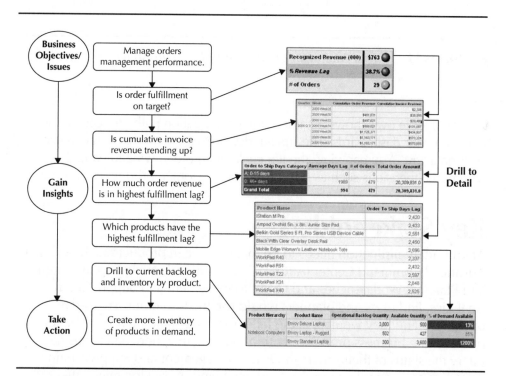

FIGURE 6-10. *Order Management analytical workflow example*

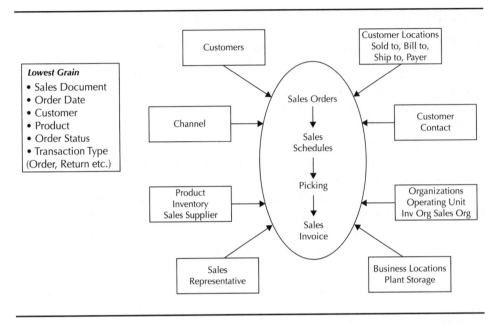

FIGURE 6-11. *Order Management and Supply Chain Analytics logical data model*

The middle oval shows a natural drill or navigation path you can set up between your dashboards. The surrounding boxes show what you can see your data "by." You can view the life cycle of an order, wing to wing, by common dimensions such as time, sales rep, customer, product, and so on.

Key Stakeholders

An important distinction needs to be made between products such as Oracle Advanced Command Center (APCC), Oracle EBS Advanced Supply Chain, and Planning Workbenches and Order Management and Supply Chain Analytics. End users and planners would use the former for day-to-day operations and they would use the latter for understanding how to better optimize the business processes within their organization. Sales reps can query the status of their orders in Order Management and Supply Chain Analytics, for example, to understand what kind of backlog might affect them at quarter and month end.

Your stakeholders would include many of the following:

- **The vice president of operations or vice president of supply chain**
  This person and their organization are responsible for shipping
  products on time and within cost targets.

- **The plant manager and warehouse manager**   These people also have
  shipping targets to meet. Also, when an order has to be expedited,
  they will be the first to feel the pain. Anything you can do to help
  them optimize the flow of orders and finished goods through their
  plant or warehouse will cut their costs.

- **The sales operations people**   These people are often the ones in
  charge of turning a customer order into something that can be
  scheduled, built, or picked.

Cross-Functional Analysis

By looking at material movements and inventory aging analyses, you can
gain better control and insight over your inventory to identify inventory- and
cost-reduction opportunities. This also allows you to connect the dots to
detect relationships between returns and supplier quality.

Metrics such as AR Balances and AR Turnover are available, so if you want
to drill into AR Transactions, you need to also stand up Financial Analytics.
Here are some examples of cross-functional use cases involving Supply Chain
and Order Management Analytics:

- Tying Procurement and Spend Analytics to Supply Chain and Order
  Management Analytics allows a company to see how a supplier's
  on-time performance affects your ability to ship goods bought for
  resale in a timely manner.

- Adding Manufacturing Analytics to the preceding use case allows
  an organization to perform the same analysis for raw materials,
  rather than just goods bought for resale. It also allows the company
  to understand the effect of delays or variability in the manufacturing
  process on shipments and revenue recognition.

- The progress of opportunities, as tracked by Sales Analytics, is often
  used to anticipate likely demand, whose fulfillment Supply Chain
  and Order Management Analytics would track. Tying these two
  together allows people to see how unanticipated changes in the sales
  pipeline have affected the company's ability to ship on time.

Subject Areas

Although the following subject areas are available out of the box, it's a minor effort to mix and match them as appropriate to meet your business needs. Only a handful of the available out-of-the-box attributes are initially exposed; during the implementation you have the flexibility of deciding which attributes belong where.

Sales Overview

The subject area "Sales – Sales Overview" provides detailed metrics on opportunity, order and invoice lines by sales organization, customer, product, time, and fulfillment details (see Figure 6-12). One would use this subject area to get a view of the two ends of the order-to-invoice process, without delving into what happened in between.

Orders, Backlog and Invoices Overview

The subject area "Sales – Orders, Backlog and Invoices" provides visibility into booking, billing, and backlog by customer, product, sales organization, time, and fulfillment details at the sales, backlog, and invoice line level (see Figure 6-13).

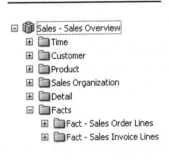

FIGURE 6-12. *Sales – Sales Overview*

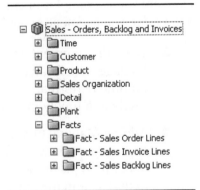

FIGURE 6-13. *Sales – Orders, Backlog and Invoices*

Order Process

The subject area "Sales – Order Process" provides the ability to analyze sales cycle details by customer, shipping location, office location, plant, product, sales organization, time, and backlog and fulfillment details (see Figure 6-14). You can analyze, for example, where your bottlenecks are occurring in your Order Management Process.

Inventory and Backlog

The subject area "Sales – Inventory and Backlog" provides more detailed measures on inventory and backlog by time, product, plant, and storage location parameters (see Figure 6-15). It can be used to understand the effect of backlogs on the inventory when the backlogs clear and can be fulfilled.

Backlog History

The subject area "Sales – Backlog History" provides the ability to report on backlog history by customer, sales organization, time, product, and fulfillment details (see Figure 6-16). You can use this subject area to detect trends and patterns over time.

Sales Receivables

The subject area "Sales – Sales Receivables" provides metrics on AR balance and turnover by customer, company, and time dimensions (see Figure 6-17). This is not as detailed as what you'll find in Financial Analytics, however, it is

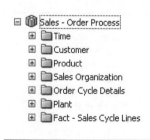

FIGURE 6-14.   *Sales – Order Process*

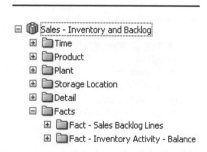

FIGURE 6-15.   *Sales – Inventory and Backlog*

FIGURE 6-16. *Sales – Backlog History*

FIGURE 6-17. *Sales – Sales Receivables*

useful for Sales Teams, for example, to understand if and when customers have paid for goods ordered and shipped or services delivered.

Customer Activity

The subject area "Sales – Customer Activity" provides a number of different types of customers (such as active, inactive, new, and dormant) by time, ship to location, sold to location, and customer parameters (see Figure 6-18). This is a good starting point to analyze and understand customer churn.

Order Lines

The subject area "Sales – Order Lines" provides the detailed ability to report on order line facets by customer, shipping location, office location, plant, product, sales organization, and time details (see Figure 6-19). It includes both

FIGURE 6-18. *Sales – Customer Activity*

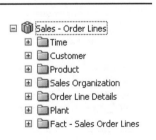

FIGURE 6-19. *Sales – Order Lines*

quantities and monetary amounts. It includes strictly detailed information and additive aggregates of it. It does not include any complex KPIs.

Sales Revenue

The subject area "Sales – Sales Revenue" provides visibility into GL revenue alongside order and invoice metrics by product, customer, time, and order detail dimensions (see Figure 6-20). It is very similar to the Sales Overview subject area; the principal difference is that this subject area includes GL revenue, whereas the Sales Overview subject area allows data to be reported by sales organization.

Orders and Invoices

The subject area "Sales – Orders and Invoices" provides measures on order and invoice details by product, customer, time, sales organization, and fulfillment details (see Figure 6-21). This subject area differs from Sales Overview in that it has details on bill-to and ship-to locations.

Backlog Lines

The subject area "Sales – Backlog Lines" provides the following details: Unscheduled Backlog, Scheduled Backlog, Delinquent Backlog, Blocked Backlog, Operational Backlog and Financial Backlog, including both quantities and amounts (see Figure 6-22).

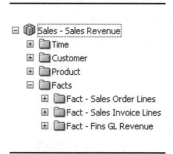

FIGURE 6-20. *Sales – Sales Revenue*

FIGURE 6-21. *Sales – Orders and Invoices*

```
□ 📦 Sales - Backlog Lines
   ⊞ 📁 Time
   ⊞ 📁 Customer
   ⊞ 📁 Product
   ⊞ 📁 Sales Organization
   ⊞ 📁 Backlog Details
   ⊞ 📁 Plant
   ⊞ 📁 Fact - Sales Backlog Lines
```

```
□ 📦 Sales - Booking Lines
   ⊞ 📁 Time
   ⊞ 📁 Customer
   ⊞ 📁 Product
   ⊞ 📁 Sales Organization
   ⊞ 📁 Plant
   ⊞ 📁 Booking Details
   ⊞ 📁 Fact - Sales Booking Lines
```

FIGURE 6-22. *Sales –*
Backlog Lines

FIGURE 6-23. *Sales –*
Booking Lines

Booking Lines

The subject area "Sales – Booking Lines" provides the following metrics: RMA Volume and Value Rate, Booked Amount, Discounted Booked Amount, Booked (Return Material Authorization) COGS, Adjustment Amount, and Number of Adjustments (see Figure 6-23). You can query on transaction-level details for specific booking lines if required.

Invoice Lines

The subject area "Sales – Invoice Lines" provides the capability for analysis on net invoiced amount, average invoice value, invoiced discount, cancellations, and cumulative invoice revenue (see Figure 6-24). You can query on the transaction level details for specific invoices if required.

```
□ 📦 Sales - Invoice Lines
   ⊞ 📁 Time
   ⊞ 📁 Customer
   ⊞ 📁 Product
   ⊞ 📁 Sales Organization
   ⊞ 📁 Invoice Details
   ⊞ 📁 Fact - Sales Invoice Lines
```

FIGURE 6-24. *Sales –*
Invoice Lines

Pick Lines

The subject area "Sales – Pick Lines" has the capability for analytics on the following metrics: On Time Pick Rate, Picked Amount, Shipped Amount, Picked COGS, Shipped COGS by Fulfillment Location, Storage Location, Office Location, Shipping Location, and On Time, Early, and Late Picked Quantities (see Figure 6-25). This subject area helps a company determine how its picking affects its ability to ship orders to customers on time.

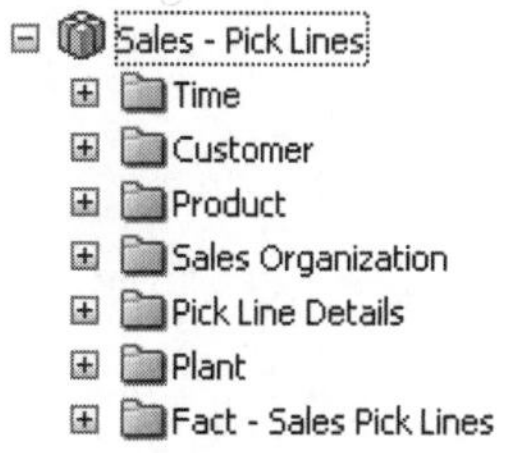

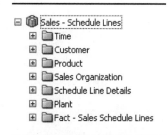

FIGURE 6-25. *Sales – Pick Lines*

FIGURE 6-26. *Sales – Schedule Lines*

Schedule Lines

The subject area "Sales – Schedule Lines" is a summary-level view on metrics such as Confirmed Scheduled Quantity, Total Scheduled Amount and Scheduled COGS by Fulfillment Location, Manufacturing Location, Storage Location, Office Location, Shipping Location, and so on (see Figure 6-26).

Inventory Balances

The subject area "Inventory – Balances" provides information that represents at a point in time information of all inventory balances and inventory values related to products whose inventory is maintained by the business organization. It includes all inventory statuses that Supply Chain and Order Management Analytics knows about (see Figure 6-27).

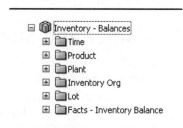

FIGURE 6-27. *Inventory – Balances*

Inventory Transactions

The subject area "Inventory – Transactions" is used to capture all the product-related (movement type) transactions that occur during a product's life cycle at an inventory location of a business organization (see Figure 6-28). Transactions are typically performed against business documents that authorize such transactions.

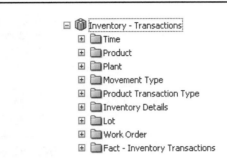

FIGURE 6-28. *Inventory – Transactions*

Finished Goods BOM (Bill of Materials)

The subject area "Inventory – Bill of Materials" provides a listing of all the subassemblies, intermediates, parts, and raw materials that go into a parent assembly, showing the quantity of each required to make an assembly (see Figure 6-29). Out of the box, only the Finished Goods Bill of Materials is supported (e.g. not Manufacturing or Engineering).

Customer and Supplier Returns

The subject area "Inventory – Customer and Supplier Returns" provides information on the product returns related to both suppliers and customers. We have seen over the past few years that managing returns, sometimes called "reverse logistics," has become increasingly costly and therefore worth more scrutiny (see Figure 6-30).

FIGURE 6-29. *Inventory – Bill of Materials*

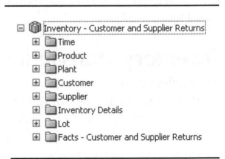

FIGURE 6-30. *Inventory – Customer and Supplier Returns*

Typical Configurations and Customizations

A useful modification you can make, if appropriate, to view on-hand inventory by Finished Goods Bill of Materials is to add the following joins to the RPD:

```
"Oracle Data Warehouse"."Catalog"."dbo"."Dim_W_PRODUCT_D_
Items"."ROW_WID" = "Oracle Data Warehouse"."Catalog"."dbo".
"Fact_W_INVENTORY_MONTHLY_BAL_F"."PRODUCT_WID"
```

and

```
"Oracle Data Warehouse"."Catalog"."dbo"."Dim_W_PRODUCT_D_
Items"."ROW_WID" = "Oracle Data Warehouse"."Catalog"."dbo".
"Fact_W_INVENTORY_DAILY_BAL_F"."PRODUCT_WID"
```

Out of the box, items in the BOM fact don't have a common dimension set up with a physical join to the w_product_d table (or to be more specific, the Dim_W_PRODUCT_D_Items alias). This is a very simple and quick modification. Also, don't forget the need to set the content level for the logical inventory fact sources.

Although you can pretty much run the out-of-the-box ETL without any configuration to get some basic information, you will quickly find yourself needing to follow the configuration steps to populate the domain values and map to the category sets, as required by the ETL. Although there are a number of steps that will take some time to follow for the initial implementation, you'll appreciate the design and architecture down the road. The key benefit is that configurations made on the source system are captured in the domain CSV files, so you don't need to customize the ETL mappings with any hard-coded logic. Down the road if there's a change in your source system, you can update the CSV file without having to open up an Informatica mapping. This not only makes maintenance easier and protects you from upgrades, but it lowers the turnaround time and implementation costs of changes. Finally, using CSV files to capture lists of values also supports the architecture designed to handle multiple data sources, and the domain values allow you to harmonize to a common display value on your dashboards. Therefore, make sure you follow the configuration steps very carefully.

Often the question is asked, "What are the impacts on changes to my source on the BI Applications?" In the case of EBS, most changes are either a screen or list of value configurations, and rarely do you find the physical data model changed. Same for JD Edwards. In the case of PeopleSoft, however, it was fairly common to customize the underlying physical data model, so this could force equivalent changes to your out-of-the-box ETL.

NOTE
Purchase orders and sales orders related to drop shipments aren't linked out of the box; this would require a customization during implementation.

What to Watch Out For

In your RPD is a key logical dimensional table you'll need in order to get a combined view of an order across many fact tables (order lines, invoice lines, pick lines, and so on). In the business model and mapping layer, review the "Dim – Sales Order Num" table. It provides OBIEE the information needed to create a logical dimensional table to join together three key fields: Sales Order Number, Sales Order Item, and Item Detail Number.

Around 2008, Simon Miller had to fly into an urgent meeting with a GPS manufacturer who was trying to produce this type of query. At the time this logical dimension didn't exist in the Oracle BI Applications. After spending about 30 minutes or so looking at the requirements, and then spending another 20 minutes explaining why you don't write SQL that physically joins fact tables together, he was able to spend five minutes setting up this logical dimension. This was documented, recommended to Oracle Product Management, and added as part of the next version out of the box. A lot of simple tweaks can be done; if you find one, be sure to let Oracle know so we can share it with other customers.

Another thing to watch out for: You're going to get lots of warning messages in the OBIEE Admin Tool consistency checker after upgrading to OBIEE 11.1.1.6.2 BP1 or higher. On one hand, you'll get messages saying you have logical fact tables not being used. On the other hand, if you try to disable those logical fact tables, you'll get an error messaging saying they don't join to any logical dimension. You can ignore those, at least in development.

If you start deleting the logical tables not being used, you lose the value of the prebuilt semantic layer. If, for example, you want to expose an attribute from the Physical layer to Presentation layer, you have a reference point of where to do it. It's a simple drag-and-drop exercise if the Business Model layer is already set up. Once you go to production, if you choose to clear out the error messages, keep a copy of the original RPD as reference for future changes.

Another thing to watch out for: With EBS 11.5.10 you could take an export of a production database, restore it elsewhere, and use it to run your ETL in a Dev/Test/QA environment. With EBS R12.x, however, stored procedures are called, so a simple table import/export strategy won't work. You need access to the stored procedures as well. This also affects your security strategy. You need a read-only version of the EBS "apps" (super) user that can also execute the stored procedures. The stored procedures mainly captured Project Number and take care of the Bill of Materials explosion. Even if you don't own or use Project Analytics, you should still run these ETL mappings, providing a placeholder should you choose to use this in the future. There is a way (in the standard Oracle documentation) to disable Project dimensions.

If you have very large numbers of products, and complex or deep BOM configurations, you might run into some ETL performance issues. This can be addressed directly with Oracle and some of the more experienced partners. Custom approaches are available, and Oracle is looking into various options. Currently, the BOM is flattened out, which can require much processing. Figure 6-31 illustrates at a high level the logic and approach used. Essentially, the logic starts at 1 and walks through the BOM until it gets to 36 in this example.

Finally, you only get one chance to capture inventory balances. Although theoretically you can go through historical transactions to try to build them from the beginning of time, in reality this is never very accurate. For example, you probably don't have the starting balance from when the ERP was stood up, nor the transactions you need from that initial go-live. Therefore, the sooner you stand up this application, the sooner you can track history. Many of the out-of-the-box dashboards require incremental loads over at least a couple of quarters before they get fully filled out with data, at least where snapshots (for example, cycle times) and balances (for example, AR and Inventory) are concerned. Snapshots and balances are taken after you implement in production, so you're not able to build a historical view of snapshots and balances (the data has long since changed, and you most likely have no initial reference point).

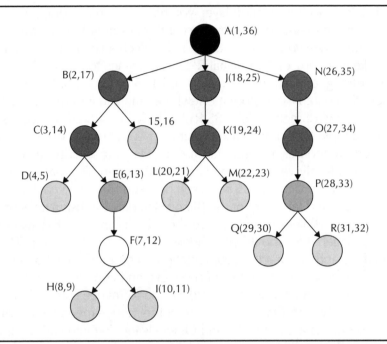

FIGURE 6-31. *BOM explosion process (follow the path for letters and numbers)*

Conclusion

Order Management and Supply Chain Analytics is one of the larger, most-used and highest value BI Applications. Some customers have reported large ROI gains within days or weeks of implementation, simply because they've never been able to see their orders, invoices, and inventory summed up in this way before, with full drilldown to details. You might be surprised at what you find. If nothing else, you'll have a higher level of visibility to your order-to-cash process to identify where and how this can be improved to increase revenue for your organization.

CHAPTER
7

Manufacturing Analytics

Initially when Siebel developed Analytic Applications there was a gap in the supply chain and order management application, specifically the work-in-progress (WIP) stage where a product is manufactured. One could look at the sales order fulfillment backlogs leading up to the manufacturing process as well as at every step of what happened after the product was built until the cash was collected. Manufacturing, though, was not covered. If you wanted to understand efficiencies of different lines of machinery, work order cycle times, yield variances from standard, or any of the many other facets that separated a lean, low-cost, high-quality manufacturing process from a less efficient one, a significant custom extension was required.

Oracle initially released Manufacturing Analytics as an extension pack for Oracle BI Applications 7.9.6.3. Manufacturing Analytics allows a manufacturing company to analyze production planning, manufacturing execution, inventory, production costing, and quality for (primarily) process manufacturing. The scope of this book is to cover Oracle BI Applications 7.9.6.4, where Manufacturing Analytics is fully integrated into the larger BI Application family.

Description of the Business Process

The manufacturing process can vary greatly, depending on whether the organization builds to order, assembles to order from subassemblies built to stock, or builds to stock based on a forecast. The process also differs between discrete, process, and high-tech manufacturing. This book cannot replace an entire book on production forecasting, scheduling, and manufacturing, so it's assumed you, the reader, already understand your requirements and want to know if the out-of-the-box functionality is a match for your environment. Figure 7-1 provides a high-level idea of the kind of coverage provided by Manufacturing Analytics, where you can analyze what happens from when the raw material comes in to when the finished goods are ready for customers. Figures 7-2 and 7-3 go into a little bit more detail on the specific coverage, along with the various inputs and outputs you can measure.

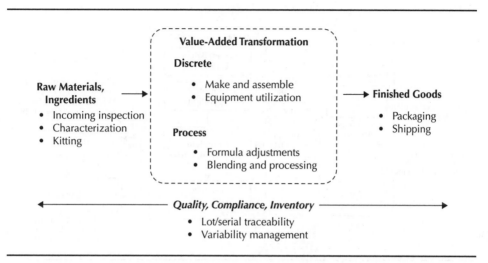

FIGURE 7-1. *High-level process covered by Manufacturing Analytics*

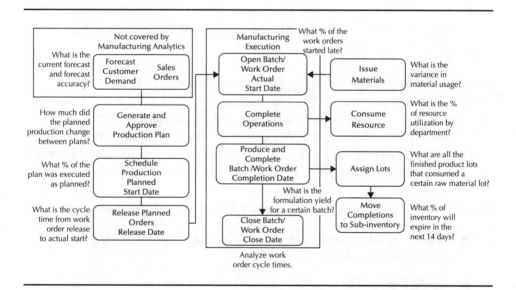

FIGURE 7-2. *Types of analytical coverage for Manufacturing Execution and Inventory*

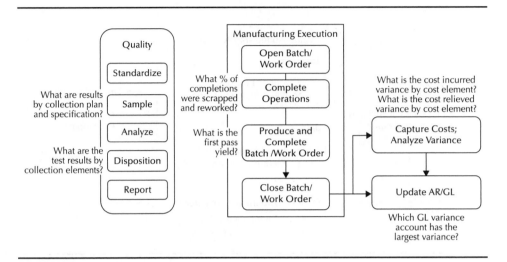

FIGURE 7-3. *Types of analytical coverage for Manufacturing Quality and Costs*

The specific processes covered by Manufacturing Analytics are the following:

Inventory Management   Previous versions of the Oracle BI Applications covered inventory transactions, bill of materials (finished goods), and inventory balances. There was no coverage for lots, Kanban and aging, material usage, and lot genealogy until Oracle BI Applications 7.9.6.4. Manufacturing Analytics in 7.9.6.4 now allows you to view available inventory after all known orders have "pegged" or reserved the amounts needed for fulfillment.

Work Orders   Work orders can be viewed from five different perspectives:

- **Aging**   A list of work orders in various age buckets; also rolled up for a summary view.

- **Cycle times**   The durations between key dates, where you can quickly identify where bottlenecks are occurring.

■ **Order performance**   Various metrics used to determine the overall success rate of the manufacturing process, including on-time completion, PPM defects, first pass yield, late work order percentage, and so on.

■ **Snapshots**   This perspective provides the ability to view trending of what's open, on hold, backlogged, past due, and so on, over time.

■ **Work order transactions**   Used to analyze start versus completed versus scrap versus rework versus backlog quantities, and so on, at a summary view or a detailed level (for example, drill down from summary into details).

Quality   Process and discrete quality are tracked in separate tables because they require different metrics and attributes. Whereas they both cover metrics such as count of tests, test quantity, and result values, process manufacturing requires different dimensions, such as time of test, sample, and lab. The coverage includes collection plans, associated collection elements, test results, nonconformance summary, and disposition actions for the different nonconformance sources and nonconformance types.

Resource Usage and Utilization   The equipment used during the manufacturing process is tracked, along with a comparison of the available capacity to the actual usage. Although this is tracked at the work order level, you can also roll up by the actual resource itself over time across all work orders. Comparisons can be made between actual versus planned. Further details around equipment downtime and an hourly breakdown would require Manufacturing Operations Center (MOC) Analytics, which provides similar coverage, for specific pieces of equipment in one location (plant specific).

Production Plans   The most current production plan is available to compare to the recent actual production, providing a planned-versus-produced comparison. This is more of an "after-the-fact" analysis to understand the historical accuracy of production plans. Proactive views of plans and various versions of plans would require a production plan to be flagged as a baseline plan. This baseline plan can be sourced directly from Advanced Supply Chain Planning (ASCP) or could also come from EBS MPS/MRP, if a customer has not deployed ASCP.

Business Benefits

The business benefits for manufacturing analytics can be divided into three buckets:

- Improving manufacturing cost and execution
- Increasing the number of perfect orders delivered
- Better management of inventory used and generated in the manufacturing process

Improving Manufacturing and Execution

Manufacturing organizations make money by controlling costs, times required, and yields obsessively. Manufacturing Analytics can help monitor trends in these and similar key performance indicators to help identify deviations quickly and aid in identifying their root causes. In that way, Manufacturing Analytics can both keep costs from drifting away from established values and help ensure that cost control programs deliver the improvements they are designed to. They can also help identify best practices from across a company's plants so they can be replicated wherever possible.

Increasing the Number of Perfect Orders Delivered

By monitoring both time needed and backlogs, Manufacturing Analytics can help companies avoid overtime and expedited shipping and still hit customers' expectations for perfect delivery. Clearly, one would have to monitor whether errors in manufacturing or supply chain were causing shipping to have to be expedited in order to understand how much expediting is required to compensate for errors in each phase of fulfilling a customer's order.

Key Stakeholders

The prime stakeholders for Manufacturing Analytics will be the vice president of manufacturing and the plant managers. They need to understand whether they are hitting both volume and cost targets and their schedules. If production forecasts are inaccurate, either manufacturing plants will have to handle the deviations or the company will not be able to ship the customers' orders on time.

Lesser stakeholders include product management, engineering, and possibly sales. As engineering and product management seek to introduce improvements in products, they will want to look at how well manufacturing has been able to hit its existing targets for cost, time, and quality to understand the likely impact on changes. Also, analysis of deviations may cause engineering and product management, in conjunction with manufacturing, to change how a product is made so it can be produced at a lower time and cost or a higher quality.

Sales teams can look at the pegging subject area to confirm inventory has been set aside and allocated for their particular orders.

Cross-Functional Analysis

Depending on how an organization is structured and uses Manufacturing Analytics, we see the following possible scenarios:

- **Sales**   In many organizations, if manufacturing can see the sales pipeline, it will have a better idea of what the manufacturing schedule will look like. This advanced view can help make production schedules more accurate.

- **Procurement and Spend**   Often, manufacturing's ability to produce will be constrained by the availability of long lead time inputs. A better understanding of vendors' ability to hit their delivery targets will help manufacturing hit its production goals and meet its commitments to customers. It will also help the organization set better "available-to-promise" limits so that it promises only what it can deliver.

- **Supply Chain and Order Management**   To analyze the entire order-to-cash cycle, one first needs to look at Procurement and Spend, Order Management and Supply Chain, and Manufacturing Analytics as a whole. This allows an organization to see the root causes of many variances in final product cost, timeliness, and quality.

- **Enterprise Asset Management**   Unplanned downtime will impact manufacturing's ability to meet its schedules. Looking at the maintenance records of assets in a factory can help assign a value to unplanned maintenance, which in turn helps an organization develop what Phillip Crosby calls "the cost of nonconformance," which is his definition of the cost of poor quality.

■ **Project Analytics** Many Oracle BI Applications have links to Project Analytics; Manufacturing Analytics is one of them, as of version 7.9.6.4. Most of the out-of-the-box subject areas include the conformed (shared) Projects dimension (for example, tracking work orders by project and task).

Subject Areas

The following subject areas are available out of the box. Starting with BI Applications 7.9.6.4, some subject areas are shared across different BI Applications from a technical perspective, even though specific BI Applications are licensed separately.

Actual Production

The subject area shown in Figure 7-4 covers what has been produced by work order: scrap amounts, daily throughput, late completed, and so on. This would primarily be used to compare performance across plants and products to identify bottlenecks between various work order dates.

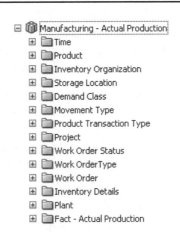

FIGURE 7-4. *Manufacturing – Actual Production*

Discrete Quality

The subject area shown in Figure 7-5 is specific to a discrete manufacturing process, used to monitor the overall quality trend. Result values and test quantities are tracked to identify nonconformances by priority, severity, status, source, and type. Tests are tied back to the Work Order, Project, Department, Inventory Lot, Specification, Collection Plan, Collection Element, Disposition, and many other dimensions.

Kanban

The subject area shown in Figure 7-6 is used to monitor Kanban inventory replenishments, automatically generated using the traditional Kanban just-in-time delivery methodology. Where physical Kanban cards are still used in the manufacturing process, you can also monitor the count of lost and damaged cards. The overall replenishment cycle time is also tracked by supplier and work order.

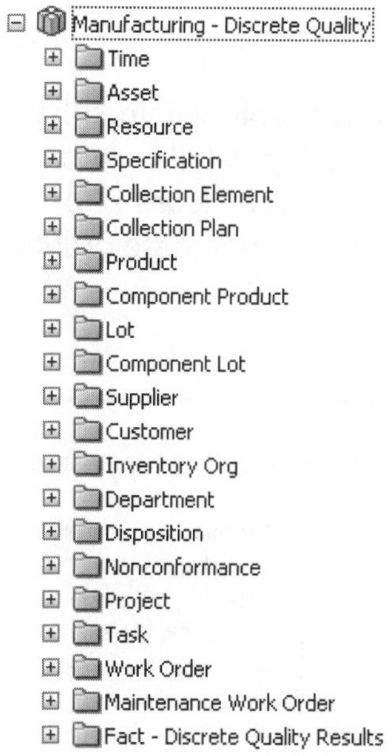

- Manufacturing - Discrete Quality
  - Time
  - Asset
  - Resource
  - Specification
  - Collection Element
  - Collection Plan
  - Product
  - Component Product
  - Lot
  - Component Lot
  - Supplier
  - Customer
  - Inventory Org
  - Department
  - Disposition
  - Nonconformance
  - Project
  - Task
  - Work Order
  - Maintenance Work Order
  - Fact - Discrete Quality Results

FIGURE 7-5. *Manufacturing – Discrete Quality*

- Manufacturing - Kanban
  - Time
  - Kanban Card
  - Kanban Document Type
  - Kanban Error Code
  - Kanban Source Type
  - Kanban Card Status
  - Kanban Supply Status
  - Product
  - Inventory Org
  - Source Org
  - Storage Location
  - Source Storage Location
  - Supplier
  - Work Order
  - Fact - Kanban Replenishments

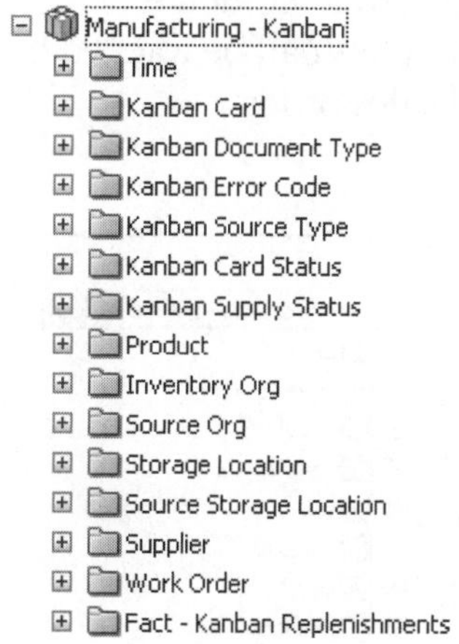

FIGURE 7-6. *Manufacturing – Kanban*

Lot Genealogy

The genealogy of an inventory lot can be tracked through the various levels and tied back to the vendor and purchase order, as shown in Figure 7-7. Out of the box, nine levels plus the end level are available (flattened out). Each level tracks the transaction date, work order name, quantities, lot level, and other attributes. This is especially important, for example, if there's a recall on a part and you need to trace the part through your supply chain.

Material Usage

Actual-versus-planned usage of materials or products are tracked by Seiban, project, and work order status, operations, type, and number, as shown in Figure 7-8. This allows an organization to identify possible inventory overages or shortfalls. In addition, it provides feedback to the inventory planning process.

Inventory Pegging

Depending on whether your organization utilizes hard or soft pegging (that is, setting aside inventory for specific orders), the pegging details can be analyzed to compare demand versus supply quantities (see Figure 7-9). Quantities can be tracked by specific work orders, plans, purchase orders, and sales orders.

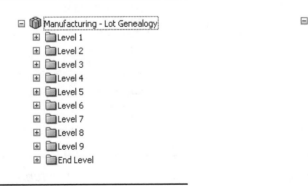

FIGURE 7-7. *Manufacturing – Lot Genealogy*

FIGURE 7-8. *Manufacturing – Material Usage*

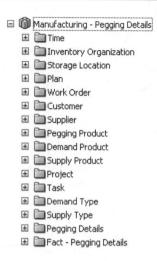

FIGURE 7-9. *Manufacturing – Pegging Details*

Plan to Produce

The subject area shown in Figure 7-10 compares the planned manufacturing amounts to what was actually produced by product, project, and demand class. This allows you to analyze metrics such as production attainment trends by week and month, along with a plan-to-produce ratio, percent, and linearity.

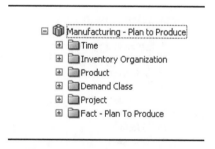

FIGURE 7-10. *Manufacturing – Plan to Produce*

Process Quality

The subject area shown in Figure 7-11 is specific to process manufacturing and is used to monitor the overall quality trend. Result values and test quantities are tracked by test specification and evaluation. This is also broken down by the size of the sample, the quantity consumed, the remaining quantity, and the count of tests conducted. Numerous dimensions are available for each test, including the date/time of the test, the lab and tester, the specific product tested, the customer, the supplier, and the resource.

Production Cost

The subject area shown in Figure 7-12 allows you to monitor and compare completion costs to actual costs to planned costs, and thus the resulting variances. This can be broken down by cost element and work order and/or rolled up by project, Seiban, and GL account.

Production Plan

With the subject area shown in Figure 7-13, you can compare the current planned value with the baseline planned value of a production plan. This can help identify downstream impacts on suppliers, projects, Seibans, and inventory balances.

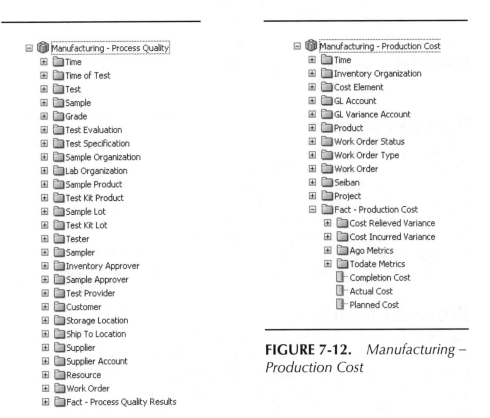

FIGURE 7-12. *Manufacturing – Production Cost*

FIGURE 7-11. *Manufacturing – Process Quality*

```
⊟ 📦 Manufacturing - Production Plan
    ⊞ 📁 Time
    ⊞ 📁 Inventory Organization
    ⊞ 📁 Product
    ⊞ 📁 Demand Class
    ⊞ 📁 Project
    ⊞ 📁 Seiban
    ⊞ 📁 Plan
    ⊞ 📁 Fact - Production Plan
```

FIGURE 7-13. *Manufacturing – Production Plan*

```
⊟ 📦 Manufacturing - Resource Usage
    ⊞ 📁 Time
    ⊞ 📁 Inventory Organization
    ⊞ 📁 Product
    ⊞ 📁 Resource
    ⊞ 📁 Resource Owning Department
    ⊞ 📁 Operation Owning Department
    ⊞ 📁 Work Order
    ⊞ 📁 Work Order Status
    ⊞ 📁 Work Order Type
    ⊞ 📁 Work Order Operations
    ⊞ 📁 Seiban
    ⊞ 📁 Project
    ⊞ 📁 Fact - Resource Usage
```

FIGURE 7-14. *Manufacturing – Resource Usage*

Resource Usage

The subject area shown in Figure 7-14 allows you to compare the actual time and cost charged with planned quantity and amount usage by resource. Resources can either be equipment or people. This is tracked by work order (number, status, type, operations, and so on) and can be rolled up by time, product, Seiban, and project. You can therefore monitor the effectiveness of the manufacturing planning process and have a proactive view of potentially negative financial impacts should there be significant cost variances. You can also monitor the overall trend of your resource usage.

Resource Utilization

The subject area shown in Figure 7-15 is similar to the preceding subject area but is not as detailed. Instead, the capacity of a resource and its percentage utilization (via time and cost usage) can be analyzed, across all work orders. Normally, you wouldn't be able to allocate capacity across future (known and unknown) work orders, so this is naturally a summarized subject area.

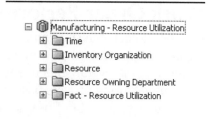

```
⊟ 📦 Manufacturing - Resource Utilization
    ⊞ 📁 Time
    ⊞ 📁 Inventory Organization
    ⊞ 📁 Resource
    ⊞ 📁 Resource Owning Department
    ⊞ 📁 Fact - Resource Utilization
```

FIGURE 7-15. *Manufacturing – Resource Utilization*

Work Order Aging

The subject area shown in Figure 7-16 allows you to analyze the aging of your work orders, how many are open, as well as the age and the value by different aging categories. You can thus identify the work orders with the highest value that are the oldest, which could also identify which orders are at risk of a customer cancelling or changing them before the manufacturing process has completed.

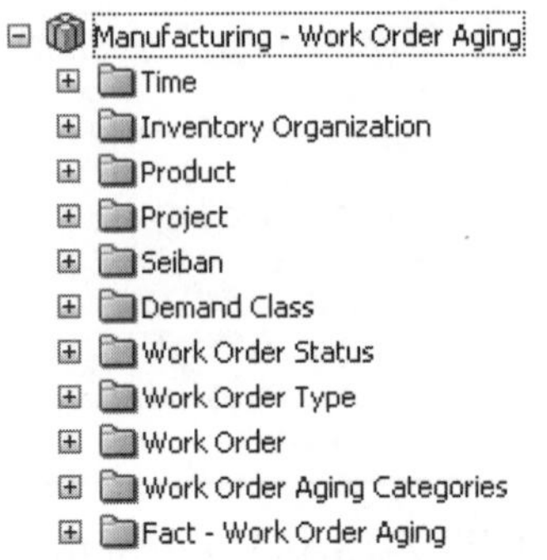

FIGURE 7-16. *Manufacturing – Work Order Aging*

Work Order Cycle Time

Cycle times are the time spent between different check points. Out of the box for Manufacturing Analytics the following cycle times are measured: Creation to Actual Start, Creation to Completion, and Actual Start to Completion. Lead time variances between standard and actual can be tracked. As with almost all Manufacturing Analytics subject areas, the subject area shown in Figure 7-17 can be rolled up by time, product, Seiban, and project and can be broken down by work order.

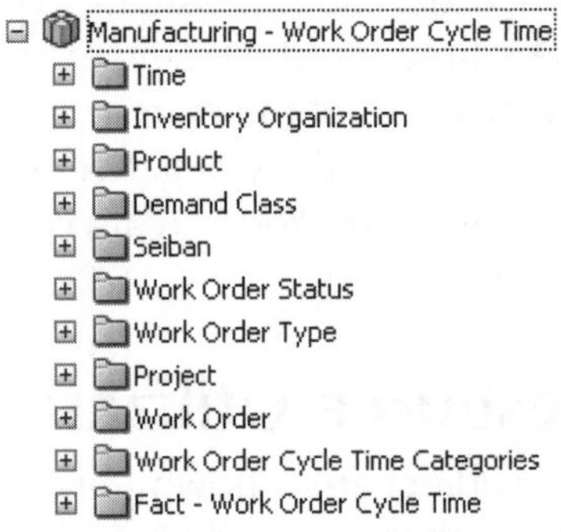

FIGURE 7-17. *Manufacturing – Work Order Cycle Time*

Work Order Performance

Use the subject area shown in Figure 7-18 for when you want to understand the overall effectiveness of the manufacturing process based on key metrics such as On Time %, Scrap %, Rework %, Parts Per Million Defects, Late Work Orders %, Yield %, and Backlog %. This is available at the lowest level of detail, with all the various dates attached to a work order and work order operations (Actual, Scheduled Start, Scheduled Completion, Released, and Required). This is the current view of any given work order and not a historical snapshot.

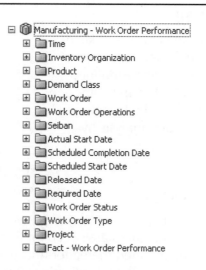

FIGURE 7-18.   *Manufacturing – Work Order Performance*

Work Order Snapshot

The subject area shown in Figure 7-19 is a snapshot of data over time, which means it won't be as useful on the first day as it will be after you've gone live and captured a number of month's worth of snapshots. Source systems won't capture the historical status of a work order, only the current state. Manufacturing Analytics freezes that view for comparison purposes. You can compare the number of open work orders, for example, at any given point in time. This is important if you want to understand trends in key metrics such as Backlog, Past Due Backlog, # of Work Orders on Hold, and so on, over time.

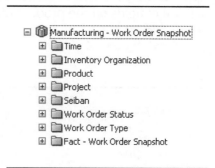

FIGURE 7-19.   *Manufacturing – Work Order Snapshot*

Inventory Aging

The subject area shown in Figure 7-20 keeps track of the inventory shelf life, with metrics such as Obsolete Quantities and Amounts, Days Left in Inventory, Days Left in Expiry, and Days Since Expired. This is at the Inventory Lot grain, and it also provides analysis by inventory buckets.

FIGURE 7-20. *Inventory – Aging*

Inventory Balances

The subject area shown in Figure 7-21 provides inventory balances by lot level. Out-of-the-box daily balances are stored for three months and then monthly snapshots are maintained thereafter (this is configurable). This is the same subject area in Oracle BI Applications 7.9.6.3 and earlier, only the lot level (lower grain) and a handful of fields on the product dimension specific to manufacturing have been added.

Inventory Transactions

The subject area shown in Figure 7-22 provides detailed inventory movement types transactions. This is the same subject area in Oracle BI Applications 7.9.6.3 and earlier, only the lot level (lower grain) and a handful of fields on the product dimension specific to manufacturing have been added.

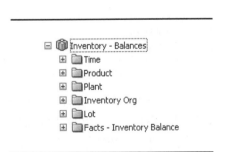

FIGURE 7-21. *Inventory – Balances*

FIGURE 7-22. *Inventory – Transactions*

FIGURE 7-23. *Inventory – Bill of Materials*

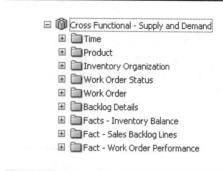

FIGURE 7-24. *Cross Functional – Supply and Demand*

Finished Goods BOM (Bill of Materials)

The subject area shown in Figure 7-23 provides the breakdown of sub-assembly items in any given finished goods bill of materials (BOM). This is the same subject area in Oracle BI Applications 7.9.6.3 and earlier. The BOM is flattened out, and you can traverse from the header to the parent, to the sub-assembly items.

Supply and Demand

Figure 7-24 shows a powerful subject area that ties together order backlogs, work orders, and inventory balances. End users, for example, can see for any given sales order the backlog, the work order assigned to address the backlog, and the inventory balances available to the work order. If, for example, an item is out of stock, the chain reaction to the work order and the backlog can be analyzed.

Typical Configurations and Customizations

If you're a JD Edwards customer, you'll have to build your own ETL adaptor to populate the staging tables. Essentially, you need to use the Oracle BI Applications universal adaptor concept. The direct mappings are not yet available from JDE tables to the BI Applications staging tables.

With the BI Applications 7.9.6.3 extension pack is a QA helper (domain) file that will need to be populated. This defines the quality collection elements gathered from each organization, along with the associated attribute column. BI Applications 7.9.6.4 no longer requires this file. Table 7-1 shows an example, should you need to implement the extension pack along with your 7.9.6.3 BI Applications implementation.

Organization ID	Collection Element	Attribute
101	Quantity	Attribute1
101	PO Quality Code	Attribute2
101	Comments	Attribute3
101	Inspection Result	Attribute4
101	Supplier Lot Number	Attribute5
101	Power Deviation	Attribute6
101	Item Category	Attribute7
101	UOM	Attribute8
101	Revision	Attribute9
101	Subinventory	Attribute10
101	Locator	Attribute11
101	Lot Number	Attribute12
101	Serial Number	Attribute13
101	Reason Code	Attribute14
101	Quantity Tested	Attribute15
101	Production Line	Attribute16
101	To Op Seq Number	Attribute17
101	From Op Seq Number	Attribute18

TABLE 7-1. *QA Helper Domain File Example Used with the Extension Pack Only*

What to Watch Out For

Depending on the full scope of your requirements, you may need to purchase and implement additional BI Applications not integrated with Manufacturing Analytics, but still use OBIEE 11*g* as a common technology and end-user interface. These are called *edge applications* (meaning outside of the core ERP system). These are typically Oracle acquisitions not yet fully integrated to the ERP.

These edge applications may include the following:

- **FTI**   Fusion Transportation Intelligence (Oracle Transportation Management source)

- **MOC**   Manufacturing Operations Center (manufacturing equipment performance)

- **APCC**   Advanced Planning Command Center (Oracle Advanced Supply Chain source)

- **P6 Analytics**   Primavera source

If you're currently on Oracle BI Applications 7.9.6.3, it's better to upgrade first to Oracle BI Applications 7.9.6.4 if you also need Manufacturing Analytics than to implement the 7.9.6.3 extension pack. The simple reason is that there's no upgrade from the extension pack to Oracle BI Applications 7.9.6.4. You'll save time in the medium and long term with this approach. Manufacturing Analytics 7.9.6.4 is much improved over the extension pack, for example the Work Order cycle time metric was added. This is of value to process manufacturers who track lots and formulas.

Also, the extension pack has limitations, such as globalization and multilanguage support. You may need special approvals even to download it. Very few customers had time to implement the extension pack before BI Applications 7.9.6.4 was released because the extension pack was a temporary stop gap.

If upgrading to 7.9.6.4 isn't an immediate option, go ahead and work with the extension pack, but hold off on customizations for as long as you can. There's much you can learn from and value you can receive by starting with the extension pack and the out-of-the-box content. You'll have a chance to work with the data, better understand what type of dashboards your plant managers and executives require, and define the next round of requirements for when you're ready for version 7.9.6.4.

NOTE
Unlike the 7.9.6.3 extension pack, there will be an upgrade path from BI Applications 7.9.6.4 to BI Applications 11g.

The Oracle BI Applications development team has been working on building a discrete Manufacturing Analytics module, which will be generally available (GA) with a BI Applications 11g version first, then as an update to the 7.9.6.x version shortly afterward.

When evaluating Manufacturing Analytics, explore the boundaries of the coverage. For example, because planned orders and work orders have a many to many relationship, you can't easily associate or link them together directly. It's important to understand how Manufacturing Analytics tracks actual work order consumption rather than the Oracle Demantra or Oracle ASCP (Advanced Supply Chain Planning in EBS) forecast. Variances therefore are based on an what was actually consumed.

Pegging is based on a Make to Order process rather than a Make to Stock process. Manufacturing Analytics, when sourced from Oracle EBS, primarily pulls data from MPS (Manufacturing Production Scheduling) out of the box. You may need some customization to pull from ASCP to pull in soft pegging and some additional planning data.

Manufacturing Analytics 7.9.6.4 captures Quality Plan data including Quality Elements from EBS (only), therefore you can monitor various quality metrics and not be limited to just scrap.

Conclusion

Manufacturing Analytics provides a holistic view of the manufacturing process—from planning, to the actual execution, to the quality and effects on inventory. By providing multiple views or angles of the process, you're able to identify major bottlenecks between process checkpoints. You can quickly identify major exceptions and outliers, by ranking and sorting various metrics. For example, what are the top ten work orders by the longest open date? What are the range of costs, quantities, and usage of inventory lots?

Finally, by tying together Manufacturing Analytics with the other Oracle BI Applications, you can form some very interesting cross-functional analysis.

For example, with organizations using specialized suppliers to handle specific tasks for a company, a given product may be shipped and received several times before being shipped to the final dealer or customer. In such cases, tracking all the movements becomes increasingly difficult without first integrating Manufacturing Analytics, Order Management and Supply Chain Analytics, and Procurement and Spend Analytics in the supply chain.

CHAPTER

8

Procurement and
Spend Analytics

Procurement and Spend Analytics tracks a purchase from the time the purchase requisition has been drafted or the replenishment order comes from the MRP (Material Requirements Planning or Material Resource Planning) until the good is received, undergoes incoming QA, and is either paid for or returned. This module also interacts with Supply Chain and Order Management Analytics because goods received are often put into inventory. It also interacts with other Oracle Business Intelligence Applications as we will discuss in the "Cross-Functional Analysis" section of this chapter. Procurement and Spend Analytics are equally applicable to the procurement of goods as to services. They are also often as applicable in a public sector or nonprofit organization as they are in a corporate setting. In addition, they are equally applicable for direct procurement and indirect procurement. Direct procurement buys direct materials and services—namely, the materials and services used to build the final product or products bought for resale. Indirect procurement procures everything else (for example, office supplies or janitorial services).

Procurement and Spend Analytics helps customers procure in two major ways:

■ They make it easier to aggregate purchases (or "spend" as procurement people call it) across the organization. When the organization understands its total spend of a commodity, Procurement can go to the market and negotiate the largest possible discount because it can confidently promise a much larger quantity purchase.

■ They make it easier to monitor the vendor's performance against the contract, allowing deviations to be detected and rectified more quickly, thus helping ensure that the savings are achieved without compromising quality or timeliness.

Description of the Business Process

For indirect procurement, typically the process goes something like this:

1. Someone fills out a requisition specifying what is to be bought.

2. Management approves the requisition (or not).

3. Procurement issues a purchase order to buy the product or service from an approved vendor, usually per a pre-negotiated contract,

or the requester buys it directly from a punch out to an approved vendor's store.

4. The vendor accepts the purchase order (or not).

5. The product or service is received.

6. The product or service is accepted or returned.

7. The invoice is received.

8. The invoice is approved for payment.

9. The invoice is paid.

Direct procurement can be much more varied. Most notably, though, it does not start with a requisition. It usually starts with the MRP system requesting a replenishment or with a vendor initiating a shipment based on rules provided by the customer (so-called *vendor managed inventory,* or *VMI*). Procurement often does not issue an individual purchase order for each MRP replenishment or VMI replenishment. A blanket purchase order is drawn down.

Figures 8-1 and 8-2 describe parts of what procurement goes through. The first figure describes what procurement does when attempting to source a category. The second figure describes how goods and services—particularly indirect goods and services—get procured. Although strategic sourcing is

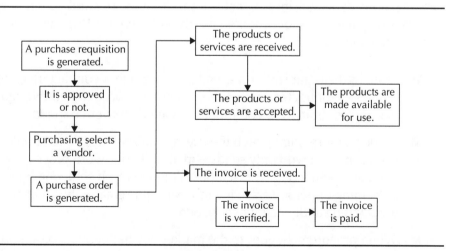

FIGURE 8-1.   *Procurement – Requisition to Check ("Req to Check")*

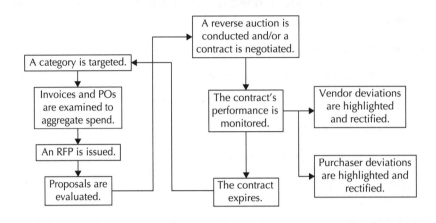

FIGURE 8-2. *Procurement – Strategic Sourcing*

not yet supported explicitly in Oracle BI Applications 7.9.6.4, the part of the process dealing with aggregating spend can be monitored. Also, parts of the process of monitoring the contract can be tracked.

Business Benefits

Organizations derive business benefits from Procurement and Spend Analytics by paying less for procured goods and services. This can arise from several sources:

- More of the organization's spend goes through a contract, reaping the lower contracted price. Often spend that does not go through an existing contract for a commodity is called "maverick spend."

- Products more often match the user's requirements. For example, does someone who only sends e-mail and does word processing need an engineering workstation? Alternatively, if someone buys something underpowered, it can wear out prematurely, for example, a truck repeatedly being overloaded.

- When procurement goes to the market, it can negotiate based on the largest anticipated spend because it knows it has collected spend from across the organization. This process is often called "strategic sourcing." The larger the spend, the better price Procurement can negotiate.

- Because it is easier for Procurement to collect spend, it can strategically source commodities it could not in the past either because it did not have time or because the effort was not worth the potential savings.

- It is easier to identify and collect rebates and discounts that do not appear on an invoice.

- Procurement can more quickly and easily identify deviations in vendor performance and take action to rectify them.

We often see that organizations can take anywhere from 0.8 percent to over 10 percent off procured materials and services tracked by Procurement and Spend Analytics. Consequently, if the people in your procurement department believe that this type of analysis can help them analyze how they spend money, the ROI on this analytic application is one of the easiest to justify.

NOTE
This benefit is in addition to the benefit described in Chapter 5 because cost center managers avoid buying goods and services they do not, or no longer, need.

Key Stakeholders

The procurement department is your major customer, all the way from individual buyers to the vice president of procurement or chief procurement officer. They own the data. They do the analysis. They are responsible for delivering the results. There may not be many users for this application, but each one can drive a huge amount of value. The value does *not* come from laying off buyers but by making them more productive. Here are some benefits if we free up time for them:

- They can source more commodities.

- They can monitor vendors' performance more closely.

■ They can monitor the market better to see whether a new competitor has come in who can give them a better price or better terms.

■ They can interact with the product development department more to ensure that products are designed with what the market can provide in mind.

If you work in a manufacturing company, also check with the plant manager. This person often has a target margin to maintain. If you can help Procurement be more effective, the plant manager will benefit.

Cross-Functional Analysis

Often Procurement and Spend Analytics is combined either with Manufacturing Analytics or Order Management and Supply Chain Analytics for a better understanding of where the purchasing process or vendors are slowing down the production and distribution processes. It can also be combined with Field Service Analytics or Enterprise Asset Management Analytics to understand the performance of repair parts and contract labor in minimizing asset downtime.

Procurement and Spend Analytics can also be paired with Financial Analytics for two reasons:

■ One can get a much more complete view of the accounts payable process than just looking at invoices and AP transactions, which are available in Procurement and Spend Analytics. Primarily, Financial Analytics adds information about balances and aging.

■ Cost center managers use Financial Analytics to identify unnecessary spend and curtail it. With Procurement and Spend Analytics combined with Financial Analytics, cost center managers can target off contract spend more specifically, not just to curtail spend but to direct their employees to target it to preferred vendors. Also, as cost center managers cut their spending, the volume that procurement can target will fall. Both procurement and cost center managers need to work together to ensure Procurement is providing vendors the best estimates of ongoing spend.

Finally, one can use Procurement Analytics with Project Analytics. PeopleSoft and E-Business Suite, for example, have very comprehensive project accounting built into their Financials and Procurement modules. These help people in project work understand what is driving their spending and their performance versus budget. It also lets them see how delays in procuring goods and services impact their ability to hit their milestones and budget numbers. To allow this feature to be used, though, people need to track project numbers in the ERP Procurement and Financials modules.

Subject Areas

Many of the subject areas for Procurement and Spend Analytics line up around parts of the procure-to-pay process. Others are used for ongoing maintenance of supplier relationships. One (Employee Expenses) is used to monitor what employees spend on their expense accounts. Together they track the information, money, and goods flow from when the goods or services are requisitioned, either by a person or an MRP system, until they arrive and are stocked or used and paid for.

Purchase Requisitions and Purchase Request Status

Purchase Requisitions and Purchase Requisition Status handle the parts of the process from the time the requisition is submitted until it is approved. They also help people track what takes the time to approve a purchase requisition. These subject areas, shown in Figures 8-3 and 8-4, look at what happens between when a purchase

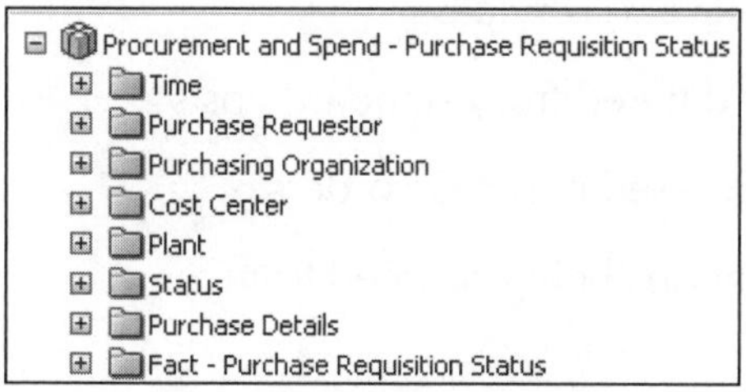

FIGURE 8-3. *Procurement and Spend – Purchase Requisitions*

FIGURE 8-4. *Procurement and Spend – Purchase Request Status*

requisition is issued and when the purchase order is issued. They look not just at the purchase requisitions themselves, but also statistics about the purchase requisition process, such as the following:

- Cycle times
- Numbers of requisitions
- Average lines per requisition

These help people in lines of business and procurement judge the efficiency of the approval process.

NOTE
Purchase Requisition Status only supports the Universal Adapter concept; therefore, to populate the current status on a purchase requisition, you would need to first write your own ETL to populate the staging tables of the BI Apps.

Purchase Orders

The subject area shown in Figure 8-5 tracks the procurement process from the time when a purchase order is issued until the goods are accepted or rejected upon receipt. It allows people from the procurement, supply chain, and manufacturing departments to understand the following:

- How long it takes to receive materials from vendors
- How the quality compares to what was expected
- How much was invoiced for goods and services
- How much the invoiced amount differed from standard costs
- How efficiently procurement processed purchase orders
- The numbers of vendors and locations being sourced from

In analyzing how procurement is saving money and is facilitating manufacturing and supply chain to do their jobs, this subject area is often at the center of the action. Take particular care, then, to ensure it is correct and verify that all expected fields are populated correctly from your source system(s).

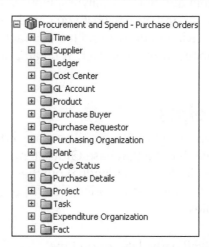

FIGURE 8-5. *Procurement and Spend – Purchase Orders*

In addition to metrics that help people understand each individual purchase order, this subject area contains many aggregate metrics that can be used to ascertain the efficiency and effectiveness of the Procurement department. These include the numbers of purchase orders, purchase order lines, the numbers of cost centers, and the purchase price variance. Oracle EBS and other ERPs support complex services procurement. Complex services procurement involves a contract for a set of services performed as part of one deliverable, usually as part of an engineering and construction or maintenance and overhaul project. However, it can be part of an IT procurement, for instance, converting a system from a legacy environment to a new environment. Often, there are milestone payments based on intermediate deliverables. Often these payments do not represent the whole value earned. Part is retained until the project is completed and the final deliverable accepted. Also, parts of the project may be financed. All these aspects of complex services procurement can be tracked with Procurement and Spend Analytics and, where applicable, Project Analytics.

For project-based services, complex services procurement can be tracked as part of Project Analytics or by itself in Procurement and Spend Analytics. You can look at schedules, overall completion rates, and the performance of in-house services and materials with Project Analytics, which you cannot do with just Procurement and Spend Analytics. However, with Procurement and Spend Analytics, over and above what you can do to monitor the orders, receipts, and invoices having to do with such a contract, you can monitor prepayments and retainage from a contract. You can also monitor the amounts financed.

Purchase Receipts

The subject area shown in Figure 8-6 provides many complex KPIs (Key Performance Indicators) that the Purchase Order Item subject area does not. It goes beyond just looking at individual purchase orders and purchase receipts to focus on KPIs that monitor price, quality, quantity, and timeliness. Here are some examples:

- Amounts received early, late, or on time

- Changes in received amounts versus a year ago

- Average days late for shipments received late

- Numbers of return transactions, return amounts, and return quantities

- Prices for goods received

Procurement people use this as they review the suppliers' performance and as they review the volumes they want to suggest to the suppliers they will buy.

This subject area also adds to the ability to track complex services procurement by including amounts and quantities of goods received that are part of a complex services agreement.

FIGURE 8-6. *Procurement and Spend – Purchase Receipts*

Purchase Cycle Lines

Like the Purchase Receipts subject area, the subject area shown in Figure 8-7 contains complex KPIs used to judge the performance of a procurement organization or of vendors supplying your organization goods and services. These include the following:

FIGURE 8-7. *Procurement and Spend – Purchase Cycle Lines*

- Percent received early, on time, or late.

- Cycle times for purchase requisition to approval, purchase requisition approval to purchase order approval, and purchase order approval to purchase receipt.

- Metrics concerning comparing prices paid to standard costs, such as PO amount at purchase price, PO amount at standard cost, and percent price variance.

- The supplier score. Although Oracle has provided a standard definition of this metric—a combination of percent received early, percent received on time, percent received late, and PO cost variance—organizations often build this according to their own definition. This definition is stored in the Business layer of the RPD. The RPD describes the mapping between the data in the data warehouse (physical layer) through the business layer into the presentation layer, which users see when they want to build queries.

These metrics are invaluable in helping the supply chain, manufacturing, and procurement people understand what drove variances from standard costs and what caused inventory shortages.

Invoice Lines

By now, we have modeled requisitioning, ordering, and receiving goods and services. The next step in the process is to receive and pay the invoices. At this point, you know whether or not people bought products from preferred vendors using contracted prices. The subject area shown in Figure 8-8 also introduces a dimension table containing information about projects and tasks. This is used to assign purchases to different projects, as discussed in the "Cross-Functional Analysis" section. Besides measuring the efficiency of the invoicing process, it also introduces metrics to measure how much spend could be addressed with better compliance. Some of these metrics include

- Payables leakage amount and year-ago payables leakage amount

- Invoice price variance, year ago, and percentage change

- Average invoice unit price and year-ago average invoice unit price

- Benchmark price and supplier benchmark price

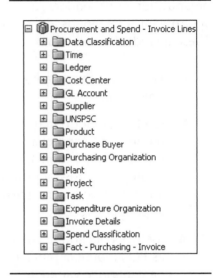

FIGURE 8-8. *Procurement and Spend – Invoice Lines*

Metrics such as these help procurement departments benchmark their performance and understand how much more effective they could be in cutting costs. Facilitating this type of analysis typically drives much more value than figuring out how to process a few more invoices a day does. Moreover, it does so without cutting employees.

Supplier AP Transactions

This subject area tracks how the organization pays its suppliers (see Figure 8-9). It contains information based on accounts payable (AP) transactions, such as the number and the frequency with which they are paid early or late. Unlike the AP subject area in Financial Analytics, this subject area does not include balances or aging. However, it is based on the same fact table. In Procurement and Spend Analytics, the Supplier AP Transactions table only has the following dimensions licensed:

- W_XACT_TYPE_D
- W_PARTY_D

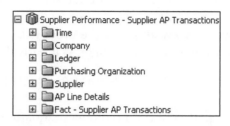

FIGURE 8-9. *Procurement and Spend – Supplier AP Transactions*

- W_LEDGER_D

- W_SUPPLIER_ACCOUNT_D

- W_AP_TERMS_D

- W_STATUS_D

- W_DAY_D

- W_INT_ORG_D

Financial Analytics has supplier AP transactions at a much finer grain.

Supplier Performance

Procurement and Spend Analytics let a procurement department conduct periodic reviews of its suppliers with much less effort than it does today. Today, it may take Procurement several days or even more than a week to prepare for a review with a supplier. During this time, Procurement should gather information about the following:

- How well the vendor has performed against its obligations regarding, timeliness, quality, and cost.

- How well the company is doing to meet its objectives as to the quantities purchased and adequacy of notice given.

We often find that, although a contract may state that the goods will be shipped, for example, 30 days after receipt of order, the customer requests delivery two weeks after the order is issued. When the shipment shows up three weeks later, is it early, late, or on time?

■ Whether price escalators or deflators are being applied appropriately.

If a procurement department can hold reviews quarterly, for example, instead of annually, they and the vendor can identify and rectify problems before they get out of hand. If Procurement can target second-tier as well as first-tier vendors, they can improve their relations with those vendors. This improvement in timeliness, quality, and cost can then help make lines of business more effective as well as lower costs. Some organizations also make supplier scorecards available to their suppliers, not as static reports, but as interactive dashboards. Providing suppliers dashboards will help ensure that the supplier and customer both have the same view of the supplier's performance. In this way, there will be fewer surprises during supplier reviews.

There are no metrics in the Supplier Performance subject area (shown in Figure 8-10) that do not appear in other subject areas. This subject area exists because it drives a particular need—namely, improving supplier performance.

Given how this subject area is used, Oracle supplies the metrics needed for this purpose, including the following:

■ Percent and quantity received early, late, and on time.

In this metric, genuine lateness is not separated from when the customer requested shipment outside of contract guidelines. Although there is no explicit support for contracts, this metric is date driven, for example, requested date versus received date.

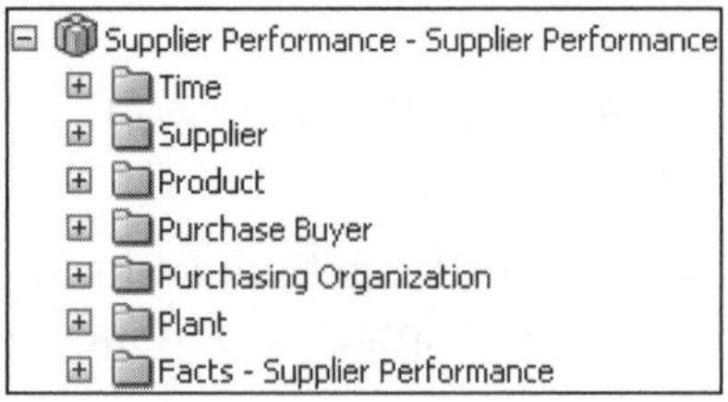

FIGURE 8-10. *Procurement and Spend – Supplier Performance*

- PO cost variance

- Percent accepted and rejected

- Purchase cycle time and receipt cycle time

- Supplier score

Procure to Pay

The subject area shown in Figure 8-11 contains only metrics found in other subject areas. It does, though, allow for monitoring the whole procure-to-pay process. It contains a subset of quantity and monetary value metrics that allow organizations to monitor the flow of goods from requisition, if any, through purchase order to receipt and invoice. For an organization looking at the whole process as an overview, from the point of view of the supplier, the product, and the receiving location, this subject area is a good place to start.

Employee Expenses

Finally, Oracle provides an Employee Expenses category (see Figure 8-12). This is useful not only by itself, but also with Project Analytics and HR Analytics. This cross-functional analysis helps identify what is contributing to a project's cost as well as what types of people may not be following corporate guidelines as to preferred airlines, hotels, and car rental companies. At Siebel, Tom Siebel had on his personal dashboard a list of the top 10 employees by employee expenses. Unless there was a very special

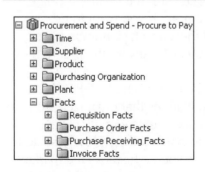

FIGURE 8-11. *Procurement and Spend – Procure to Pay*

FIGURE 8-12. *Employee Expenses*

situation (for example, working on a consulting project far away from home), it was a very uncomfortable list to be on.

This subject area looks at actual, approved, and requested expenses and items related to filing expense reports, for example, time to file, time to approve, and time to reimburse. More importantly, Employee Expenses allows expenses to be sliced by many dimensions, including the following:

■ Cost Center

■ Employee and Employee Organization

■ Approver

■ Expense Source

■ Project and Project Expenditure Type and Task

■ GL Account

■ Payment Method

■ Adjustment Reason

■ Time

Typical Configurations and Customizations

Procurement and Spend Analytics can be implemented in a fairly straightforward manner. Mostly, you must make sure that the appropriate hooks are enabled in the ERP system. For example, if you want to tie expenses to projects, ensure that project numbers and task numbers are coded on the ERP. If your organization uses p-cards, ensure the p-card files are fed into the ERP.

People often enrich their data with UNSPSC codes. The UNSPSC is an organization under the auspices of the United Nations that organizes products into product families. This lets procurement departments identify close substitutes and also identify products related to one another. Closely related products should be easier for the same buyer to source because the markets should be similar. This can be done manually, by asking vendors to do it, or by sending out the data to a third-party provider. Procurement and Spend Analytics supports UNSPSC codes.

Strategic Sourcing

Although strategic sourcing is not yet formally supported, you can use the existing Procurement and Spend Analytics to help a procurement department with a strategic sourcing initiative. You can use the existing Purchase Orders or Purchase Receipts subject area to gather information on the entire spend for a commodity, the vendors currently providing it, and their current timeliness, quality, and cost performance. This information helps Procurement know how much it can advise vendors to plan for as it draws an RFP or ITT in British English, (Request for Proposal and Invitation to Tender, respectively) for a commodity. Procurement departments often spend months gathering the spend before putting out an RFP. Historic spend data provided by the Purchase Orders or Purchase Receipt subject areas can also highlight which vendors should be short listed and which should not be offered the opportunity to bid.

Also, you can use the Supplier Performance subject area to collect the information needed for supplier reviews easily.

What to Watch Out For

Because you cannot control easily what your suppliers or engineers call a part, there may be a lot of duplication within your product files. As we have described before, the presence of dirty data in your ERP is no excuse to delay implementation. It is almost always better to make better decisions based on dirty data than superficial decisions based on no analytic environment. Also, you can use Spend Classification Analytics to fill in product categories and other missing attributes based on Oracle Data Mining.

Also problematic is having suppliers set up multiple times, either within a single ERP or across multiple ERPs. To view global spend by supplier, for example, there needs to be a way to link all the suppliers together. When your suppliers have the exact same name, OBIEE will automatically aggregate and group the spend by supplier. When names and other attributes are different, however, then a Master Data Management (MDM) strategy needs to be deployed. A quick way to handle this initially is to implement a cross-reference table and use this as a lookup to populate a supplier hierarchy on the existing Supplier dimension.

A common area of confusion concerns the scope of the type of spend tracked by Procurement and Spend Analytics. Mobile phone bill details, for example, are not tracked. This type of detail, even if provided in electronic (EDI) format, is not kept in the ERP procurement process or in employee expense lines.

A common question that comes up concerns support for Oracle EBS iStore. It has been our experience that this is simply an ecommerce front end to the Oracle EBS Procurement back end. Therefore, requisitions and purchase orders generated through EBS iStore would be pulled into Procurement and Spend Analytics.

Spend Classification

Spend Classification is a relatively new BI Application. It does not look like other BI Applications in that it does not consist of the usual four elements—namely, a data model, prebuilt ETL, metadata, and prebuilt dashboards, reports, and alerts. Also, unlike other BI Applications, it is highly tied to the Oracle database because it uses Oracle Data Mining as its data-mining engine. It, however, is not necessarily tied to an ERP Oracle produces. It can be run from data extracted from any ERP. It provides added functionality to people with Procurement and Spend Analytics, which is why we include it in this chapter. This is licensed separately; Procurement and Spend Analytics are a pre-requisite. Despite this application being relatively expensive per seat, an organization will not need to buy very many seats of it. Only the few power users who will build the models need have seats. Note that although this application uses Oracle Data Mining as its data-mining engine, you can still run it if your procurement systems were not written by Oracle and do not run on the Oracle database. In that sense, it keeps with the design specifications of all other Oracle BI Applications—that they not be confined to Oracle applications or database customers.

Description of the Business Process

When someone introduces a new product, often they will put in "Miscellaneous" or "Unknown" for a product category, or leave it blank. In any event, this description does not help Procurement consolidate spend. Without a good view of the organization's spend, Procurement lacks the knowledge it needs to go the market and negotiate for the best possible terms. Spend Classification uses Oracle Data Mining to attempt to classify purchases.

Spend Classification can use the UNSPSC taxonomy, the taxonomy used in EBS, or a custom taxonomy.

Operation

Figure 8-13 illustrates the process flow for spend classification. As with most data-mining products, one first picks a set of data to "train" the data-mining algorithm. This data should be checked to ensure that the categories are both correct and consistent across the enterprise. For instance, if one unit of a bank considers an ATM (cash point) machine a piece of computer hardware, another should not consider it part of a building, just because it is built into a wall. This data set can either be extracted from data warehouse tables or uploaded from Excel. Often people will extract data from the data warehouse, classify it by hand, and then upload it to the spend classification engine. This sample of data needs to be broad enough that the Spend Classification engine can see examples of the types of goods and services that go into all major categories the enterprise uses. This data can come from purchase requisitions, purchase orders, or AP transactions. If a category is not represented in the training data, Spend Classification will not be able to guess how to classify it when someone goes to classify it on

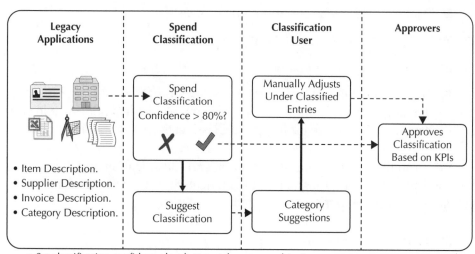

• Set classification confidence levels to match program objectives.
• Experts examine a very small number of exceptions.

FIGURE 8-13. *Process flow for Spend Classification*

a full run. Also, all descriptive fields should be filled in, allowing the Spend Classification engine to fill in the most descriptive fields on its full run.

Once Spend Classification has processed the training data, you can run the data mining engine on a larger set of data. Spend Classification will classify records where it finds a good enough match between the contents of its training data set and the record in question. It may fill in all fields—a "well-classified" record. It may fill in a subset of fields—a "semi-classified" record. If it cannot find a sufficiently high match for any field, it will mark the record as "unclassified."

Once a classification run is complete, we recommend going through and checking a subset of the classified and unclassified records. This offers you the opportunity to override what Spend Classification has chosen. These revised records can then be classified as "approved." Spend Classification will then use these to improve its model, which in turn allows it to improve its matching ability.

How to Classify the Data

Begin by splitting the data set into three parts—for training, validation, and testing. Then, for each language that the product data contains, download the training data set and cleanse it manually:

- Make all abbreviations and names consistent.
- Categorize items consistently.
- Use names in your taxonomy
- Identify any missing leaf nodes in the taxonomy and add records to the training data set for these. The more complete the leaf nodes are in your taxonomy, the more useful Spend Classification's results will be.

Next, run the training dataset through Spend Classification and then run the validation data set through Spend Classification. Check the results of the validation data set by performing the following tasks:

- Correct the results as needed.
- Fill in any missing fields.
- Label these records as "Approved."

After validating the model, test it with the test data set. This helps ensure that any changes made during validation stand up to an independent set of data. Then repeat this for all languages.

Run the validation data set and check the results. Spend Classification provides several graphs that show how successfully Oracle Data Mining was able to classify the records in the data set you gave it, given the training data set you provided and the degree of confidence you specified when you ran the model. It also shows the number of levels of hierarchy it was able to fill in. Then, you can manually override any results the data-mining algorithm made where you see mistakes. These overrides will be added to the model to help it improve in the future.

Advanced Model Creation

If you want to build your own model rather than use either the EBS or UNSPSC model, this feature lets you build your own. It does assume, though, that you have some familiarity with data-mining algorithms. A wizard guides you through the process of setting up the model. You specify the columns within a table to be used (input) and enriched (output) as well as the algorithm to be used for your training data set. Oracle does not give guidance as to which algorithm should be used. This is best left for scenarios not well handled by the default taxonomies.

Integration with E-Business Suite iProcurement

In iProcurement, you can use the results of a Spend Classification exercise to add category information to individual non-catalog items. In the profile options, set the Oracle Data Mining (ODM) model, the URL for the Web Service for the Spend Classification, and enable category classification on the non-catalog request page. Then perform the following steps:

1. Navigate to Shop.

2. Navigate to Non Catalog Request.

3. Add the item to the cart.

4. When the Category Selection Region displays, click Assisted.

By integrating Spend Classification with iProcurement, you can be assured that what has been discovered in Spend Classification becomes part of EBS and the two stay synchronized.

Final Thoughts on Spend Classification

We often find that well over half of purchase records have incomplete or almost totally missing information about the product being purchased. For Procurement to be able to conduct good strategic sourcing, it needs to have accurate figures about how much the organization is spending on different goods and services. Only then will it be able to use the organization's entire buying power to get the best possible pricing. Also, only then will it be able to highlight where people are not buying on contract. When people do not buy on contract, our experience is that they pay about 15 percent more than the contract price. Spend Classification, especially when integrated into iProcurement, allows Procurement to understand how much people are spending and to monitor whether they are using the approved pricing. This helps to reap the 0.8- to 10-percent decrease in costs that truly effective procurement can bring to an organization.

Conclusion

Every organization—whether public sector or private sector, for profit or nonprofit—buys products and services. Ensuring the organization gets the maximum value for what it pays helps the organization expand its goals. Helping procurement ensure vendors deliver products at the agreed combination of price, quality, and timeliness helps the rest of the organization do what it is tasked with. The justification for this analytic application is one of the easiest to develop.

One of our customers was a small chain of Catholic hospitals. The CEO, a nun, summarized the issue well: "No money, no mission," she said. With Procurement and Spend Analytics, you and your procurement department can help free up more money for your organization's mission.

CHAPTER
9

HR Analytics

In some sense, HR Analytics should be the most ubiquitous analytic application. After all, what organization does not have employees or contractors? These employees and contractors bring a wide range of talents to bear to help an organization meet its mission. As they spend more time with the organization, they gain more skills specific to the organization. As long as they remain qualified to do their jobs, retaining these people should be a priority. So should monitoring their skills, certifications, and career development. Even making the case when an employee's skills do not match what is required and the employee must be moved on or counseled out of the organization should be a priority for the organization to function well. HR Analytics helps organizations manage these vital tasks.

In 7.9.6, Oracle added the Absence Management, Recruitment, and Learning Enrollment and Completion subject areas. These subject areas enhanced the value of HR Analytics by letting the organization track how it was sourcing employees, who was absent, and what classes they were taking and completing. As will be discussed later, using HR Analytics to track where employees come from, how they perform once hired, and whether they stay turns out to be one of the easiest business benefits to quantify in monetary terms. Similarly, being able to track excessive absences and determine root causes are also relatively easy-to-quantify business benefits.

Description of the Business Process

HR Analytics has moved beyond its original monitoring of the "hire-to-retire" process by including learning and absence management. It has also extended this process to become "recruit to retire." Figure 9-1 and Figure 9-2, respectively, show a picture of the recruit-to-hire process and the hire-to-retire process.

The hiring process is familiar to most of us:

- A requisition is requested.

- If approved, a requisition is opened.

- The requisition is posted, usually internally first. If someone seemingly qualified applies, we go to the applicant management subprocess. If no one seemingly qualified applies, either the job is posted, according to company practice, on the organization's website or the job requisition is given to one or more staffing firms, internal or external recruiters, or employment agencies to fill.

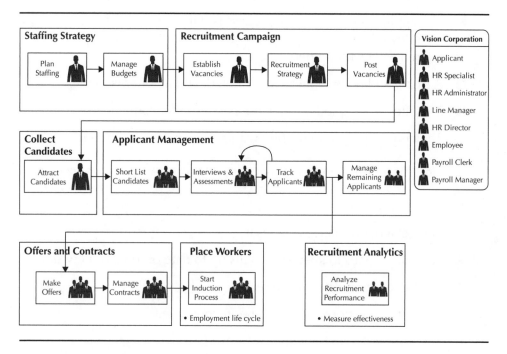

FIGURE 9-1. *The recruit-to-hire process*

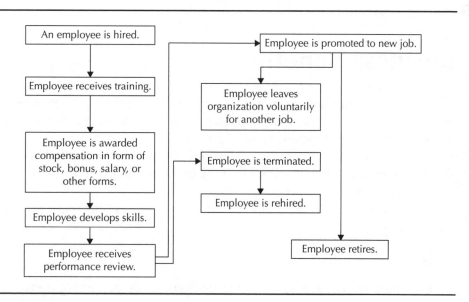

FIGURE 9-2. *The hire-to-retire process*

- The applicant management process is started. Candidates are interviewed, proficiency tests are administered, and background and reference checks are performed.

- A salary and benefit package is drafted, and an offer is made.

- The offer is accepted or rejected, perhaps after some negotiation.

- The new employee joins the organization and is onboarded.

Similarly, most of us know what happens after one joins an organization:

- You do your job.

- You get a performance appraisal.

- You take classes to keep your skills up to date or to learn new skills.

- You get promoted or transferred.

- You get raises, bonuses, and other recognition.

- You are entitled to benefits.

- Eventually, you retire, resign, get laid off, or get fired.

In addition, organizations often have to answer to governments about diversity measures.

Business Benefits

To date, the easiest business benefit to quantify is what the HR people sometimes call "minimizing regrettable turnover"—namely, getting people you want to stay not to resign. The authors' research shows that the cost to replace someone is between 80 and 120 percent of an employee's expected annual pay. The Hackett Group says the cost is even higher: It is between 80 and 120 percent of an employee's fully loaded costs (in other words, total pay plus benefits and overheads).

Total pay comes in several forms, so do not forget to count them all. They may include

- Wages or salaries.

- Commissions. We assume commissions at 100 percent of quota for people in sales.

- Overtime, for hourly employees.

- The expected value of bonuses.

Then add a percentage for benefits and overheads, if you want to use the Hackett metric, rather than our more conservative metric. Benefits and overheads can range from 30 percent to over 60 percent. The head of HR can help you with this number.

How could hiring costs be this big? Here are some of the direct costs the organization will incur:

- The hiring manager's time filling out the requisition

- Their management's time approving or denying it

- Managerial and HR time reviewing resumes and interviewing candidates

- Travel and living expenses for the candidate to visit the employer

- Recruiters' and employment agencies' fees

- Background check fees

- Placement test fees

- Hiring bonuses

- Relocation expenses

- Nonrecoverable draw

- New employee training costs

- Part of the employee's salary prior to the employee being fully up to speed

In addition to the direct costs, there is the value that client-facing people add, which we do not include in the preceding calculation:

- For people in a sales function, their share of the value of revenue they bring in. This includes people in outside sales, inside sales, and customer service reps with selling responsibilities.

■ For people in service, their billings, whether actual billings to customers or the imputed value of billings for repairs done as part of a service contract or warranty.

One of us was reviewing this breakdown with a prospect in the financial services industry. He had an IT person and an HR person on the phone. The IT person scoffed at the 80-to-120-percent number as far too high. The HR person said, "For client advisors, that's about right."

HR Analytics helps HR and hiring managers mitigate regrettable turnover in several ways (see Figure 9-3):

■ It helps identify recruiting channels and recruiting methods that provide employees who succeed and stay. Different channels have different chances of providing people who are likely to stay and thrive. Management needs to identify the most productive channels and reward and nurture these. This analysis can help identify when a "more expensive" channel is really worth the added expense.

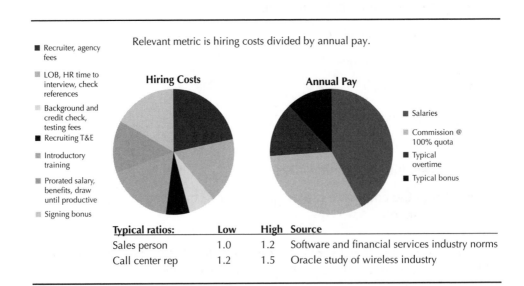

Relevant metric is hiring costs divided by annual pay.

■ Recruiter, agency fees
▨ LOB, HR time to interview, check references
▨ Background and credit check, testing fees
■ Recruiting T&E
■ Introductory training
■ Prorated salary, benefits, draw until productive
▨ Signing bonus

Hiring Costs   **Annual Pay**

■ Salaries
▨ Commission @ 100% quota
■ Typical overtime
■ Typical bonus

Typical ratios:	Low	High	Source
Sales person	1.0	1.2	Software and financial services industry norms
Call center rep	1.2	1.5	Oracle study of wireless industry

FIGURE 9-3. *Cutting regrettable turnover reduces costs to replace*

Considering the cost of turnover, choosing a channel that provides people who are more likely to stay and thrive should provide much more value than just ensuring that the hiring cycle is executed efficiently. Consider this the difference between "doing things right" (analyzing the efficiency of the recruiting process) and "doing right things" (hiring preferentially from channels that demonstrate the greatest rates of success). We have not discovered anyone else's recruiting analytics that allow this type of analysis.

■   Nothing is worse than hiring an employee and finding that the job is not what the employee thought it would be. We had one client who ran a call center and found that the job simulation provided a watered-down version of what the job was like. Also, the interviewers were not setting expectations properly on the numbers of calls that people would have to answer or the short time between calls. After experimenting with different interviewing scripts and job simulations, they got candidates who were not suited for the job to drop out of the hiring process sooner, thus minimizing our client's cost. Those who were left understood better what the job entailed and stayed longer.

■   One client wants to use HR Analytics to identify what it calls "Bosses from Hell." This client has a definition for the term. The characteristics include bosses whose internal postings attract few, if any, applicants, bosses with higher-than-average turnover among their subordinates, fewer-than-normal numbers of transfers to other units (the manager has veto power over a person transferring in this organization), longer time-in-grade within the work unit, and several other metrics. They feel that if they can identify Bosses from Hell and get them training and counseling before they poison the atmosphere of the work unit, regrettable turnover can be cut.

■   Careers can be managed more by the numbers, ensuring that people throughout the organization get the chance to develop and manage their careers, helping them to feel that the organization values them as employees. Also, training can be correlated to regrettable turnover to show what training programs contribute to longevity.

We also saw one organization that was having problems with absences. This organization ran a chain of clinics and had doctors on staff. When it found itself shorthanded, it had to contract with outside doctors at a much higher rate. It found a consistent pattern of doctors calling in sick on days when the local football team was in town, thus increasing the cost to the employer. The chain of clinics spanned several metropolitan areas, meaning all the doctors were not affected on the same weekends. HR Analytics allowed them to see the problem and take steps to fix it.

Key Stakeholders

We have repeatedly found that to get and keep funding and enthusiasm for a BI project, it is imperative to line up people who will win if the analytics are implemented and succeed. This may sound self-evident, but we do not see IT people who want analytics implemented line up their support nearly enough. Then the project becomes an IT-only project with no cost justification. Also, often the business people who will use the project feel that IT is forcing them to accept something they do not want. Take the time to locate these people and figure out how they can win.

First, line up key line-of-business executives, meaning "anyone except HR." These people pay the bill in terms of reduced productivity when employees leave in higher-than-acceptable numbers. They have to put up with reduced productivity when they make a poor hiring decision, a decision that would have been less likely to happen if HR and line-of-business executives knew which channels produced people who were more likely to stay and succeed. Does this mean that an IT executive is, for the purpose of HR Analytics, a line-of-business executive? Yes. However, please cast your net more broadly than that. Look for executives who have a hard time attracting or keeping qualified people. Look for executives in the areas of the organization that drive the company's strategy. Look for executives in areas that are growing. These may be call center managers, sales vice presidents, R&D vice presidents, VPs of operation, or wherever your organization needs to attract and keep good people to advance its mission. Ask them what it would be worth if they could cut their regrettable turnover. Ask them what it would be worth if they could be better assured that the people they extended offers to and who accepted would be more likely to succeed and stay. If you cannot get a succinct answer from one line-of-business executive, look elsewhere. You're probably talking to the wrong people.

Second, look at senior HR executives. These people bear some of the cost of recruiting and therefore will be interested if HR Analytics can cut their recruiting costs by cutting the number of people they have to recruit in the first place. They also are usually in charge of monitoring the progress of any diversity initiatives. Note that diversity initiatives may not resemble what we are used to seeing in western cultures. They may be set up to give preference to citizens or indigenous people as opposed to expatriates. Keep the following points in mind:

- The value from monitoring diversity programs arises, first, from ensuring that the organization complies with all applicable regulations and is able to defend itself if called upon to justify its actions.

- Second, the value arises from being able to execute any diversity initiatives the organization has laid out for itself. Usually, the weakest value proposition arises from quantifying the time saved from speeding up the monitoring of diversity initiatives.

Also, if your organization has unions, HR Analytics can help monitor that hiring and layoff policies are executed as required by the collective bargaining agreement, saving or minimizing the money that would be required to contest grievances.

Finally, some companies have separate learning departments dedicated to ensuring that employees are trained to be able to do not only their current jobs, but also the jobs the organization expects they will need to do in a few years. The people in these departments will want to understand what training employees take and, ideally, how it affects their job performance. To the people in these departments, the value, at minimum, should be finding out which training programs do not provide employees with the required measurable skills and replacing them with programs that do.

Cross-Functional Analysis

Because employees are core to much of what happens in most organizations, many cross-functional analyses include HR Analytics. These can include monitoring the performance of frontline personnel as recorded in parts of a CRM system and tying it to training programs, tenure, compensation, or sources where these people were recruited. HR Analytics can also be used with Project Analytics to understand the ability of different people to perform similar tasks in different projects and how that relates to their training, tenure,

Metric	Additional Applications Required
Revenue per employee Costs per contingent worker Expenses per employee Contribution per employee Net margin per employee AP invoices per AP clerk per day AR invoices per AR clerk per day	Finance (note that this can be calculated at a total enterprise level only)
Number of inbound interactions per CSR Number of outbound interactions per CSR Close rate (for trouble tickets) per CSR First call resolution per CSR	Contact Center
Leads per sales rep	Sales
POs, both value and count, processed by buyer per day	Procurement

TABLE 9-1. *Sample Cross-Functional Metrics and the Additional Applications Needed to Enable These Metrics*

compensation, and other attributes. It can also be used in conjunction with Financial Analytics to ensure the correct expense data is used to calculate profitability per employee. Also, at one organization, we have seen HR Analytics combined with Manufacturing Analytics to analyze whether completed courses correlate with reduced accidents, increased productivity, reduced overtime, or increased quality.

In addition, if your organization has purchased other analytic applications, many compound metrics are either newly exposed or can now be analyzed by the characteristics of the employees that make them up. These are detailed in Table 9-1.

Subject Areas

Release 7.9.6 added much new content to HR Analytics. In addition to three new subject areas—Recruitment, Learning, and Absences—Oracle enhanced the existing Compensation and Workforce Profile Subject Areas. For those of you who wondered where Retention went, it got rolled into Workforce Profile. This release also increased the number of levels of hierarchy for the organization to 15 and the number of levels of supervisory hierarchy to 18.

Absence

This subject area, shown in Figure 9-4, contains data, not only on absences, but also on headcount. Besides counting the absence hours or days, both notified and unnotified, it also counts the number of absences and computes frequencies of absences. These can be tracked down to the date the absence occurred. HR professionals also view absence trends as predictors of employee engagement, which often drives productivity and retention. Also, because this subject area contains headcount facts, many

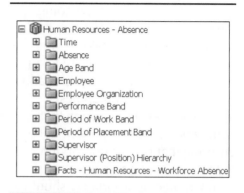

FIGURE 9-4. *Human Resources – Absence*

types of analysis can be performed that compare the incidence of absence to criteria dealing with the composition and structure of the workforce. Headcount facts describe counts of employees, contractors, full-time employees, part-time employees, supervisors, and almost any other way you can *count* employees. HR Analytics also lets you aggregate employees into full-time equivalents. Therefore, although HR Analytics calls the metrics "counts," in reality they can be more complex than simply counting people. This complication also affects how aggregations are performed. This subject area also includes time of service metrics. By combining these, one can understand the effects of both demographics and seniority on the frequency of different types of absences and, given their predictive value in determining engagement and retention, the likely effect in the future if absences are not addressed.

Compensation

The subject area shown in Figure 9-5 concerns itself with the whole body of compensation, including salaries, overtime, bonuses, deductions, and net pay. It also provides a subset of the metrics used in the U.S. Statutory

Compliance subject area dealing with compensation. With this subject area, one can track compensation to see whether total compensation is equitable across different groups of employees (for instance, across geography and job family) doing the same job. People also use it to compare compa ratio (i.e., the ratio of an employee's salary to an appropriate average or benchmark) across divisions, geographies, and so on. Besides ensuring that compensation drives performance, ensuring that people contributing to the organization's success are compensated appropriately should also cut regrettable turnover by removing one cause of people leaving. As HR professionals know, people leave for many reasons, but effective administration of compensation should help the organization husband its resources and devote them to people who provide a disproportionate share of the contribution to the organization.

FIGURE 9-5. *Human Resources – Compensation*

Learning Enrollment and Completion

Learning Enrollment and Completion, shown in Figure 9-6, tracks people's use of company-sponsored training programs. It tracks enrollment, the taking of classes, the grades they get, and how long it takes them to get through a program of learning. It handles web-based training and instructor training as well as in-house and company-approved third-party training equally. It can also help evaluate what groups of employees are taking what classes. In this way, both line of business and HR management can understand variations in the uptake of classes and of different groups' performance in

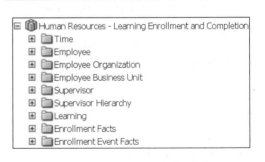

FIGURE 9-6. *Human Resources – Learning Enrollment and Completion*

the training programs. Also, management can assess effectiveness of training programs by tying training to job performance, particularly for front office or production employees (that is, employees whose productivity is relatively easily measured). They can also assess whether higher cost types of training (for example, lab versus lecture or instructor led versus web based) give outcomes that justify their higher cost.

Performance

There are two sets of facts in the subject area shown in Figure 9-7: performance facts and headcount facts. As discussed in the section on the Absence subject area, headcount metrics contain counts of employees. Performance metrics, on the other hand, contain the costs and revenues of these employees. The costs are payroll costs and contractor costs. The fact that revenue metrics do not make sense for most public sector and nonprofit organizations should not detract from this subject area's value. The ability to understand where the money is going should help the organization tie the cost per person to whatever measures exist of the value that that unit makes to the organization's mission.

Recruitment

This subject area, shown in Figure 9-8, covers the cycle from when the organization decides it needs to hire someone until that person joins the organization. We showed a diagram of this process earlier. This process lets line of business and HR people manage the pipeline and the time it takes to get someone on board. Have you ever taken a job only to have another employer come back to you

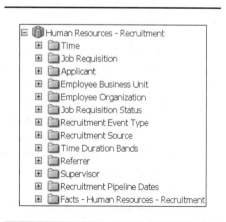

FIGURE 9-8. *Human Resources – Recruitment*

FIGURE 9-7. *Human Resources – Performance*

and say, "If only you had waited another month, we would have hired you?" If so, you should understand what can happen if an organization takes too long to hire someone they really want.

Recruitment also lets people understand the effectiveness of an internal recruitment program. It is an article of faith that internal referrals have a higher likelihood of success than people hired from the outside. After all, if I refer someone and that person does not turn out well, my reputation suffers, too. Also, if certain areas attract no or very few referrals, that may be as telling as if they post internally and no one applies.

In this subject area, one has several collections of facts:

■ **Applicant facts** These describe headcounts of the applicant pool. Organizations can then look at whether different segments of the applicant pool for both contingent and permanent employees are rising or falling and compare that to the numbers of requisitions in the pipeline. By measuring these metrics, one can ensure that requisitions are filled promptly and see whether campaigns to attract new people are providing the numbers of applicants needed. These facts also contain two metrics that are not counts: interview score and screening score.

■ **Quality of Hire facts** This narrow fact table contains counts and scores on the new employees' performance as they complete their initial service to the organization.

■ **Requisition facts** These facts measure counts and cycle times of people and events dealing with the hiring process. In this collection of facts, you can find cycle times for most events in the hiring process, from when the application is drafted until an applicant accepts or rejects a job offer. All cycle times date from when the requisition was open. Therefore, if you want to measure the time between two other events, just subtract the two relevant ones to get the cycle time you want. Oracle also measures the age of requisitions in months. In addition, one has counts of requisitions throughout the hiring process and the numbers of openings. These differ because a requisition may contain requests to hire for multiple openings. When taken together, the organization can see how well it is moving people through the hiring process and where the bottlenecks are, whether in attracting people to fill openings or getting them interviewed and screened or in making a decision on whether or not to hire them.

■ **Recruitment Cycle Time facts**   These facts look at the same cycle times as the requisition, except they look at them from the point of view of the applicant, not the requisition.

■ **Recruitment Event facts**   At each of the events described in the diagram of the process shown in Figure 9-1, HR Analytics keeps track of how many people are at that stage at a point of time and how many people exited the process there. By comparing different stages in the process, an organization can tell where people are leaving the process and compare that to historical norms.

■ **Recruitment ratios**   This fact table contains many ratios that describe the organization's ability to move people through the recruiting process and the success of the employee referral program.

The organization's ability to move people through the recruiting process shows how efficiently the organization can recruit people and can identify where people are dropping out of the process. Together with the Recruitment Cycle Time facts, these ratios can paint a rich picture of how well oiled the recruiting machine is. However, to tell how well these people do once hired, one has to marry these metrics with the Quality of Hire metrics described earlier.

Employee referrals are considered to have a higher likelihood of succeeding than people from the outside because referrers stake part of their reputations on the quality of the people they refer.

U.S. Statutory Compliance

When I speak of "employees" in this section, this includes full-time and part-time employees and contractors. This subject area, shown in Figure 9-9, is used for people who need to report to the U.S. Government on their compliance with programs that monitor the diversity, immigration status, and veterans' status of a workforce. The language proficiency of employees is also monitored. In this subject area, the dimensions are more important than the facts. The facts all fall into four categories: headcounts, times between events (for example, hire to leave), pay averages, or ratios of counts. These are used to help an HR department ensure that its practices do not violate various laws. They can also be used to help monitor performance with internal diversity programs or with union contracts. This and the Workforce Profile have largely the same dimensions. This has a Period of Work dimension that Workforce Profile does not have. They only have one fact table in common: Time in Service Facts.

```
☐ ⬡ Human Resources - US Statutory Compliance
    ⊞ 📁 Time
    ⊞ 📁 Age Band
    ⊞ 📁 Employee
    ⊞ 📁 Employee Organization
    ⊞ 📁 Employee Business Unit
    ⊞ 📁 Performance Band
    ⊞ 📁 Period of Work Band
    ⊞ 📁 Period of Placement Band
    ⊞ 📁 HR Event Type
    ⊞ 📁 International Assignment
    ⊞ 📁 Supervisor
    ⊞ 📁 Supervisor (Position) Hierarchy
    ⊞ 📁 Facts - Human Resources - US Statutory Compliance
```

FIGURE 9-9. *Human Resources – U.S. Statutory Compliance*

This subject area contains the following fact tables:

- Terminations and Hires

- Performance Facts

- Headcount Facts

- FTE Facts

- Salary Facts (just base salary)

- Compensation Facts (includes all compensation, not just salary)

- Gender and Race Specific Headcount Facts

- Gender and Race Specific Salary Facts

- Time in Service Facts

We have not spent much time on reports provided because organizations typically modify these. However, this subject area provides many of the reports needed for U.S. Government Equal Employment Opportunity, Affirmative Action Program, and VETS-100 reporting. Oracle does not advise using these reports for actual reporting to the U.S. Government, but it is useful to be able to monitor performance according to these formulas between reporting deadlines, ensuring that when it comes time to submit reports to the government, there are no surprises.

Workforce Profile

This subject area, shown in Figure 9-10, is used to describe the profile of the workforce and let HR professionals and line-of-business managers track the progress of employees through the organization. As stated in the prior section, the U.S. Statutory Compliance and Workforce Profile subject areas share almost all the same dimensions. In addition to the ones included in the U.S. Statutory Compliance subject area, this includes dimensions dealing with the length of service band and the previous location, employee organization, position, job, pay grade, and supervisor.

FIGURE 9-10. *Human Resources – Workforce Profile*

Together, these two can help HR professionals get a view not only of the profile (via Workforce Profile) but also of the progress (via U.S. Statutory Compliance).

Workforce Profile includes these facts:

- HR Event Facts
- Performance Band
- Workforce Profile Facts
- Span of Control Facts
- Time in Service Facts

Typical Configurations and Customizations

HR Analytics allows you to load all your history and build up your snapshots over time. This is a very complex task, so fortunately the logic is prebuilt. Unlike Inventory Balances, AR Balances, and AP Balances, this is achievable from a data perspective. HR Analytics is one of the prebuilt BI Applications where you're almost guaranteed to have a mix of sources. HR departments typically use many systems to track information, both Oracle and non-Oracle. For example, outsourced payroll data, Kronos time cards (customization required), recruiting systems, performance management systems, and so on. If this is the case, you should probably implement in phases, one data source at a time, starting with Workforce Profile.

HR Analytics requires careful study of the prebuilt ETL and metric calculations because of heavy reliance on domain values. Also, many ETL mappings are required to get to the final fact tables exposed to end users. Overall, the types of measures provided can be broken down into the following categories:

- Balance versus event measures

  - Point in time versus period

  - How many _____ happened in the last year/quarter/month?

  - How many _____ do I have now? A month ago? A quarter ago? A year ago?

- Deriving event measures

  - Using event dimension to break down by event types

  - Combining with balance measures broken down by event types

- Aggregation (SUM versus AVG)

  - Headcount/FTE

  - Period of Service

  - Performance Rating (%)

The ETL process is diagrammed in Figure 9-11 to illustrate how complex the process is to capture and track Workforce Events. There are layers, for example, of fact tables that are used for ETL processing but not exposed for reporting purposes.

Oracle HR Analytics ETL processes are well documented via a technical white paper available on My Oracle Support. You can find the document entitled "Oracle Business Intelligence Applications Implementing Human Resources Analytics with PeopleSoft Adaptors [ID 1326742.1]." The diagram in Figure 9-11 is from that document. Also available are "Oracle Business

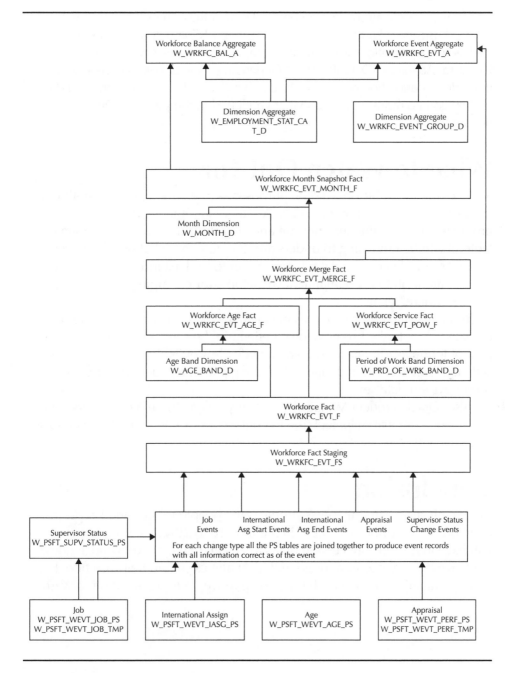

FIGURE 9-11. *High level flow ETL flow to populate tables needed to track workforce events*

Intelligence Applications Implementing Human Resources Analytics with Oracle E-Business Suites Adaptors [ID 1326766.1]" and "Oracle Business Intelligence Applications Implementing Human Resources Analytics with Universal Adaptors [ID 1269240.1]." Depending on your data source, one of these documents should be kept close at hand as a detailed reference guide as they go into more detail than what you'll find in the standard Oracle documentation.

What to Watch Out For

Some of the fact tables have dual purposes—for example, storing both job requisitions and recruitment events. Another example is the workforce profile where both the current state and snapshots are stored in the same table. It can be confusing to understand the data model at first; however, when it's populated with data, it gets easier to understand over time. Pay careful attention to the semantic layer setup—for example, the logical table source "where" clause.

You'll need to ensure your testing includes the proper matching up of domain values to the business logic defined in the semantic layer—there are a lot of formulas to review, so plan accordingly. You'll also need to allocate sufficient time to read and follow the configuration instructions for your source system data set.

Also, Oracle Product Management is very willing to help customers, so if you need additional help, feel free to contact your Oracle BI sales team to set up a meeting.

Conclusion

An organization can only be as strong as the people it hires and keeps. In addition, as baby boomers retire in the next 10 to 20 years, organizations will have to develop succession plans to ensure that their knowledge does not leave the organization for good. HR Analytics should help you find, keep, and cultivate the employees that will help move your organization forward.

CHAPTER
10

Enterprise Asset
Management Analytics

I n the Oracle BI Applications 7.9.6.3 extension pack in March 2012, Oracle first shipped Enterprise Asset Management Analytics (herein EAM). Oracle shipped it under controlled availability. It became generally available with Oracle BI Applications 7.4.6.4, which was released in January 2013. As of the release date, adapters are available for Oracle EBS 11g, and some versions of Maximo. Check with Oracle for which versions of Maximo are supported because this is in flux as of press time. In version 7.9.6.4, Oracle has incorporated a Universal Adapter, which means you can load data from any source. Of course, the prebuilt adaptors require less effort to implement. Universal adaptors are described in detail in Chapter 3.

EAM tracks all the costs and labor required to keep an asset fit for service. As such, we see it applying in any industry where the availability of high-priced assets is critical to success. This includes the following industries:

■ Utilities

■ Mining

■ Transportation, including refuse collection and recycling

■ Heavy manufacturing

■ Telecommunications companies

■ Oil and gas, including exploration, production, refining, and oil field services

Note that these can apply to parts of the public sector, for example, a transit authority, or the maintenance function of a public works department, the police or military.

Description of the Business Process

As part of the business process, one schedules maintenance, performs maintenance by employing parts and labor, completes work orders, accounts for the costs of performing the maintenance, and determines root causes.

Figure 10-1 covers the entire EAM process flow, from maintenance plan to work order completion.

We also see EAM interacting with other Analytic Applications for cross-functional analyses. Here are some examples:

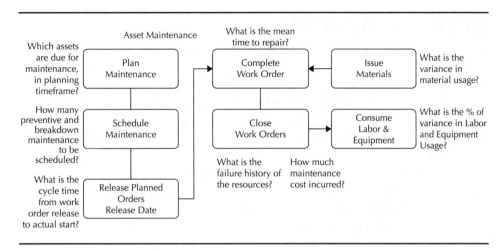

FIGURE 10-1.   *EAM analytic needs*

■ Maintenance wants to understand whether certain spare parts or maintenance contractors are responsible for a disproportionate share of breakdowns. It may be necessary to combine Procurement and Spend Analytics with EAM to answer this.

■ Manufacturing wants to understand to what degree asset failures are impacting plant throughput or quality and, thus, the ability to fulfill orders on a timely basis. Depending on the answer, preventive maintenance schedules may be altered or other maintenance practices changed. To get the answer to this, one may have to combine EAM with Manufacturing Analytics and even Procurement and Spend Analytics or Supply Chain and Order Management Analytics.

■ Maintenance and finance want to tie cost variances to GL accounts. To do so would require both EAM and Financial Analytics.

■ Maintenance and HR want to understand the impact of training and certification on mean time to repair (MTTR) and mean time between failures (MTBF) for maintenance workers. To answer this question would require HR Analytics as well as EAM. Where certification is mandated by law, there may be legal reasons to monitor certification of who is performing certain maintenance.

Business Benefits

At the top of everyone's list should be keeping assets operating safely. When a machine breaks down, it can cause injury or death. We do not know how to quantify the monetary value of safety, but in any company with big equipment we have ever worked in, the number-one priority for every manager has always been safety. If you look at major industrial accidents, poor maintenance has played a prominent role in many of them, probably second only to carelessness.

Because EAM has been on the market for such a short period of time, we do not have any good quantitative benchmarks as to what people can save or make with Enterprise Asset Management Analytics. Therefore, we can only describe the benefits qualitatively:

- The biggest monetary value in EAM should maximizing uptime. The value of keeping a plant up as close to 100 percent as possible almost always outweighs the cost of maintenance. If it does not, the asset usually costs too much to maintain and should be replaced.

- For production-related assets, the biggest value lies in increasing the capacity of the production line, and thus the amount of revenue the asset can generate. Ask what it would be worth if one could improve the output of a production line by 1 percent by decreasing planned and unplanned downtime.

- Also, with improved asset uptime, if production cannot be increased (for example, snow plows), then assets can be sold or retired, generating income and lowering future maintenance costs. Alternatively, would your customer be willing to pay more to have the task performed more quickly?

- An asset has reached the end of its useful life when one of three things occurs:

  - It does not serve and cannot be modified to serve the needs the organization has for it.

  - The net present value of ongoing maintenance costs, both material and labor, exceeds the total cost of replacing it.

  - One can no longer get spare parts for the asset.

Determining when an asset has reached the end of its useful life can help an organization save money either by helping to make the business case for replacing the asset or by helping to decide that the asset can be kept because these conditions have not been met. Note that these criteria may have no relationship to the depreciation period. The depreciation period is an accounting construct that may or may not have any relationship to what happens in the real world.

■ A lower-cost spare part that does not perform well in service is false economy. The value of the part keeping the asset in service is almost always greater than the difference in cost of a cheap spare part and one that maximizes uptime. Also, repeated failures may indicate that there is a quality problem with spare parts, one that needs to be addressed with the vendor before uptime or safety is compromised. This cost becomes part of what Phillip Crosby calls "the price of nonconformance."

Key Stakeholders

You should have two big stakeholders: the organization that uses the asset and the organization that maintains it. The asset owner has two major problems to solve:

■ *How to keep the asset up.* By helping monitor mean time between failures (MTBF) and mean time to repair (MTTR), EAM helps asset owners understand whether their assets are delivering the uptime needed to do what the organization wants.

■ *How to keep the total cost of ownership of the asset down.* The asset owner has a budget for the maintenance of the asset. EAM helps this person understand how much money is being spent keeping the assets working. It also helps them work with the maintenance organization to understand the root causes of failures—whether the asset is being used improperly, parts are not providing the lifetime expected from them, the asset is being overworked, or the people providing the maintenance are not doing the job properly.

The maintenance organization usually has a budget for maintenance that is the mirror image of what the asset owner has. Maintenance is supposed to provide a minimum MTBF and a maximum MTTR within a budget for labor and materials. EAM can help this organization meet its objectives.

Cross-Functional Analysis

Most commonly, we would expect Enterprise Asset Management Analytics to be used with Procurement and Spend Analytics to help tie the timeliness, cost, and quality of spare parts to the cost effective uptime of an asset. If spare parts are delivered late, the asset will be inoperative longer. If the quality is below standards, the asset will break down more often than expected. If the price is too high, the cost to operate the asset will be too high. We expect there will also be interaction with HR Analytics as people seek to determine whether the mean time to repair is influenced by the training a repair technician receives. We expect, also, to see analyses that tie Enterprise Asset Analytics to Manufacturing Analytics to see how the maintenance an asset receives impacts the uptime of a manufacturing line or the quality of products it turns out. We expect there will be interactions with Project Analytics to see how the frequency or duration of downtime affects the ability of a project team to deliver its work on time.

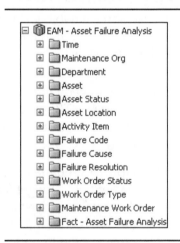

Subject Areas

EAM consists of eleven subject areas.

Asset Failure Analysis

This subject area includes facts about the amount of downtime and the cost to fix a given asset as well as the MTTR and MTBF for the asset (see Figure 10-2). It describes this for

FIGURE 10-2. *EAM – Asset Failure Analysis*

each work order, asset, time period, maintenance organization, and failure. It also tabulates the cause and resolution of failure. One would use this subject area to understand root causes of failures and to look for patterns of failures across assets and maintenance organizations.

Asset History

This subject area looks at the history of the costs incurred in acquiring and maintaining an asset (see Figure 10-3). It would be used to help understand when an asset is costing so much to maintain that it should be replaced. Because it also separates preventive from other maintenance, this subject area can be used to help understand how much of the maintenance is predictable.

Asset Maintenance Cost

This subject area ties the activities and work orders used to maintain an asset to the GL accounts where this information is kept for financial accounting purposes (see Figure 10-4). It separates the costs into labor and materials. It also separates breakdown maintenance from preventative maintenance as well as estimated costs from actual costs and variances.

FIGURE 10-3.   *EAM – Asset History*

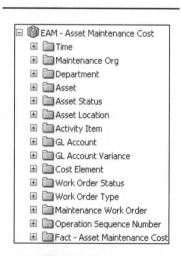

FIGURE 10-4.   *EAM – Asset Maintenance Cost*

Asset Maintenance Work Orders

This subject area contains facts about individual work orders and when they
occurred, how long they took, and how many there were (see Figure 10-5).
It is used primarily to help gauge how well a maintenance organization
fulfilled its workload and to help understand where gaps and bottlenecks are
delaying the completion of work orders.

Asset Meter Reading

This subject contains meter readings for each asset at the time of each work
order (see Figure 10-6).

Asset Quality

This subject area contains test results for every part or component that is
tested as part of every asset (see Figure 10-7). It contains names of suppliers
and lot numbers of parts. It has maximum and minimum specifications
for the test results. This subject area should be useful as people apply
the principles of statistical process control as they look at trends of test
results as predictors for the need for preventive asset maintenance to avoid

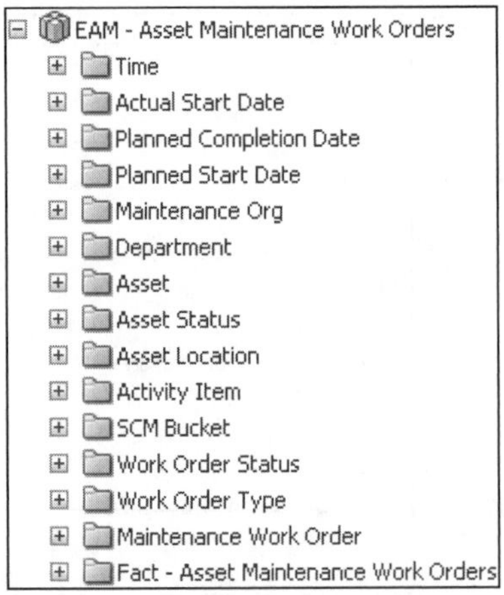

FIGURE 10-5. *EAM – Asset Maintenance Work Orders*

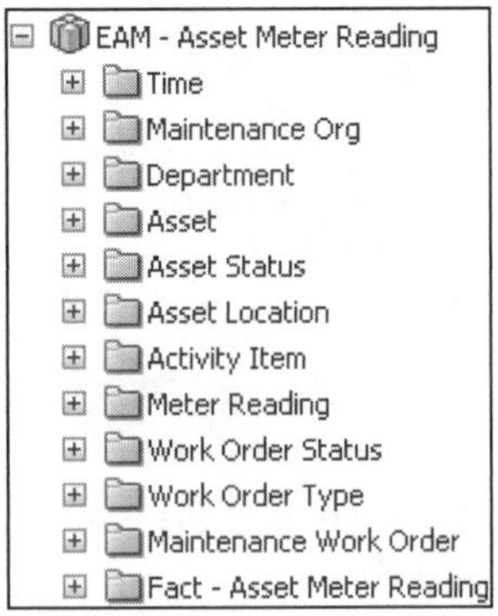

FIGURE 10-6. *EAM – Asset Meter Reading*

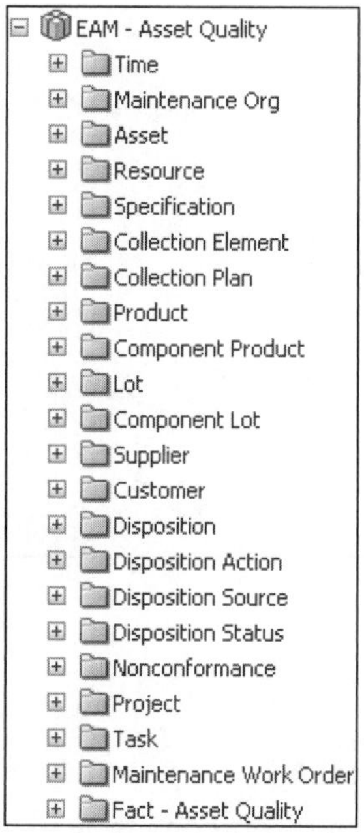

```
EAM - Asset Quality
    Time
    Maintenance Org
    Asset
    Resource
    Specification
    Collection Element
    Collection Plan
    Product
    Component Product
    Lot
    Component Lot
    Supplier
    Customer
    Disposition
    Disposition Action
    Disposition Source
    Disposition Status
    Nonconformance
    Project
    Task
    Maintenance Work Order
    Fact - Asset Quality
```

FIGURE 10-7. *EAM – Asset Quality*

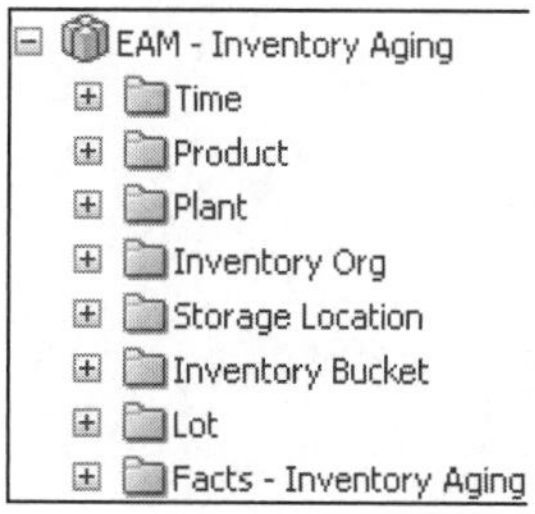

```
EAM - Inventory Aging
    Time
    Product
    Plant
    Inventory Org
    Storage Location
    Inventory Bucket
    Lot
    Facts - Inventory Aging
```

FIGURE 10-8. *EAM – Inventory Aging*

breakdowns. Coupled with Procurement and Spend Analytics, this subject area should help Procurement and Maintenance work together to identify which repair parts lead to the lowest total cost of ownership for the organization. For organizations that supply maintenance services to third parties, this subject area also contains information about the customer who owns or operates the asset.

Inventory Aging

This subject contains inventory aging information about spare parts and supplies (see Figure 10-8). It allows people to track not just the age of inventory items, but also how much had to be scrapped or written off as obsolete. We have seen organizations that keep large numbers of spares on hand to protect against any extended downtime. This subject area can help better ensure that this type of premium service is run to minimize scrap.

Maintenance Material Usage

This subject area tracks how much material is used in executing a work order, including both standard and actual usage for a particular type of repair (see Figure 10-9). Variations in usage between similar repairs and deviations from standards should signal further investigation.

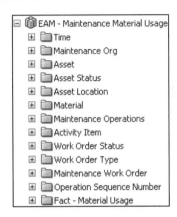

FIGURE 10-9. *EAM – Maintenance Material Usage*

Maintenance Resource Availability

This subject area is used to help understand whether a resource was available to execute a work order (see Figure 10-10). It also helps understand the utilization of the resource. The operator of a resource can then see how efficiently the resource is used. However, this does not tie back to individual work orders. To understand that, the operator would look at the Maintenance Resource Usage subject area.

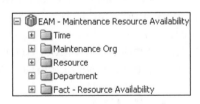

FIGURE 10-10. *EAM – Maintenance Resource Availability*

Maintenance Resource Usage

This subject area tracks the maintenance work order, step by step, tying in the parts, labor, and resources used to execute a work order (see Figure 10-11). It holds hours, costs, and efficiencies. This subject area would be used to understand the base, step-by-step interactions between people, parts, resources, and assets in executing the process needed to fulfill a work order.

MRO Inventory

This subject area contains the inventory balances and values for spare parts and supplies (see Figure 10-12). It also allows for inventory to be blocked, unblocked, consigned, in transit, in inspection, and obsolete. It also specifies reorder points and replenishment points.

FIGURE 10-11. *EAM – Maintenance Resource Usage*

FIGURE 10-12. *EAM – MRO Inventory*

Common Configurations and What to Watch Out For

EAM Analytics is a very new product. It was just released in January of 2013. It is too soon to tell what pitfalls people might run into. We can only suggest you check with Oracle's support website for patches, bug reports, and so on, as organizations start implementing this product. You're not on your own; you'll benefit from the experiences of other customers as they too roll out this Analytics Application.

Conclusion

To make an organization leaner, its management wants to keep the value of assets to a minimum. To keep it as productive as possible, these assets need to be available for use as close to 100 percent as possible. To make the best use of the organization's resources, money and time used to maintain these assets need to be spent as efficiently as possible. Enterprise Asset Management Analytics helps organizations reach these goals. It is equally applicable for the owners of assets as it is to third-party servicers of assets. As Oracle goes forward, this product should prove to be a valuable part of the portfolio of BI Applications for its target markets.

CHAPTER
11

Project Analytics

The Project Management Institute estimates that 20 percent of worldwide GDP is spent on projects (per www.pmiteach.org). That puts project-related spending at over $12 trillion per year. Besides private sector project spending, which we will cover later, many people sell to governments according to a government contract. That work, even if it would not be considered project work for business-to-business transactions, is often considered project work if the purchaser is a government. All projects need to track the time spent on labor and material expenses. These need to be tracked versus milestones, and from the inception of the project to its completion, which may take several years.

We have all seen projects that went way over budget and took way longer than they should have. They all did so one day at a time. Tasks slipped. Scopes changed. Things cost more than they should. Managing multimillion dollar, multiyear projects is difficult. Project managers need more than just a project management tool such as Primavera or Microsoft Project. They need to be able to analyze where the labor and expenses are going. They need to evaluate subcontractors. They need to see how delivery times for procured materials affect project schedules.

ERP systems are geared to collect information needed to close the books. They often gear their reporting to a year at a time, which does not serve the needs of projects that cross year boundaries and may take years to complete.

In general, we see two groups of industries that find Project Analytics useful:

- Organizations that bill for projects, such as job shop manufacturers, professional services firms, and government contractors.

- Organizations that undertake and pay for projects (that is, project owners). These can include both public sector and private sector organizations.

Both people who bill for projects and project owners have to interact with procurement departments to monitor the procurement department's and the vendors' ability to get the right goods at the right price for the project so that the project is not delayed and does not run over budget. We find that these projects fall into several groups:

- IT projects
- Engineering and construction projects

- R&D projects

- New product launches, including both the manufacturing ramp-up and the marketing and sales parts of launching a new product

Because Project Analytics handles both billable and nonbillable projects, both groups benefit.

The payoff from Project Analytics is not only closer management of the project, but also the ability to audit the project's progress and survive an audit to be able to justify the resources spent on a project. Without a product like Project Analytics, audits can be very time consuming and error prone. For government projects, there can be consequences of not being able to prove what expenses were charged to the projects, such as disallowing the expenses and not being allowed to bid on follow-up projects for periods measured in years. Clearly, avoiding these consequences is worth spending money on.

Description of the Business Process

Making the process shown in Figure 11-1 work involves attention to the detail in all the boxes. Project Analytics' job is to help monitor all the details involved in this process so that projects can be executed successfully.

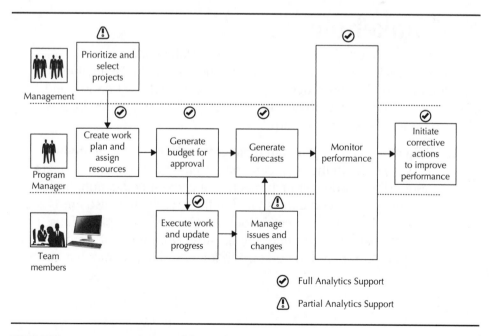

FIGURE 11-1. *A project's life cycle*

Business Benefits

As of 2013, the Project Analytics product is still relatively new. We do not have the experience with it that we do with many other BI Applications. Consequently, the benefits we describe are qualitative.

First, users can focus on closer control. As deviations from plan are detected, they can be addressed more cheaply than if they are allowed to go unnoticed.

Second, better resource allocation is possible. A professional services firm makes money when its resources are billable. A better view of a portfolio of projects should allow better deployment of resources. Also, when resources are needed to fix a deviation, project executives can view across a portfolio of projects to see where a resource can be drawn from while minimizing the impact on the entire portfolio of projects.

Complex projects often require complex reporting back to funding agencies. The project will reap a major benefit from being able to keep up with the reporting to the standards the funding agency requires. The project will reap a minor benefit from being able to do so with fewer people. Our experience is that very few people think of the quality of the reporting until a project audit occurs. By then, fixing the reporting quality has become very expensive.

Key Stakeholders

As we have described above, lining up the key stakeholders before launching a BI project raises the likelihood of success more than almost anything we have found. In project analytics, look for the people whose bonuses and reputations are on the line to deliver projects on time and within budget. Here are some of the major groups.

- **Project managers, program managers, and project executives**
  These people, in the project management chain of command, are responsible for delivering projects to a given specification, budget, and timeline. In companies that bill their work, they also are responsible for the project's profit margin. These people will use Project Analytics to monitor the day-to-day progress of a project and track that compared to budget and forecast. For program managers

and project executives, they will also look at where they can trade off resources to handle deviations efficiently.

- **Project accountants**   In large projects, these people control the day-to-day approval of invoices and monitor the project for deviations from plan. They report deviations back to the project and program managers for them to take action on.

- **Executives in companies that bill for projects**   These people need to monitor the profitability of the portfolio of work the firm is engaged in. They also need to monitor their receivables so their cash flow stays strong.

Ensure you engage these people as you build the case for Project Analytics and develop requirements for this product.

Cross-Functional Analysis

Besides the analytics you can get from Project Analytics, you should look at analytics that tie in Procurement and Spend Analytics. Also, provided of course that you code project numbers on invoices, you can tie projects to accounts payable and accounts receivable in Financial Analytics. This allows invoices and payments or collections to be added to the business process described in the prior section.

Figures 11-2 and 11-3 illustrate the tie-in with Financial Analytics. Figure 11-2 shows project invoices from Financial Analytics. Project invoices would be used in conjunction with Project Analytics to show how invoices generated as a result of certain milestones being achieved would tie into overall company profitability. Figure 11-3 shows how this subject area then appears in OBIEE and can be incorporated into dashboards and reports.

Figures 11-4 and 11-5 illustrate the tie-in with Procurement and Spend Analytics. Figure 11-4 shows the Procurement Performance dashboards and that the Commitments by Project area is hidden. It could be exposed as part of an effort to have Procurement and the project manager collaborate on how vendor performance was affecting project performance. Figure 11-5 shows the dashboard that would be displayed once it was exposed.

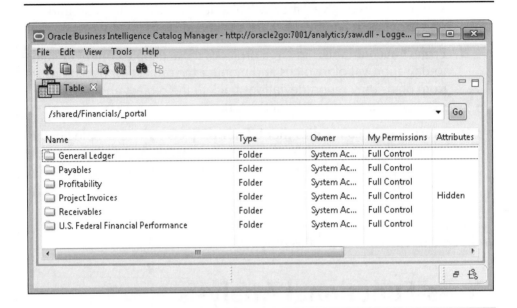

FIGURE 11-2. *Project invoices in Financial Analytics*

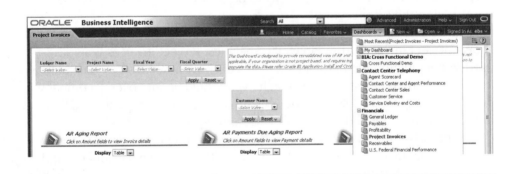

FIGURE 11-3. *Project invoices in OBIEE*

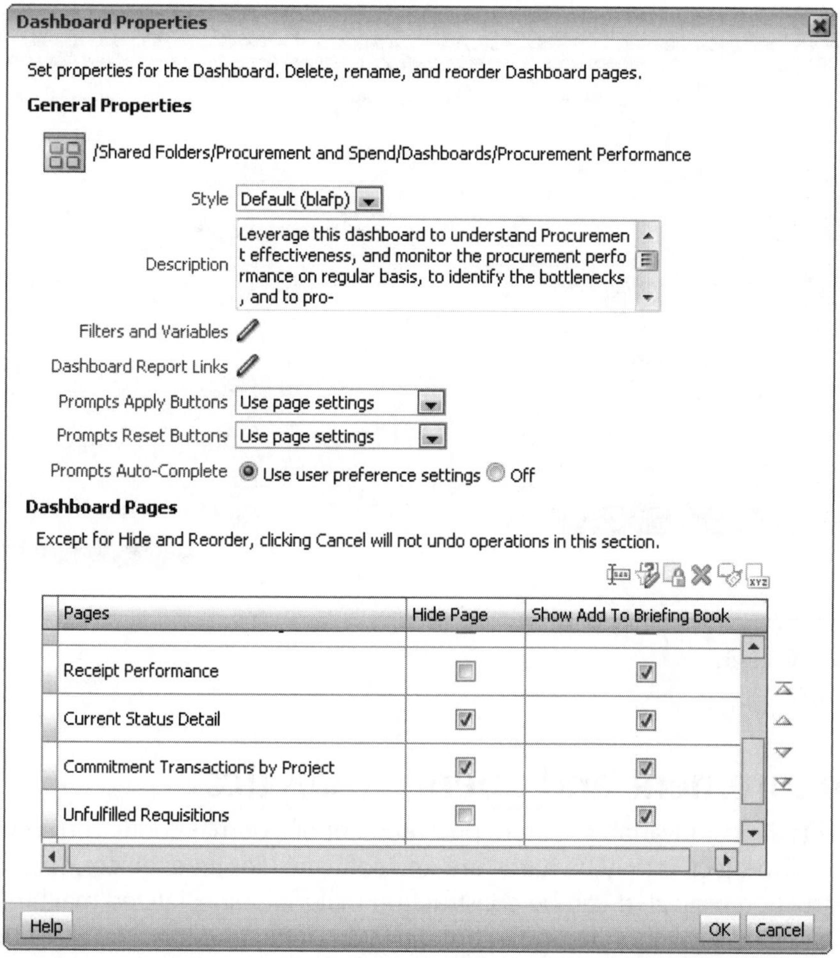

Dashboard Properties   ☒

Set properties for the Dashboard. Delete, rename, and reorder Dashboard pages.

General Properties

🔳 /Shared Folders/Procurement and Spend/Dashboards/Procurement Performance

Style | Default (blafp) ▾

Description | Leverage this dashboard to understand Procuremen ▲
t effectiveness, and monitor the procurement perfo ☰
rmance on regular basis, to identify the bottlenecks
, and to pro- ▼

Filters and Variables 🖉
Dashboard Report Links 🖉
Prompts Apply Buttons | Use page settings ▾
Prompts Reset Buttons | Use page settings ▾
Prompts Auto-Complete ⦿ Use user preference settings ◯ Off

Dashboard Pages

Except for Hide and Reorder, clicking Cancel will not undo operations in this section.

Pages	Hide Page	Show Add To Briefing Book
Receipt Performance	☐	☑
Current Status Detail	☑	☑
Commitment Transactions by Project	☑	☑
Unfulfilled Requisitions	☐	☑

Help   OK   Cancel

FIGURE 11-4.   *Hidden Commitment Transactions by Project dashboards*

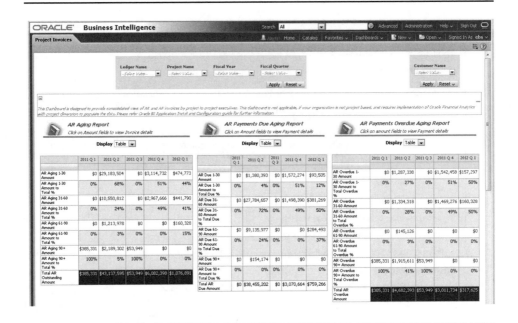

FIGURE 11-5.

Procurement and Spend Analytics

Projects almost invariably require procurement of external goods and services. For an IT project, it may be hardware and software. For an engineering and construction project, it can be construction materials, specialized machinery that is rented for a short period of time, or subcontracting services. For a new product introduction, it can be specialized tooling, advertising, or new raw materials. If these materials are late, they can impact the project timeline. If they cost more than planned, they can impact the project budget. In addition, once a purchase order is issued, the organization is usually legally committed to make the purchase. Therefore, the project manager needs to know not only what invoices have been received, but also what purchase orders are outstanding. If a deadline slips, one must understand how this will affect outstanding commitments. For example, can purchase orders for promotional materials be cancelled if a deadline slips? Will material show up on site before it is needed? Only by combining Procurement and Spend Analytics can one see the full picture of what is at stake.

To gain this insight, the project team needs access to critical data contained in Procurement Analytics. E-Business Suite and PeopleSoft both allow for project information to be entered; thus, project data can be combined easily with procurement data.

Financial Analytics

As described in Chapter 5, accounts receivable and accounts payable are mirror images of each other. Accounts receivable transactions and aging can be tied to projects. Similarly, accounts payable transactions and aging can be tied to projects. This allows for a complete view of a project's cash flow, for both the project owner and an organization that bills for projects. Accounts receivable can also be tied to projects in a similar manner.

Subject Areas

Project Analytics contains eight subject areas:

- Budgets

- Commitments

- Forecasts

- Costs

- Billings

- Agreements and Funding

- Performance

- Revenues

These areas cover, for an organization that bills for its work, everything from the agreements that allow a project to begin through the execution of the work, to the billing and collection for the work done. Handling the winning of the contract, however, is typically done through Sales Analytics. For a project owner, Project Analytics handles everything from the agreement to the completion of the work. AP transactions can also be tied to projects to allow the business process to be followed through payments. However, this requires Financial Analytics to be licensed.

Metrics and KPIs

As in other chapters, we are spending more of our time discussing KPIs and metrics at the expense of dashboards. Building new metrics—particularly those that must be built in the data warehouse rather than in the business layer of OBIEE—is much more difficult than building new reports. Also, the metrics required typically change less from one company to another than the structure of reports do. Many standards organizations, such as the PMA (Project Management Association) in the case of project management, specify best practice metrics. They do not specify report layouts. Oracle, therefore, decided to put its effort into building a library of KPIs, rather than chasing the poltergeist of the ideally formatted report. Wherever accepted formats for reports exist, though (for example, balance sheets, income statements, and cash flow statements), Oracle has built them.

Almost all metrics are available from inception to date, month to date, and year to date. We cannot stress enough how important having inception-to-date metrics is. Whether you're recouping costs, assessing project profitability, or undergoing a project audit, inception-to-date metrics drive the analysis. The ability to calculate these without having to worrying about what fiscal or calendar year the activities or charges occurred in separates what can be done from a project accounting system from what is done in an analytic system.

Budget

This subject area, shown in Figure 11-6, tracks metrics having to do with budgets, including revenues, margins, labor and equipment time, many different kinds of costs, and work breakdown structures. Budgeted costs tabulated include people, equipment, and capitalizable costs. These are available for the original and current budget, and they can be viewed from inception to date, month to date, or year to date, as well as for arbitrary collections of dates. Because the budgets can be stored at a task level corresponding to a work breakdown structure, budget-to-actual calculations can be computed on a very detailed level, allowing for fine-grained comparison of costs and analysis of

FIGURE 11-6. *Project – Budget*

where deviations are occurring. Capital resource costs can also be tabulated the same way to let one see whether a machine or other capital resource is not performing up to expected levels.

Commitments

The commitments subject area, as shown in Figure 11-7, helps project managers understand what purchased resources have been requested or committed. It ties the procure-to-pay cycle into a project and lets project managers understand what materials or services the project can expect to pay for. It also lets them see what materials have arrived and are outstanding, what have been accepted or rejected, and what have been invoiced by the vendor. Both quantities and monetary amounts are stored. Project managers use this, not only to track their

FIGURE 11-7. *Project–Commitment*

progress against a budget, but also to understand what they will be liable for. For example, in a new product launch, a product launch team often wants to spend the entire budget for marketing the new product in the last months and weeks before launch to generate the maximum buzz in the marketplace. When a launch is only a few weeks away, having to wait for accounts payable to record invoices leads to a picture that can be a month or more overdue. Understanding what has been committed to lets the product launch team spend up to the limits of their budget, confident they will not exceed their budget. Otherwise, they may leave 10% of their budget unspent for contingencies without knowing whether those contingencies are likely to arise.

Commitments can be tied to given projects and tasks, suppliers, internal organizations, and customers. As with all other Oracle BI Applications, the vendor, customer, and internal organization tables are conformed with other BI Applications.

Forecasts

The Forecasts subject area is shown in Figure 11-8. Forecasts allow project managers and project executives to compare actuals, the estimated totals at the time the project is complete, the *estimate at complete* totals, and the estimated totals needed to be spent from now until the project is complete, the *estimate to complete* totals. It calculates these totals for costs, effort, and revenues. These are collected inception-to-date, year-to-date, quarter-to-date, and month-to-date. It also contains forecasted margins and margin percentages. This subject also contains information on the various budgets that have been built for a project. People use this subject area to see how budgets change over time and to ascertain whether the budget left will be sufficient to finish the project at current run rates. This allows forecasts to be maintained for different types of resources, whether equipment, employees, suppliers, jobs, or materials, and to tie them to tasks to help determine whether certain resources are or are likely to become overloaded.

Costs

This subject area differs from the Forecasts subject area in that it only includes actuals, but it includes them in much more detail. For instance, it breaks out billable from non billable costs, raw costs from fully burdened costs, and people costs from equipment costs. It also includes capitalizable costs. As with Forecasts, it tabulates costs inception-to-date, year-to-date, quarter-to-date, and month-to-date. It also tabulates month ago and quarter ago costs to facilitate trends in projects that should be running at a steady

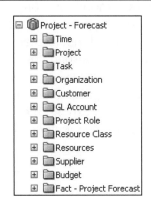

FIGURE 11-8. *Project–Commitment Forecast*

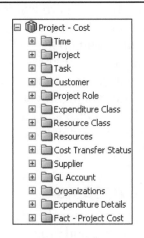

FIGURE 11-9. *Project–Cost*

state or at a predictable trend. With one
exception, it has the same dimensions as the
Forecasts subject area, namely it has details
of individual expenditures. Someone worried
about day to day project administration would
use this subject area to keep track of costs
accruing to the project and, where applicable,
how these costs could be billed to a customer.

Billings

Organizations that bill for project work
would use this subject area. Consequently, its
dimensions around project are much richer than
project related dimensions in other subject areas,
like Forecasts or Commitments. These allow
projects to be tracked, not just by the project
hierarchy, but also by a rich set of project types,
like public sector versus private sector, project

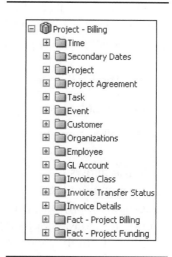

FIGURE 11-10. *Project–Billing*

initiation and close dates, project manager, and project priorities, just to name
a few. In addition, it allows secondary dates to be tracked, namely the dates
the tasks or milestones were approved, the date the invoice was released,
and the date the payment was billed through. As with other subject areas, it
provides inception-to-date metrics, year-to-date, quarter-to-date, and month-
to-date metrics. These include items of concern only to organizations that bill
for projects, like write offs, numbers of approved, unapproved, billed, and
unbilled invoices, as well as retentions and withholdings. An organization
that bills for work uses these to help predict and manage its cash flow. These
can also be matched up with amounts specified in agreements to see how the
billing is proceeding with respect to what was anticipated when the contract
was signed.

Agreements and Funding

Before beginning the discussion of this subject area, it is useful to discuss what
an "agreement" means to people in project work. An *agreement,* which some
organizations call a *master services agreement,* or *MSA,* is a blanket contract
specifying billing rates, legal terms and conditions, remedies, and so on.
Individual projects either reference the MSA or are added as amendments
to the MSA. All project accounting systems have the concept of agreements
built into them.

The Agreements and Funding subject area, shown in Figure 11-11, applies to people who bill for projects. It lets people compare

- The funding levels agreed to

- What has been billed

- What remains

FIGURE 11-11. *Project – Funding*

It also allows these funds to be aggregated to an agreement level. Because it allows people to compare many past projects to what is happening today, lessons from prior projects, whether or not they were completed successfully, can be applied to today's projects. If an organization also purchases Financial Analytics, a more detailed comparison can be done to individual accounts receivable invoices and payments.

The metrics in this subject area allow for the tracking of funding against, not just projects, but also agreements and individual tasks within a project. They allow people to ensure that change notices get written for individual tasks and that expenditures for individual tasks do not go over the agreed budgets. They also allow for the calculation of overall agreement profitability.

In addition, these metrics allow tracking all the way from the agreement to the invoice so that project accountants and project managers understand where they stand in turning an agreement into cash for themselves as well as into value for the client.

This subject area also contains many count-based metrics, including the following:

- Numbers of projects and tasks with

    - Funding agreements

    - Initial funding

    - Additional funding

    - Cancelled funding

- Total numbers of

  - Agreements

  - Expired agreements

  - Unexpired agreements

Performance

This subject area, shown in Figure 11-12, brings together actual, budget, forecast, cost, and estimate-at-completion numbers along with variance and percent-complete metrics as well as a count of the number of projects to allow for fine-grained tracking of a project, program, or portfolio versus its budgets and forecasts. This subject area also splits out metrics into both monetary- and time-based categories and allows separate tracking of equipment, labor, billable, capitalizable, nonbillable, burden, and raw costs. Raw costs are direct costs incurred to the project, including salaries and travel expenses. This subject area also allows tracking of receivables, revenues, and margins.

FIGURE 11-12. *Project – Performance*

The Performance subject area, we anticipate, will be the most highly used subject area for people who track the progress of projects. It permits tracking of the buckets of cost described previously at a task level and at all levels of hierarchies for the task. It allows tracking of individual resources to permit fine-grained analysis of project deviations.

Revenue

Organizations that bill for project-related services will use the Revenue subject area, shown in Figure 11-13. People who contract with them, however, would not use this area. Once the work is done, the contractor must bill the customer for the work. This work may have milestones before work can be billed. Parts of the revenue may have to be written off. These

FIGURE 11-13. *Project – Revenue*

amounts are tracked in all currencies you have decided to employ in your implementation of Oracle BI Applications. It includes both billed and unbilled revenues and allows these to be tied to GL accounts.

Typical Configurations and Customizations

If projects are coded into PeopleSoft or Oracle EBS according to EBS or PeopleSoft's standard processes, the information comes over in a fairly straightforward manner. If not, those customizations will have to be mirrored in the ETL used to populate the data warehouse and the metadata used to populate the business layer.

What to Watch Out For

Oracle has several types of project analytics. Hyperion has Project Planning Analytics. Primavera has P6 Analytics. Oracle BI has Project Analytics. How do you decide which to use? Table 11-1 compares each product.

Product	Usage
Hyperion Project Planning Analytics	■ The main data source is Hyperion Planning. ■ Track a project through the planning and approval process, not once the project is launched. ■ Track the requirements of the project as the scope becomes clearer, but before it is approved.
Primavera P6 Analytics	■ The main source of data is Primavera project management. ■ Track labor and equipment resources. ■ Track cost, but not revenue data. ■ Need to change the project plan in Primavera based on the results of analyses. ■ Need to do resource leveling.
Oracle Project Analytics	■ The main source of data is the ERP. ■ Track the financial performance of a project after it is launched. ■ Track revenue as well as labor and equipment resources and costs. ■ Monitor the performance of contracts versus agreements or contracts, not just plans. ■ Integrate project management with procurement, HR, or other analytic applications and their stakeholders.

TABLE 11-1.   *Comparison of Uses of Oracle's Three Types of Project Analytics*

Across customers, we commonly see that work breakdown structures (WBSs) don't always line up unless there's a formal integration in place between EBS and Primavera. Typically, the WBS for EBS is only required for financial tracking, whereas the full WBS is maintained in Primavera.

Although P6 Analytics (Primavera) and Project Analytics are not integrated out of the box, it shouldn't be too hard in theory to integrate or at least link the physical data models. If nothing else, both can be merged to compare reports side by side on the same dashboard.

Another thing to watch out for is AR and AP transactions that span more than one project, because only one source transaction can be mapped to a single project in Project Analytics.

Conclusion

Almost every organization has project work, whether IT implementation, construction, R&D, or new product introductions. Many of these projects have a material impact on the organization's financial performance, whether they are delivered on time and within budget or they run over. Many of these require detailed choreography of people and materiel to provide the required result. Just having a good project management system is often not enough. The results have to tie back to the financial systems of record. Project Management Analytics can help detect deviations before they become so large that they jeopardize the project.

CHAPTER
12

Sales Analytics

S ales Analytics tracks the progress of a sales campaign from the time a lead is recorded in the sales force automation system until an order is received. As such, in a business-to-business sales cycle, it usually follows Marketing Analytics, where the lead is identified, and it precedes Supply Chain and Order Management Analytics, where the order is recorded and either shipped or queued for manufacture. It is typically used for business-to-business or business-to-government sales cycles. Business-to-consumer sales cycles are typically not complex enough to require tracking in a sales force automation (SFA) system.

Sales Analytics was one of Siebel Systems' first analytic applications. Tom Siebel, the president, recognized that, unlike ERP applications, it is much more difficult to get salespeople to enter reliable, timely, and complete data than it is to force, for example, order-entry clerks to enter orders. Siebel realized that to increase adoption of the SFA system, he had to provide salespeople something in return. That "something," he decided, was dashboards that would help them, not just their managers, manage their territories. (Remember that a primary audience for Sales Analytics is the individual, quota-carrying salesperson.) Siebel Systems also decided that Sales Analytics would be more valuable if it could be combined with Marketing Analytics, to allow sales results to be tied more directly with the marketing process, and also with Service Analytics, so salespeople could identify where post-sales issues might contribute to customer satisfaction problems, which detract from a sales team's ability to sell more products and services to a given client. Siebel Service also provided the ability for a company to track the sale of service contracts on the products that sales had sold them. Service Analytics applied to Service Sales also served as a warning to sales. If the customer was not willing to renew the service contract, the ability to sell more products might be in jeopardy. Siebel Systems also later extended these linkages to include Supply Chain and Order Management Analytics to allow complete visibility to the entire lead-to-order-to-cash cycle. More recently, Oracle has developed Price Analytics to help optimize and add discipline to the quotation and pricing process.

Because Sales Analytics is one of Oracle's oldest BI Applications and because sales force automation was central to Siebel's value proposition, this application allows for a very detailed view of the sales process. It lets salespeople and managers go from viewing an entire sales territory to individual deals quickly. It provides many metrics to let salespeople and managers see how many deals are leaking out of the pipeline and how big they are. They also have built-in ties to lead generation (that is, marketing) and fulfillment (that is, supply chain/order management). We see most subject areas taking the broader view of sales than just what the subject area would indicate. For instance, CRM Sales Quotes looks at orders and shipments as well as quotes.

In recent years, people seem to have lost sight that customer relationship management (CRM) is much broader than just SFA. Salespeople will be helped if marketing can analyze whether their campaigns turn, not just into leads, but into leads that close. They will be more effective if they can get an early warning into customer satisfaction problems by looking at the incidence of problems their customers report and their customers' willingness to renew service contracts. Also, the company will be more successful if it can understand how much of the price goes into its pocket and how much goes to various, often overlapping, types of discounts.

The horizontal Sales Analytics model is shown in Figure 12-1 and is described in the next section.

Oracle also sells and supports versions of Sales Analytics for the following verticals:

- Consumer Packaged Goods (CPG) or Fast Moving Consumer Goods (FMCG) outside North America

- Pharmaceuticals

- Telecoms

- Finance

- Insurance

Pharmaceutical and CPG Sales Analytics incorporate third-party sales data to allow sales reps to see how the retail channel is performing in response to messages that sales reps leave with doctors, hospitals, and CPG retailers and how promotional programs affect sales. These products track a different sales process than standard Sales Analytics. In these two industries, the salesperson visits retailers, doctors, or other healthcare providers and offers information to them on the benefits of the company's products to attempt to influence these people to favor their products. They do not explicitly take orders. Their success is measured by data—either from third parties or from the retailers themselves—that shows how much of the company's products have sold

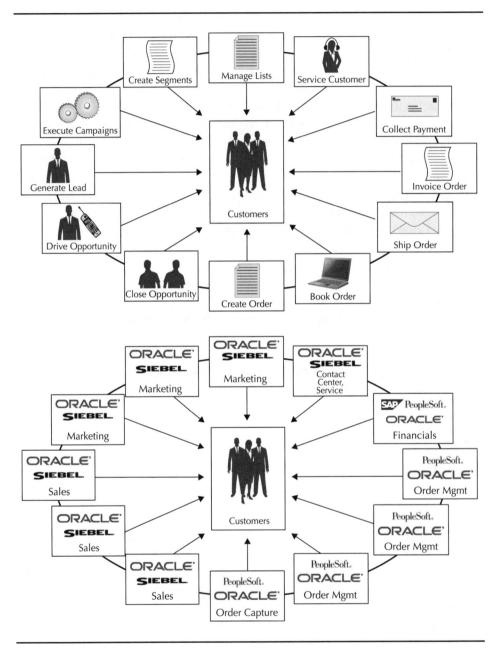

FIGURE 12-1. *Horizontal Sales Analytics model*

to end consumers. In CPG, success is also measured by how many stock-keeping units (SKUs) the retailer carries and how much shelf space the retailer devotes to the company's products.

CPG Sales Analytics also includes Trade Promotion Analytics, which allows companies who sell through retailers to track the effect of promotions the manufacturer does with the retailers. Even though this product is designed for the CPG industry, if your industry meets these three characteristics, it can probably benefit from Trade Promotion Analytics:

- Sells through third-party retailers.

- Has a source of data that tracks sales from the retailers to the end consumer, whether third-party syndicated data or data provided by the retailers themselves. An example of the latter would be Vendor Managed Inventory sales data.

- Tries to influence sales by providing incentives for the retailer to feature the manufacturer's products, for example, by giving them prominent shelf space, featuring them in the in-house television channel, or featuring them in their advertisements to the public.

CPG Sales and Pharmaceutical Sales Analytics are integrated into the rest of the Oracle BI Applications. In other words, they have conformed dimensions, use the same tech stack, and have the same naming conventions.

Description of the Business Process

The best definition we have found that separates the sales function from the marketing function is a derivation of the definition first popularized by Theodore Levitt of the Harvard Business School: "The job of marketing is to identify prospects that have the desire and money to buy the company's products and services and make them known to sales. The job of sales, then, is to close the sale in such a way that maximizes the lifetime value of that relationship to the company." Note that nothing in this definition stops marketing from creating a desire where none existed in the past. Also, note that nothing in this definition specifies whether the vendor or third parties do the selling. Because this chapter is concerned with Sales Analytics, we will pick up the trail once Marketing generates awareness or a lead. Figure 12-2 begins once the lead is generated or the prospect makes itself known to Sales.

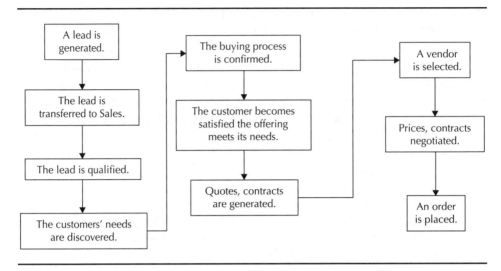

FIGURE 12-2. *The lead-to-order process*

Despite this definition, many organizations require their sales teams to place cold calls, supplementing the job classically assigned to a marketing function. Sales Analytics provides a way to analyze cold-calling programs.

Once a lead is identified, it generates one or more "opportunities." An opportunity is a sales campaign designed to sell a prospect a collection of related goods or services. Note that many opportunities may be pursued simultaneously with the same customer. These may be through different sales channels, for example, inside sales, outside sales, or resellers. These may be in different territories. They may be for different product or service lines. They may also be sold to different subsidiaries of the customer. A good sales organization will want to understand all the activity it has with a given customer. When it does, it is in a better position to generate a deal that successfully bundles many products or services together, helping to keep the customer from treating the vendor's offerings as commodities. Also, combining the offerings can minimize the customer's work because the customer only has one set of legal contracts to approve and one set of negotiations to undertake.

As the opportunity is pursued, it goes through several sales stages. These stages have different names, often depending on the sales methodology being used. The device used to track the process of an opportunity through Sales Stages is called the *sales funnel*. It is called this because at each stage, a certain percentage of opportunities is expected to drop out, as the customer whittles down the number of vendors it is looking at or the vendor realizes the opportunity either is not well qualified for what the vendor has to sell or is not likely to generate profitable business for the vendor.

Figure 12-3 is a picture of a sales funnel chart. Other than the fact that Edward Tufte, the author of *The Visual Display of Quantitative Information*,

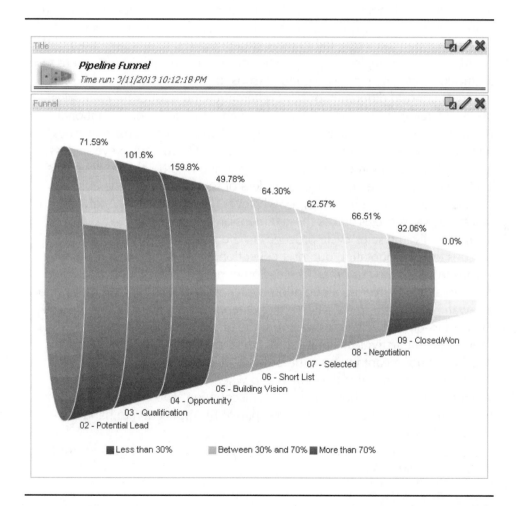

FIGURE 12-3. *Sales funnel chart*

would never approve of this chart because one cannot tell the relative heights of the bars, it conveys a lot of information to the sales organization. Typically, these charts are shown in color. In the typical color scheme, green bars mean that the salesperson or sales manager has enough opportunities in a given sales stage to meet the sales quota, assuming only normal attrition as one goes through the funnel. Red bars, on the other hand, mean that there are not enough opportunities in that stage of the pipeline. In the future, when those deals are expected to close, there will not be enough revenue to meet that period's quota. This pattern lets the sales rep understand where deals have to be progressed more quickly to fill in the gaps in the sales funnel or when management can be expected to step in. They also alert management ahead of time of when sales may fail to meet expectations.

Also, within a single company, different sales teams may use different sales methodologies. There may be good reasons for this; for example, different products are sold differently or have different characteristics for their sales cycles. Different sales methodologies, though, often arise for less rational reasons (for example, a division was acquired and never changed its sales methodology to match the new parent's sales methodology). Nevertheless, for management to forecast sales correctly, it needs to be able to aggregate likely sales across the company, regardless of sales channel, geography, product line, sales methodology, or whatever. Therefore, Sales Analytics must rationalize sales cycles across these dimensions.

Eventually, the sales cycle proceeds to the point where the sales team decides to put a quotation out for a collection of products or services it wishes to sell to the customer. The customer may or may not have solicited this quotation. Delivering a quotation, which is legally binding on the vendor, is a watershed event in the sales cycle. Often in sales organizations, we see the lead-to-quote cycle separated from the quote-to-order cycle. Table 12-1 shows how the activities change across this boundary. The order of the activities is not meant to imply the order in the sales cycle.

When the proposal is developed and when the price is negotiated, the vendor should worry about the level of discounting. This area is complex enough that Oracle has developed a separate BI Application to handle it—Price Analytics.

Table 12-1 lists the major events in the lead-to-quote and quote-to-order parts of the sales cycle.

Lead to Quote	Quote to Order
Lead qualification	Negotiation of terms and conditions
Proof the vendor's offerings meet the customer's needs	Negotiation of price, including discounts
Sponsorship identification	Review of customer's credit or lining up of financing
Budget identification	Negotiation of timing to deliver the product or service
Proposal development	Closing the deal

TABLE 12-1. *Lead-to-Quote Cycle Versus Quote-to-Order Cycle*

Business Benefits

Sales Analytics helps the organization increase its revenue. This revenue can arise from several sources:

- Increasing the percentage of opportunities a sales team wins

- Increasing the average number of products in a deal

- Increasing the number of new customers the sales department sells to

- Decreasing the number and size of the discounts needed to win a deal

- Decreasing customer churn, that is, the number of customers who quit buying from the vendor

- Decreasing the time it takes to close an opportunity successfully

The first study of business benefits we ever took part in was for sales and marketing analytics at a CPG company. We studied the company's implementation of custom-built data marts for sales and marketing. The increase in gross profit that people at the customer's site would acknowledge amounted to 0.4 percent of sales. In other words, for each billion dollars of sales, *gross profits* increased $4 million per year.

At a pharmaceutical company, we found the divisional vice president of sales was willing to take a one-time 2-percent increase in sales quota to fund the purchase and implementation of pharmaceutical sales analytics in his division. Why? He believed, after the discussions we had had with his sales and marketing teams, that he could increase sales by 8 percent. He felt that putting commissions on 2 percent of sales at risk for the possibility of getting commissions on an extra 6 percent of sales was worth the risk. Since, for many sales organizations, the rate of commission rises after one achieves 100 percent of sales quota, the increase in pay was probably much more than 6 percent of his variable pay.

How does Sales Analytics do this?

- It helps salespeople and their managers see what deals are stalled. The salesperson can see that a deal is stalled and change tactics. A sales manager can coach a salesperson that the current sales strategy is not working and suggest or mandate a change. If they can get a deal moving forward, they can increase the percentage of deals they win and decrease the time it takes to close a deal. Therefore, ask about how better understanding of a sales pipeline could increase win rates or cut the length of sales cycles.

- Best practices from across a sales force can be identified. Sales management can then describe to other teams what the best practices have achieved, allowing other teams to increase their win rates or average deal sizes or cut their sales cycle times. For instance, a particular sales organization may be executing the sales process more effectively. Another may have discovered particular collections of products that can be sold together, raising average selling prices. Another may have discovered a way to communicate product value propositions to minimize discounting. As sales management discovers these advances, it will want to communicate them across the sales force to raise the entire unit's performance. Sales Analytics can help identify practices that work and can monitor whether, after these practices are communicated to the rest of the sales force, other sales teams are following these newly discovered practices.

- When a salesperson is not making his/her quota, management needs to coach the salesperson as to how to improve. If the salesperson continues to underachieve, the sales manager has to terminate the salesperson. This is a fact of life in sales. Salespeople and sales managers understand this. Sales Analytics can provide, not anecdotes, but a rich set of data to document the salesperson's performance. The sooner underperforming salespeople can be coached to improve or counseled out of the organization, the more the organization as a whole can sell.

■ Very little in an organization is more important than hitting one's sales numbers or, if that cannot be met, alerting management as early as possible when sales will experience a shortfall or when sales will greatly exceed expectations. If sales will fall short of expectations, supplies have to be curtailed to keep inventory from piling up. In more extreme cases, layoffs or job sharing will have to be planned. Also, investors have to be alerted. If sales will greatly exceed expectations, supplies have to be procured and products built. In a services business, subcontractors have to be lined up. After all, if sales takes an order and the rest of the organization cannot fill it promptly, both the company and the customer lose. Sales Analytics helps improve sales forecast accuracy through the sales funnel, as described previously. By comparing prior results to prior forecasts, management can understand who habitually undershoots or overshoots sales targets and pass more reliable estimates up the chain. These comparisons also provide the basis for management to understand the source of sales reps' forecasting errors and take steps to fix them.

We anticipate that implementing Sales Analytics will usually *not* save the organization any money. In fact, it may increase the organization's costs. After all, they have to buy the software and implementation services, as well as pay to keep the system going.

Key Stakeholders

The prime stakeholder is the sales department, from the head of the sales department all the way to the individual, quota-carrying salesperson, including both inside and outside salespeople. Each year management sets higher expectations for the sales force than the year before. Often, they add or change the products a sales rep may sell or the accounts they call on.

Also, each year, customers' procurement departments are asked to do more with less. Therefore, they need to make sure the vendor is earning every bit of sales revenue they get. Therefore, anything you can do to help Sales increase the revenue they can bring in will be appreciated.

Sales Operations may also be a stakeholder. These people ensure that the orders are correct and can be shipped easily. Therefore, although it may sound like these people would be interested in Supply Chain/Order Management Analytics only, they look at the sales pipeline as a leading indicator of their workload and of what they are likely to have to ship. Therefore, good pipeline visibility helps these people process orders promptly. Until an order is processed—and for people who sell tangible merchandise, the product is shipped—the company cannot recognize revenue. Particularly near the end of the quarter, the pressure to get product shipped is intense because management wants to show that revenue as part of the quarterly revenue it reports to shareholders. Therefore, providing sales ops what it needs so it is not a bottleneck for recognizing revenue helps increase sales.

Lesser stakeholders are the product management and marketing organizations. Product Management often develops the sales collateral, sales training, and other material the sales force uses to sell a product line. They should be interested in whether the material they provide is effective. Again, they can consider themselves as effective if the material they provide increases revenue. Often, Product Management also sets pricing policies. They should want to understand what new pricing policies are doing to the lengths of sales cycles, win rates, and discounting. A whole subject area called "CRM Sales Products" is dedicated to gathering the statistics that product managers need to carry out their jobs.

Marketing, as described earlier, should be interested in getting qualified leads to sales. They, therefore, should want to understand how those leads develop into opportunities, quotes, and closed sales. Also, if the lead-to-close ratio is lower than expected, analysis of the sales pipeline should help people understand whether the issue is with something in the marketing campaign or in the sales force's ability to execute on the leads that marketing is providing. Without the type of detailed information that Sales Analytics can provide, particularly when combined with Marketing Analytics, we see a lot of finger pointing because both sides are relying on anecdotes to justify their position.

Cross-Functional Analysis

The ability to combine Sales Analytics with other types of analytics separates Oracle's Sales Analytics from other sales analysis solutions, such as those that come with SaaS solutions. Looking at Sales Analytics in this type of a silo only perpetuates the single pillar thinking that management is often looking to eradicate by introducing Analytics. Also, what happens if a new acquisition is announced that uses another SFA system or another division decides to adopt another SFA system? Without a single sales analytics solution, the synergies management wants to see will be delayed and minimized.

We see Sales Analytics most commonly combined with Marketing Analytics to provide a complete view of how campaigns translate into leads and then into orders. This, then, can be used to develop a return-on-marketing investment calculation.

Also, we see Sales Analytics being able to be combined with Supply Chain and Order Management Analytics to get a complete view of the lead-to-cash cycle. It lets them see how long it should take to turn a lead into cash and how many leads it takes to generate a given amount of cash. Finally, combining these lets sales and operations understand how changes in pipeline affect operations' ability to execute and how operations' execution dovetails with what sales is promising the customer.

Finally, we see Sales Analytics being combined with HR Analytics. A value proposition of HR Analytics is to understand what recruiting channels or other characteristics drive success among new hires. With Sales Analytics, sales management can gauge salespeople's progress in meeting their goals in detail. This allows sales management and HR to gauge their ability to hire effective sales reps. We understand that hiring good sales reps is more art than science, but looking at objective characteristics still does seem to have significant predictive value.

Subject Areas

These subject areas address both an overview of the sales process as well as many of the subsets of the sales process, for example, quotes or orders, as described earlier. They are designed for the individual sales reps, sales managers, product managers, and sales operations—in short, all the stakeholders described previously. Because all the data is sourced from one place, as one rolls up sales, customer, or product hierarchies or drills down them, the numbers will match.

CRM Customer Overview

This subject area, shown in Figure 12-4, does not look at individual activities, orders, shipments, and so on. Instead, it looks at activities, opportunities, and booked and shipped revenue by customer, employee, geography, customer contact, and time. It allows a salesperson or manager to get a snapshot of a territory, account, or salesperson and then gauge the overall effectiveness of the sales pipeline and revenue. It also looks at trends of these over time. It calculates many

FIGURE 12-4. *Sales – CRM Customer Overview*

counts of activities and opportunities by these dimensions so one can look at the intensity of the sales effort. It also keeps many monetary metrics to gauge both the pipeline and actual sales. In addition, it looks at wins and losses as well as time-based metrics, such as the duration of the sales cycle, the number of days in a given stage, and the length of time it takes to complete an activity. This subject area is a good place for a salesperson or manager to start to understand the overall health of a territory, account, or pipeline. Also, if you have data-quality problems, this subject area will show the anomalies quickly. Because the salesperson who enters the data is the same person who will use the results, the salesperson has an incentive to clean up the data to make the dashboards this subject area generates more valuable and increase the size of his/her commission check.

CRM Forecasting

If you have ever worked in a sales organization, you probably understand that very little is more important than timely and accurate sales forecasts. These drive management decisions on what volumes of products to make or buy. They drive marketing programs to try to fill the top of the sales funnel if demand slips. They drive what the CFO tells the financial analysts on the earnings call. They drive Procurement to accelerate or decelerate the purchase of long-lead-time items. In short, the better the forecast is, the more smoothly the lead-to-cash machine runs and the happier the CEO and CFO are at the board of directors meeting or on the earnings call. The forecasts are, in turn, driven by analysis of what deals stand where in the sales cycle and what probabilities of closing can be assigned to each deal based on where it stands in the sales cycle and other management judgment.

This subject area, shown in Figure 12-5, looks at revenues, including best case, worst case, and most likely case. It also looks at forecasted revenue. A "forecasted" deal is one where the salesperson commits to management that "this deal is very likely to close." This subject area compares various current revenue numbers to the prior forecast and to similar forecasts from last quarter and last year. It also compares the forecasts to actuals from prior periods and sales quotas. In the case of forecasted revenue, it also looks at costs and margins expected for forecasted deals.

However, the forecast does not live in a vacuum. The numbers of leads, opportunities, and activities as well as the progress of an opportunity through sales stages are leading indicators of how much revenue to expect and when. Therefore, these metrics are included in the CRM Forecasting subject area.

CRM Orders

This subject area, shown in Figure 12-6, combines three areas of metrics:

- Order Revenue

- Order Execution

- Order Discounts and Margins

The first, Order Revenue, discusses how much was ordered, looking at both orders and line items within orders. It looks at monetary amounts as well as counts and averages.

FIGURE 12-5. *Sales – CRM Forecasting*

FIGURE 12-6. *Sales – CRM Orders*

The second, Order Execution, should be of the greatest use to your sales operations and even supply chain people. It monitors the progress of when an order is taken until it is approved and, later, shipped. It looks at a subset of the metrics that order management considers to determine order accuracy and shipment timeliness. Because Sales Analytics is a CRM analytic application and not an ERP analytic application, it assumes the data is available in the SFA system. If you want to use this application, but your data is only stored in the ERP system, you will have to use the Universal Adapter to get the data into this application. There are no adapters to Sales Analytics for E-Business Suite, PeopleSoft, JD Edwards, or SAP. If you are implementing Supply Chain and Order Management Analytics, orders are stored at a lower level in that application. Therefore, it may be preferable to get orders from Supply Chain and Order Management Analytics. If you only have Sales Analytics and need order information, which is only stored in the ERP system, you will have to source it using the Universal Adapter.

The third, Order Discounts and Margins, looks at order revenue, discounts, and margins. What use is it to sell something if you do not make money on it? This subject area looks at whether the company made money selling the product. It does not attempt to allocate costs or anything sophisticated. It takes the costs fed from the CRM system. These are usually COGS at standard costs plus perhaps other standard costs such as variable marketing costs. This subject area is useful particularly if your sales force is compensated on margin rather than revenue. It can also tabulate, at a high level, how much revenue is lost to discounting. It, however, is no substitute for Price Analytics.

CRM Pipeline

This subject area, shown in Figure 12-7, differs from the CRM Forecast subject area in that it looks at the pipeline in more detail. It looks at expected revenue, for example, by sales stage, partner, and sales method. It also differs from CRM Overview in that it can look at data on an individual opportunity. A salesperson or sales manager uses this subject area to assess the health of a pipeline and to determine where to intervene to move deals ahead that have stalled or to identify sales pipelines that do not have enough

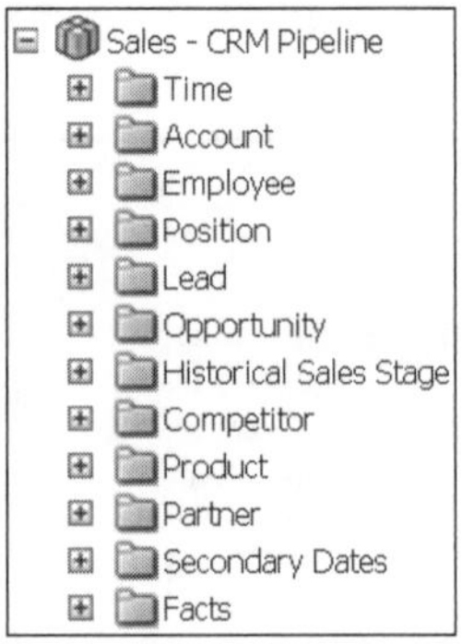

FIGURE 12-7. *Sales – CRM Pipeline*

revenue in them. It looks at both monetary values, such as the total value of opportunities or the expected amount to be closed from the opportunities in the pipeline, as well as counts, such as numbers of wins and losses and numbers of opportunities and leads. It also looks at cycle time metrics, such as the time an opportunity has stayed in a certain stage, the numbers of deals that have moved since the warehouse was updated last, and the time an opportunity has stayed open. There is a sayings in sales: "Time kills all deals." Management and salespeople need to work their opportunities either to close them or decide they are not worth closing.

Finally, this subject area has several metrics around leads. This subject area starts to measure how leads are turning into pipeline and then into closed deals.

CRM Products

This subject area, shown in Figure 12-8, looks at orders and revenue from the points of view of orders and products. It does not track pipeline, and it only briefly looks at customers. Therefore, this subject area should be of the most use to product managers, sometimes called brand managers. It looks at sales of "overlapping products," which indicates how well the organization is cross-selling. Sales of overlapping products can also indicate the opportunity to bundle products together to help keep customers from commoditizing a vendor's offerings. It also

FIGURE 12-8. *Sales – CRM Products*

looks at discounts and shipping delays, all of which can help indicate issues with the product offering that a product manager should investigate. Because this subject area also has order facts, product management and sales can collaborate as to why certain products are not selling as well as they should or why certain products are being discounted excessively.

We have seen in several organizations that product management and sales form a matrix organization, with products being one dimension of the matrix and geographies, vertical markets, or other collections of accounts being the other axis. Where a cell of that matrix is not meeting its sales or margin targets, management will put in place a profit improvement team consisting of sales and product management people to rectify the issues with that product in the particular collection of accounts. This subject area will facilitate the work of that team and allow fine-grained improvement of the business.

CRM Quotes

This subject area, shown in Figure 12-9, is primarily concerned with the quoting process. It looks at the numbers of quotes, the discounts given, and the numbers of products, opportunities, accounts, and so on, quoted. It also compares these to year-ago and other base periods. It looks at the numbers and revenue of quotes that were lost and the numbers that resulted in orders. It looks at the margins and costs of the products and orders quoted. It does not separate out different types of discounts, as Price Analytics does.

CRM Sales Activity

This subject area, shown in Figure 12-10, has no monetary facts in it. It just counts activities and service requests. It just tracks who is doing what activity and how quickly people are closing these sales activities and service requests. It is up to management and salespeople to ensure that the activities are adding value and that management is not measuring activity when it should be measuring progress. We suggest using this subject area in conjunction with the CRM Pipeline subject area to ensure that the activities are resulting in opportunities moving through the pipeline and are being closed or qualified out quickly.

FIGURE 12-9. *Sales – CRM Quotes*

FIGURE 12-10. *Sales – CRM Sales Activity*

CRM Usage Accelerator Current

Sales Analytics depends on the accurate, timely, and complete entry of data about all entities in the sales process, whether they are activities, opportunities, quotes, customers, business partners, or whatever. Without this data, one cannot assess whether the pipeline is likely to generate the expected amount of revenue. This inability, then, degrades the quality of the forecast provided to management as well as the sales team's ability to decide where to allocate resources to maximize the value of the pipeline.

If Sales Analytics is the carrot to get salespeople to enter activities and other information about the progress of their accounts, the Usage Accelerator subject areas are the sticks. Management can use these to see who is using the SFA system. They can see not only when activities were performed but when the records were created. They can see when the last time an activity was logged in the CRM system. They can see the last time anyone touched an account. They can see which accounts have no coverage. This subject also allows for some rudimentary checking of the completeness of certain customer attributes. However, it is no substitute for the Master Data Management Customer Hub subject area or a good customer MDM solution.

Besides being used as a stick, the CRM Usage Accelerator Current subject area, shown in Figure 12-11, can be used to generate tickler files and lists of activities to be undertaken. It also provides evidence to management and to IT as to the degree of adoption by the sales force.

CRM Usage Accelerator Summary

This subject area, shown in Figure 12-12, has only a subset of the attributes of opportunity and account that are in the Usage Accelerator Current subject area. It also has the statistics about who is using the SFA system and how recently. It contains the statistics about who is generating quotes in the SFA system. It also contains most of the same facts in the Usage Accelerator Current subject area.

FIGURE 12-11. *Sales – CRM Usage Accelerator Current*

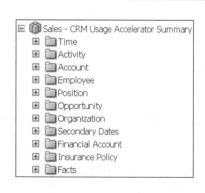

FIGURE 12-12. *Sales – CRM Usage Accelerator Summary*

Other Areas

There are also subject areas for many verticals, such as financial services, insurance, pharmaceuticals, CPG (FMCG), and vehicle sales. For financial services and insurance, mostly these subject areas rename attributes and metrics from the horizontal application to industry-specific areas. The vehicle sales subject area introduces more attributes to describe the vehicle being sold (for example, numbers of doors and engine displacement). CPG and pharmaceutical sales differ greatly because the sales rep does not actually take orders; instead, they try to influence people in the distribution channel to stock or recommend their products. Also, they differ because they incorporate third-party data that tabulates end-user sales. These days, we see very few people implementing the vertical subject areas. If we see this phenomenon change, we will expand this section of the book in a later edition.

With Fusion CRM, the new subject areas include forecasting and territory management. These will be handled in a later edition of the book.

Typical Configurations and Customizations

Many Oracle partners offer adapters to Salesforce.com. Even Oracle Consulting has one. These adapters allow people who prefer to use Salesforce.com to get the benefits that come from being able to link the results of a sales force automation system to marketing, HR, or order management functions, as described in the "Cross-Functional Analysis" section.

Typically, we see people having to configure Sales Analytics for the particular sales methodologies and sales stages they use. Where they tie the sales stages to probabilities of closing, this mapping also has to be developed.

What to Watch Out For

Often management, to save a little money on licenses, wants to roll out Sales Analytics only to sales managers and above. Resist this temptation. If managers get Sales Analytics and salespeople do not, management will be able to ask salespeople questions they cannot easily answer because they do not have access to the same data. At this point, one of two things may happen. First, they may blame you for providing management a rod to beat them with. Second, they may slow down or stop entering data into the SFA system because they know that they will be asked about it and they will be hard pressed to respond. If anything, roll Sales Analytics out to salespeople first and train them well. Meet them often during user acceptance testing. Help them interpret their graphs and reports. Then roll it out to managers. In this way, salespeople will be in a position to answer the queries coming from management and will be able to answer many of them easily. And besides, salespeople are on the front lines of providing your company revenue. Give them the tools they need. They have a tough job.

Below is a list of the major areas we have seen where people have seen problems. Pay attention to these to ensure a successful deployment.

- The ETL provided has both horizontal and vertical mappings, and the BI Applications installer also provides an option to select either/or RPD content. Make sure you line up accordingly to your Siebel instance, if that's your source. Most customers have Siebel Horizontal, which does not require any vertical BI App content.

- If you are planning on rolling out Pharma Analytics, pay careful attention to your data volumes required for Syndicated Data. This has grown so large over the years that it's becoming less practical to bring the data into your network on a timely basis. Various partners are offering SaaS types of solutions for this analysis, which makes sense, but the flip side is it can be challenging to line up third-party data to your data, simply due to volumetrics and the laws of physics.

- Don't try to measure everything with Usage Accelerator; you can paralyze your sales force by asking too much. Instead, strategically focus on key areas where data entry appears to be weak.

- The data model is set up to associate on a single primary salesperson attached to a sale; customizations will be required if you need to split a sale across more than one salesperson.

- Pay careful attention to your ERP and CRM integrations before making assumptions on what type of analysis you can do. For example, shipping information would need to be brought back to your CRM application from your ERP for a complete picture from CRM.

■ The Order information and dimension is different from Order Management and Supply Chain Analytics. This is because ERP applications have many more detailed attributes than the view required for CRM. Oracle chose to keep those two separate, probably with good reason. With proper ERP and CRM integration, this shouldn't be much of an issue, though.

■ The Order Item Attributes dimension comes from the fact table rather than being set up as a junk dimension. This causes overhead in maintenance because for each logical version of the fact table (for example, year ago, quarter ago, and so on), you need to have a matching version defined as a dimension as well. This can create some design overhead as well when setting up aggregates. It also requires additional setup in the RPD to avoid strange-looking, poor-performing SQL to be generated.

The two order facts are Order Header and Order Lines. The main difference between them is that Order Header isn't at the product grain.

For the most part, the metrics on both Order Header and Order Lines equally exist on both tables. However, if you find some KPIs that exist only at an Order Lines or Order Header level (for example, tax or shipping), you should look at ways to handle them in the RPD. For example, you can split them into different logical fact tables. After all, they're in the same logical fact table out of the box, but one is really an aggregate of another.

Conclusion

Every company depends on selling products and services to stay in business. Where these companies have inside or outside sales forces that turn leads into opportunities and opportunities into orders, Sales Analytics is appropriate. Moreover, if one has Siebel SFA and has not modified it too terribly, this application can be installed fairly quickly. On the other hand, because salespeople enter the data and because the data quality of many of the fields cannot be checked easily, the SFA system is likely to have poor quality data in it. The biggest key, we have found, to improving that data quality is to ensure that salespeople are among the first users. They will fix their mistakes once they see they can run their territories more easily and effectively with Sales Analytics.

CHAPTER

13

Service Analytics
and Contact Center
Telephony Analytics

S ervice Analytics is probably the most commonly used CRM analytic application, and it's used to help service organizations understand and analyze many aspects of service and contact center performance. It was the first core prebuilt BI Application that provides prebuilt adaptors for both ERP (EBS) and CRM (Siebel).

Service Analytics is critical when there's a need to maximize the investment you've made in the service modules of your source systems. It provides insight and analysis into service orders, agreements, and customer contact history. It is primarily used to help a service organization improve service levels, increase customer satisfaction, and to maximize both productivity and resource utilization. The ideal output/benefit is that it should help strengthen the loyalty of your customers through an improved experience. Another financial objective might be to help transform your service organization into a profit center by turning inbound service calls into outbound selling opportunities. Research has shown people are much more receptive to receiving an offer after having had their problem solved than they are upon receiving a cold call.

Service Analytics provides motivation to fully leverage an underlying service module in your ERP or CRM application because it offers a reward to an organization for diligence in documenting service requests and maintaining current and accurate information. Service Analytics is equally applicable for a contact center as for a depot repair or field service organization. In fact, in this document, we will use the term "field service" to refer both to service organizations where the technician goes to where the asset is and where the asset comes to the technician in a depot. It can provide the same type of statistics and improve the utilization of both types of service personnel.

Contact Center Analytics is a complementary application that captures the telephony type of data from your IVR (interactive voice response) and switch data. This allows you to capture the customer experience from the time they dial your number to when they hang up, from the perspective of what buttons they push, how long they had to wait, and the overall call time. Also captured are the details around the wrap-up time of the agent, when they were available for calls, and when they took calls. A hand-off and a link from the telephony equipment and software to the service software via computer telephony integration (CTI) are also available, assuming this is installed and integrated at your organization.

Description of the Business Process

A simple (basic) service module offering will provide some sort of IVR service (for example, "Push 1 for English" or "enter your phone number"), an application to capture the required information from the customer, and a knowledge base to help resolve the customer's issues. Most service organizations should have adopted CTI many years ago; however, some have yet to do this. CTI provides a "screen pop" using a customer's call display phone number to retrieve the information about that customer, thus saving time having to perform a manual search/lookup. Most organizations should also have adopted by now an external-facing web-based version of their knowledge base for customers to search on their particular issue.

More advanced service organizations have adopted a multichannel approach, providing online "click to call" services, online chats, mobile services, field services, SLA agreements, self-service RMA (Return Merchandise Authorization), and warranty services. The most mature organizations are capturing customer feedback via social networks, using this to reach out to customers proactively and monitor real-life customer experiences. Unfortunately, this makes things much more difficult to monitor from an analytics perspective because data must be pulled from many source systems—not just service, but finance, shipping, logistics, HR (training and staffing), and potentially many other areas. Ideally, your Service Analytics application should be supported by other BI Applications in order to get a complete picture, as illustrated in Figure 13-1.

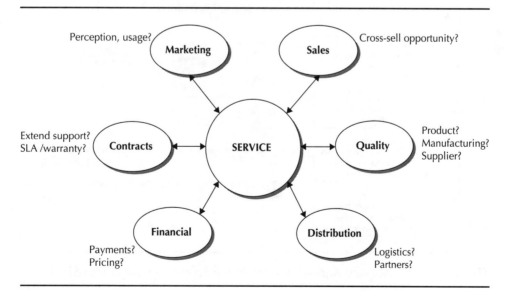

FIGURE 13-1. *Customer service touches many business processes.*

NOTE
In Figure 13-1, the outer ovals are representative of business processes rather than a mapping to a specific BI Application.

Service Analytics along with Contact Center and Telephony Analytics track the details of the physical call (IVR path, talk time, wait time, wrap-up time, and so on) and ties this to who called, why they called, and what the end result was. If the call is tied to a service contract, then a financial perspective is also available. Because the agent(s) involved in the customer contact is recorded, this can be cross-referenced to their HR profile.

An example of the type of analysis commonly performed is shown in Figure 13-2.

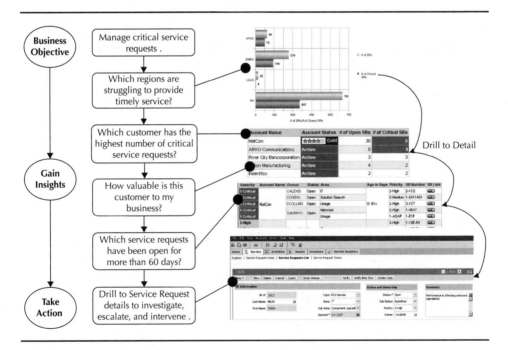

FIGURE 13-2. *Service Analytics workflow with drilling directly to Siebel*

Business Benefits

Service executives often need to balance the driving out of costs and efficiencies while maintaining a high level of customer satisfaction and revenue. For example, there's often a high cost associated with employee turnover when you take into consideration the cost and time to recruit, hire, train, and mentor a replacement employee. For instance, Siebel conducted a study of call center operators and found that customer service representatives, who were paid about $12.50 an hour at the time, cost $40,000 to replace.

There's also the cost of "lost opportunity" while open headcount is getting filled. On the other hand, there's often a practical limit on the costs to retain employees, where the company's viability could be put at risk due to salaries, perks, and so on. How can these sort of things be balanced out? How much tenure is required to meet an SLA and provide a sufficient level of customer satisfaction? Are there enough peaks and valleys of call volumes at predictable times that would warrant staffing schedule changes? Can temporary employees provide good enough service during peaks? A fuel oil distributor we know uses this approach to handle the fall and winter peak. A good place to start would be to look at world-class service organizations—what metrics do they monitor and how do they compare to their peers?

Figure 13-3 is an example of this, using an (admittedly simplistic) illustrative sample of four key metrics specific to a contact center. There are many others, and your organization will have or need to choose your primary comparative metrics based on your organizational goals and type of service.

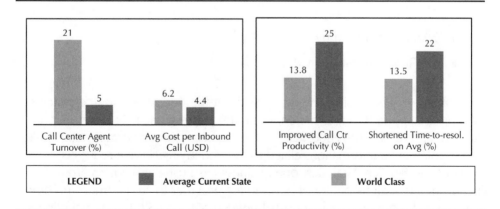

FIGURE 13-3.   *Choose the key out-of-the-box metrics to start with and then expand.*

If better analytics, for example, can help lower the average cost per inbound call by $1.00, it's not hard to show a rapid payback period for Service Analytics. In this example, 100,000 calls per month for a year could theoretically cover the software, hardware, implementation, and maintenance costs for some organizations. Of course, performance varies from customer to customer; the point is simply that business cases for this prebuilt BI Application can be easier to define than for other BI Applications.

Your organization may want or need to measure and improve countless other metrics. Here are some examples:

- Cost per Inbound Call
- First Call Resolution
- Abandonment Rate
- Agent Utilization
- Agent Turnover
- Service Costs
- Average Handle Time

All this can serve as input for your planning processes, such as the following:

- Warranty Provision Modeling
- Staffing Planning
- Spare Parts Planning
- Services Profitability What-If

None of this is possible, however, without the underlying source systems helping to capture the information, route the request, escalate when/where needed, and resolve the issues. Each of these steps generates flags, status codes, and supplemental information related to the underlying service request(s).

For Field Service Analytics, one business case usually revolves around increasing first-call resolution. For a service provider to "roll a truck" (in other words, send it out on a call), it costs between $50 and $200, not including spare parts or technician time to perform the repair. For an organization with 100,000 service calls per year, increasing the first-call resolution just a few points can easily pay for the cost of Service Analytics. If the organization that owns the assets is repairing them, you also need to factor in the value of the increased uptime of the asset because fewer repairs need to be redone.

Also, service providers want to increase the ratio of what in North America is called "wrench-on-bolt time to windshield time", in other words, the percentage of time spent actually servicing assets. Better understanding of the routes traveled and the clusters of repairs can help optimize this ratio, thus further improving technician productivity. Unless your organization is growing, though, to reap the benefits, your organization has to lay off technicians.

These two value propositions apply to public sector entities who maintain equipment, such as transit authorities, publicly owned utilities, and the repair departments of police, fire, and public works departments.

Finally, Service Analytics helps the people who have to sell service contracts understand when to call customers to remind them to renew their service contracts. The metrics people typically look at are churn and upsell or cross-sell percentages. To compute the impact on churn, do not look at churn. Look at 1/churn, or the average lifetime of a customer. If I can drop churn from 20 percent to 18 percent by better follow up, then I have increased the average lifetime from 5 years to 5.56 years. If the average annual profit on a service contract is $1,000, then my total profit is $560 times the number of customers I have. If I can upsell a percentage of these people to a more comprehensive service contract (for example, more equipment or more hours per week) and price the service contract profitability, I can incorporate the revenue from better upselling. The profit improvement would be the percentage of people upsold multiplied by the number of contracts up for renewal in a year multiplied by the profit on the upsold product.

Key Stakeholders

To do a good job at building the commitment for Service Analytics, one needs to build buy-in from people whom the service analytics will affect. We will separate these people into the three use cases for Service Analytics:

- **Contact Center Analytics**   In the contact center, you will want to talk to contact center managers and their bosses. The call center exists to serve the needs of a business function, such as service or customer care. Consequently, you will want to talk to opinion leaders and even the person who leads the function that the call center serves.

- **Field Service Analytics** In field service, you will want to talk to the VP or Director of Service. This person will help you understand the structure of the department and identify the people with the biggest business challenges that could be relieved by better analytics or the people seen as opinion leaders.

- **Services Sales** In services sales, you will need to talk to the head of the services sales area. This person probably works in the sales department. In some companies, this person works in the service department. This person can then direct you to people who sell or renew service contracts.

These people will help you understand the goals of the service function. They will help you understand the metrics they need to run their businesses. You should also help them understand the metrics Service Analytics provides. There may be metrics they are not aware they can get.

Cross-Functional Analysis

Sales and Service Analytics naturally fit well together. A classic example is a scenario where a sales rep is alerted of an escalated service request (SR) for an important customer who's about to sign a deal. There's a natural association between a sales pipeline and current open service requests. Also, the sale or renewal of a service contract may go through a sales cycle tracked in Sales Analytics, just as the sale of the original equipment did.

Also, a natural association exists with HR although you can only tie the employee dimension together. You can cross-reference the level of service delivered with the tenure and completed training, for example, of that employee. You can identify possible training plans, areas for coaching and mentoring, and even possible staffing issues.

Also, if your field service people are servicing your own equipment (for example, for a utility or trucking company) as opposed to your customer's equipment, there should be a tie-in with Enterprise Asset Management (EAM) Analytics. Both are looking at repair histories. Service Analytics looks at this from the point of view of the maintenance department. EAM Analytics looks at it from the point of view of the asset. As part of the same use case, there is also a tie into Procurement and Spend Analytics. Both the asset owner and the maintenance staff want to track the performance of purchased spare parts to see whether certain vendors' parts are failing prematurely. Moreover, the procurement department needs to know if it needs to bring these failings to the vendor's attention. After all, buying an inexpensive spare part is false economy if it wears out more quickly.

We had one customer postulate that there should be a tie in between Project Analytics and Service Analytics. This customer believed, but did not have the ability to verify, that taking shortcuts in an IT system implementation or building construction should result in higher service needs after the asset has been put into service. We have not been able to verify this, but it sounds plausible.

Subject Areas

The following subject areas are available out of the box and can be modified as required to add and remove attributes.

CRM Activities

The CRM Activities subject area, shown in Figure 13-4, covers five areas: counts of activities, cycle times associated with completed activities, costs of activities, travel, and a few counts associated with service requests themselves, not the activities within them. It does not cover transaction-level data. It looks at activities covered by service contracts, billable activities, and nonbillable activities. People look at numbers of activities to understand what products generate the bulk of activities or what people are performing the activities.

Thus, people can try to understand whether the overloaded people are inefficient or overburdened. People look at costs to understand which activities contribute to the costs being incurred. People want to look at travel because when a technician is traveling, he or she cannot be fixing

FIGURE 13-4. *Service – CRM Activities*

something. Therefore, management needs to understand what contributes disproportionally to travel. Finally, being able to tie all these activities back to service requests (SRs) helps because a customer does not care how many activities have to be incurred. They just want their problems solved.

CRM Agreements

An *agreement* is a service contract between the service provider and the customer. Because the CRM Agreements subject area covers many of the metrics associated with the agreement (for example, entitlements, invoicing, effective dates for the agreement, and revenue) as well as many of the metrics associated with SRs and activities incurred under the agreement, this subject area is quite large (see Figure 13-5). It would be used both by the people in charge of underwriting the service contract as well as the people performing services against it.

As with product sales, management may run the service organization as a matrix, with the people who develop and underwrite service contracts on one axis and the people who service the contracts on the other axis.

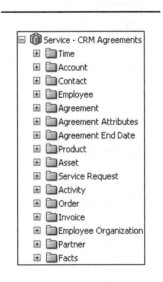

When a cell in the matrix is not meeting its expectation, management may put together a profit improvement team to investigate why. This service area does not cover the selling of service agreements, only the invoicing and servicing of them. It also covers activities undertaken that are not part of service contracts and invoicing for them, for example billable service calls.

In addition, this service area has information about orders. For companies that sell products either with warranties or with service contracts bundled with them, orders serve as a leading indicator as to how much service work will be needed in the future. As with other CRM applications, Service Analytics assumes that order information is available in the CRM system. If it is not, you will have to use the Universal Adaptor to take order information from the ERP system and bring it into Service Analytics.

FIGURE 13-5. *Service – CRM Agreements*

CRM Assets

The CRM Assets subject area, shown in Figure 13-6, looks at service from the viewpoint of the asset (that is, the product covered by a warranty or service contract). As with other subject areas, it looks at numbers of SRs and activities, but it looks at them in conjunction with an asset. It also looks at mean time between failure and mean time to repair.

CRM Customer Satisfaction

The CRM Customer Satisfaction subject area, shown in Figure 13-7, compares metrics around service requests, such as the number of SRs, open SRs, and closed SRs, and the average duration an SR was open with the results of customer surveys to attempt to correlate customer satisfaction with the frequency of SRs and how long it took to close them. It can also handle surveys that are particular to a given SR as well as those that span a period of time.

CRM E-mail Response

The CRM Email Response subject area, shown in Figure 13-8, covers e-mail responses, including both sales and service-related e-mails. These may be e-mails that request service, e-mails that turn into leads, or e-mails that turn into orders. It measures the number of leads and service requests generated, the amount of revenue expected, and the amount of time to escalate this or turn it over to sales. People expect quick responses to e-mails. Therefore, the amount

FIGURE 13-6. *Service – CRM Assets*

FIGURE 13-7. *Service – CRM Customer Satisfaction*

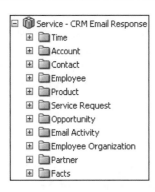

FIGURE 13-8. *Service – CRM Email Response*

FIGURE 13-9. *Service – CRM Orders*

of time it takes to turn a lead over to a sales rep or partner and the amount of time it takes to turn an e-mail into a service request will affect the amount of revenue that can be closed and the degree of customer satisfaction.

CRM Orders

The CRM Orders subject area, shown in Figure 13-9, is largely the same as the CRM Orders subject area in Sales Analytics. The Service version lacks only opportunity, marketing, and employee position information, which affect how the product was sold but not how the order was received or fulfilled. As with Sales Analytics, Service Analytics assumes order information is available in the CRM system. If you want to use this subject area, and you only have order information in the ERP system, either you will have to use Supply Chain/Order Management Analytics to get order information or you will have to use the Universal Adapter. Service personnel would use this subject area to determine what has shipped as a leading indicator of what has to be serviced in the future.

CRM Products

As with CRM Orders, the CRM Products subject area is largely the same as CRM Sales Products (see Figure 13-10). The Service version lacks employee position, geography, and some of the information about the account, for example, contact and industry information. However, it has service-related statistics about products, such as mean time between failures and mean time to repair.

```
☐ 🎁 Service - CRM Products
   ⊞ 📁 Time
   ⊞ 📁 Account
   ⊞ 📁 Contact
   ⊞ 📁 Product
   ⊞ 📁 Employee Organization
   ⊞ 📁 Partner
   ☐ 📁 Facts
       ⊞ 📁 Product Facts
       ⊞ 📁 Order Facts
```

FIGURE 13-10. *Service – CRM Products*

CRM Service Requests

The CRM Service Requests subject area, shown in Figure 13-11, looks at service requests as well as how they are logged, serviced, and closed. It tracks service level agreements (SLAs) and compliance with them, as well as workloads and numbers of open and closed service requests. It looks at average times to resolve service requests. There is also a fact table for critical service requests. You can look at these at the individual service request level as well as aggregates of them.

```
☐ 🎁 Service - CRM Service Requests
   ⊞ 📁 Time
   ⊞ 📁 Account
   ⊞ 📁 Contact
   ⊞ 📁 Employee
   ⊞ 📁 Product
   ⊞ 📁 Asset
   ⊞ 📁 Service Request
   ⊞ 📁 Order
   ⊞ 📁 Employee Organization
   ⊞ 📁 Partner
   ☐ 📁 Facts
       ⊞ 📁 Service Request Facts
       ⊞ 📁 Service Request History Facts
       ⊞ 📁 Opportunity Facts
```

FIGURE 13-11. *Service – CRM Service Requests*

Customer Service Overview

The Customer Service Overview subject area, shown in Figure 13-12, falls in the call center part of Service Analytics, not the field service part of Service Analytics. It contains summary-level metrics about how many calls were answered, abandoned, and so on; the number that were transferred from the interactive voice response (IVR); the length of queues; the time to answer calls; the average handle time; the chat time; and the e-mail response time. Therefore, this subject area can be used for multichannel

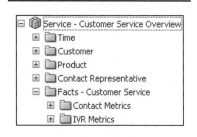

```
☐ 🎁 Service - Customer Service Overview
   ⊞ 📁 Time
   ⊞ 📁 Customer
   ⊞ 📁 Product
   ⊞ 📁 Contact Representative
   ☐ 📁 Facts - Customer Service
       ⊞ 📁 Contact Metrics
       ⊞ 📁 IVR Metrics
```

FIGURE 13-12. *Service – Customer Service Overview*

contact centers. Typically, call center managers are rated on their ability to keep average handle times within bounds. Therefore, expect this subject area to be of particular interest to contact center managers. Unlike the Enterprise Contact Center Overview (discussed next), this subject area does not have any revenue metrics.

Enterprise Contact Center Overview

The Enterprise Contact Center Overview subject area, shown in Figure 13-13, is a superset of the Customer Service Overview service area. It also contains revenue metrics associated with sales contact centers.

IVR

The IVR subject area, shown in Figure 13-14, covers detailed IVR transactions, including navigation path, entry and exit menu durations, and so on. It can be used to help tune the IVR so fewer people decide to abandon their calls and ask for a CSR (Customer Service Representative).

Service Delivery and Costs

The Service Delivery and Costs subject area, shown in Figure 13-15, is used for sales call centers. It is used to understand how much and how well inside sales people are selling and the costs of sales. Besides monitoring sales rep productivity, it can also be used to understand what products are most appropriate for a given call center to sell, both because of the nature of the product and because of the types of people who succeed in selling it.

Service - Enterprise Contact Center Overview
- Time
- Customer
- Product
- Channel Type
- Contact Representative
- Facts - Enterprise Contact Center
  - Call Metrics - Call Volumes
  - Call Metrics - Average Times
  - Chat and Email Metrics
  - IVR Metrics
  - Contact Center Sales Metrics

FIGURE 13-13. *Service – Enterprise Contact Center Overview*

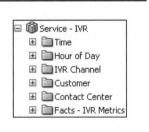

Service - IVR
- Time
- Hour of Day
- IVR Channel
- Customer
- Contact Center
- Facts - IVR Metrics

FIGURE 13-14. *Service – IVR*

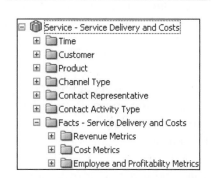

FIGURE 13-15. *Service – Service Delivery and Costs*

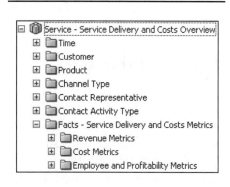

FIGURE 13-16. *Service – Service Delivery and Costs Overview*

Service Delivery and Costs Overview

The Service Delivery and Costs Overview subject area, shown in Figure 13-16, is a subset of the Service Delivery and Costs subject area. It lacks Average Call Sales Value, Sales Closure Call Volume, Sales Closure Call Time, Average Hourly Sales Call Value, and the Average Trunk Call Cost metrics.

ACD/CTI

The ACD (Automatic Call Distribution)/ CTI (Computer Telephony Integration) subject area, shown in Figure 13-17, covers detailed switch data, including ANI (Automatic Number Integration) and DNI (Dialed Number Integration) as well as detailed metrics on call volume, total times, and average times. Also covered are chat and e-mail metrics and associated dimensions such as Time (and hour of day), ACD Details, Customer, Product, Channel Type, Call Reason, Routing Strategy, and Contact Representative. This subject area can be used to help tune routing algorithms to increase first-call resolution. It can also be

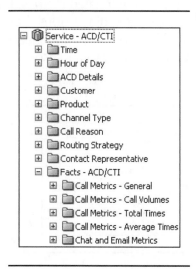

FIGURE 13-17. *Service – ACD/CTI*

used to help understand where lengthening queues are leading to greater call abandonment as well as to plan staffing levels to match call volumes.

Agent Activity

The Agent Activity subject area, shown in Figure 13-18, covers agent activity, including details on schedules, shifts, breaks, logins, and so on. It includes metrics pertinent for analyzing agent activity from a schedule perspective and associated dimensions such as Time (and hour of day), Channel Type, Contact Representative (attributes, skills, and so on), and Contact Activity Type. It can be used to understand what agents are performing less productively than expected. It can also be used to monitor compliance with areas such as adherence to numbers and durations of breaks, attendance, and amount of time spent logged in.

Agent Benchmarks and Targets

The Agent Benchmarks and Targets subject area, shown in Figure 13-19, covers contact center agent performance against targets and benchmarks for relevant call KPIs. In addition to targets and benchmarks, it looks at total and average metrics around call volumes and call times and maximum values for various time-related metrics. It ties these to associated dimensions such as Time (and hour of day), Customer, Product, Channel Type, Call Reason, Routing

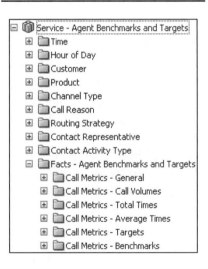

FIGURE 13-18. *Service – Agent Activity*

FIGURE 13-19. *Service – Agent Benchmarks and Targets*

Strategy, Contact Representative (attributes, skills, and so on), and Contact Activity Type. People use this subject area to understand causes of delays or increases in time spent handling customers' problems. The problems typically arise because the numbers of calls has risen, the types of calls have changed, the IVR routing strategy has changed, or the mix of skills the customer service representatives possess has changed.

Agent Performance Overview

The Agent Performance Overview subject area, shown in Figure 13-20, is very similar to the Agent Benchmarks and Targets subject area. This subject area lacks the targets and benchmarks. It summarizes data to the month. It also includes metrics around chat and e-mail traffic. It would be used to understand agent performance in a multichannel contact center over time and to determine root causes of deviations in performance.

Contact Center Benchmarks and Targets

The Contact Center Benchmarks and Targets subject area, shown in Figure 13-21, is very similar to the Agent Benchmarks and Targets subject area. This subject area lacks the statistics listing the maximum and total values of certain metrics. It also does not contain attributes around employee

FIGURE 13-20.   *Service –*
Agent Performance Overview

FIGURE 13-21.   *Service – Contact*
Center Benchmarks and Targets

language proficiency. However, it contains dimensions describing the geographic location of the call center and its parent. One would use this subject area to understand whether deviations in performance arose from the location or hierarchy of the contact center.

Contact Center Marketing

The Contact Center Marketing subject area, shown in Figure 13-22, provides coverage on the detailed impact of marketing campaigns on contact center performance. It includes information pertaining to campaigns such as dates and names. It also covers metrics such as Campaign Handle Time and the associated dimensions such as Customer, Product, Channel Type, Contact Representative, and Campaign. People would use this to understand the effect of a given marketing campaign on call center volumes and performance. It could be used to help predict the need for more agents or agents with specific skills, depending on the campaign being run and how similar it is to other campaigns in the past.

Contact Center Performance Overview

The Contact Center Performance Overview subject area, shown in Figure 13-23, is very similar to the Agent Performance Overview subject area. This subject area lacks information to tie a call to a specific employee or supervisor. However, it includes information on the geographic location of

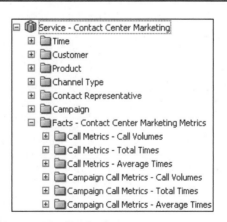

FIGURE 13-22. *Service – Contact Center Marketing*

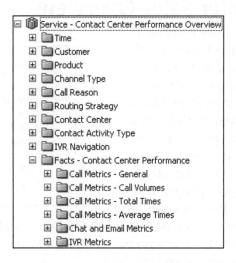

FIGURE 13-23.   *Service – Contact Center Performance Overview*

the call center and IVR performance. It would be used to determine root causes of deviations that were caused by the call center or its IVR.

Contact Center Sales

The Contact Center Sales subject area, shown in Figure 13-24, is used to track the performance of a sales-oriented contact center. It includes metrics such as revenue per call, revenue per minute, close rate, revenue per employee, and total sales revenue.

It contains associated dimensions such as Customer, Product, Channel Type, and Contact Representative. It is used to understand the performance of inside sales representatives and sales contact centers. The nature of the metrics being calculated assumes these are one-call closes, not complex sales cycles. If a sale requires many calls to close, it would probably be a better candidate for an SFA (sales force automation) system, such as Siebel Sales, than a contact center system.

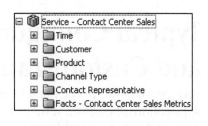

FIGURE 13-24.   *Service – Contact Center Sales*

Contact Center Sales Overview

The Contact Center Sales Overview subject area, shown in Figure 13-25, is very similar to the Contact Center Sales subject area. This subject area lacks Sales Closure Call Time, Sales Closure Call Volume, and Average Call Sales Value metrics. However, it contains many metrics used to measure the performance of the contact center in handling marketing campaigns. It would be used to measure the performance of a sales-oriented contact center, particularly if closure rate was not a primary metric or marketing campaigns caused much of the variation in load.

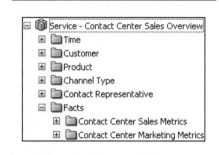

FIGURE 13-25. *Service – Contact Center Sales Overview*

NOTE
The CRM Real Time subject areas are not discussed because they're not recommended for anything other than basic data validation. They're a set of OBIEE subject areas that run directly against Siebel. They're not actively maintained by Oracle, and there's a high likelihood of your encountering performance issues. Real-time reporting out of Siebel is much better served via BI Publisher and web services as a source.

Typical Configurations and Customizations

Service Analytics and Contact Center Telephony Analytics are separate applications; however, it makes sense to implement them together. In fact, we feel they're so closely partnered we combined the discussion of both into the same chapter. There are no prebuilt adaptors to any specific ACD (Switch) and IVR applications; therefore, the Universal Adaptor concept is required. You need to set up a process to extract flat file data from your ACD and IVR sources, and possibly transform to the CSV format required by Contact Center Telephony Analytics. There's flexibility on the grain of data that can be fed into the data sources, too, for example, minute, hour, and contact center representative information.

Most customers will likely expose more attributes in the subject areas than what is available out of the box. This is a drag-and-drop exercise. A balance can be found between having enough attributes (facts and dimensions) and having too many. The goal should be to provide enough information without overwhelming the end users. As a point of design, some subject areas combine both Telephony and Service, and some do not. This is affected by the type of integrations you have on the source side.

What to Watch Out For

This application is geared more for an inbound contact center than outbound, based on out-of-the-box metrics. This application is also primarily geared for Siebel CRM sources. Although EBS CRM is supported, the EBS adaptor only covers a small part of the data model (Service Request Transactions). This is due more to the limited coverage of EBS CRM compared to Siebel CRM.

In the out-of-the-box RPD (OBIEE semantic layer, a binary file ending with an RPD extension, used by the OBIEE Server), the physical Asset dimension isn't aliased; it might be a good idea to complete this design to ensure consistency with the rest of the metadata. If you need Survey Assessment (Analysis of Survey effectiveness) details, there's a deprecated subject area called "Customers" that is available with the full (unpruned) RPD, which can be generated and exposed with the BI Applications Installer.

When bringing in telephony information, you might need to look at date/ time conversion to your data warehouse universal time from your local time, for consistency in reporting across dashboards. Every telephony system has different output capabilities and formats, so this will require some analysis and research to understand how the hand-off should work from your hardware to your input CSV files.

Another area of confusion concerns the possible overlap with real-time telephony information available with your ACD and IVR. In reality, there isn't overlap because this real-time information is only useful during a shift, to indicate the effectiveness of the planned staffing schedule. Service Analytics tracks the history, where you can review longer time periods more holistically.

Another area of confusion is that Service Analytics is not meant to be used to plan staffing schedules.

In the data model, there's no "junk" activity dimension (for example, w_activity_d, only w_activity_f). Logically, there's an activity dimension table that points to attributes from the physical fact table. Should you need to create an aggregate of your activity fact, you'll need to take this into your design consideration.

Conclusion

Both Service Analytics and Contact Center and Telephony Analytics allow you to combine data from your CRM applications and your telephony equipment to provide a "cradle-to-grave" view from the time your customer dials your service support line all the way through to issue resolution. The key benefits can be summarized as follows:

- **Service effectiveness**   Helps you monitor, analyze, and manage your various contact and service centers based on key performance metrics such as service request aging and average resolution time, thereby increasing overall customer satisfaction while reducing costs

- **Employee effectiveness**   Helps you better understand contact center representative performance to enable improvements in your employee productivity, effectiveness, training programs, and overall retention

- **Customer insight**   Helps provide CSRs with a more complete view of your customer's account profile, potential value, and propensity to buy more products, thereby enabling faster resolution of issues and increased cross-selling rates

CHAPTER
14

Making It Yours Without
Ruining the Foundation

Now, you have decided that buying an analytic application that meets the bulk of your needs will get your organization more benefits, more quickly, at a lower risk. You have picked an area to start on. You realize that to make this analytic application work best for your organization, you will have to tailor it to your organization's needs. Like most software, you realize there must be a right way to tailor it that expands the software's usability, while preserving its reliability and ease of upgrading.

You realize, also, that there is a wrong way to tailor it that will render it as difficult to maintain and upgrade as a fully custom data warehouse without the benefit of it being set up exactly the way you need it today. What's more, you realize that although "if you build it, they will come" might work well for baseball fields, it often does not work well for analytics. Users have to understand how to use this new creation and move it forward as their needs change. Finally, from time to time, the vendor of your ERP and CRM systems will change their underlying applications, and you will have to react.

This chapter helps you identify the twists and turns in this portion of the journey, and it overlaps a little bit with Chapter 3, which covers architecture in detail. There's a fine line between what would be considered a configuration and what would be called a customization. Chapter 3 touches on what you need to understand before you purchase; this chapter is more useful as you're deep into an implementation and need to customize. Oracle has extensive documentation around required implementation steps and customization best practices, and this chapter should therefore be used as a supplement only, to provide the context of "why" you're doing what you're doing.

Approaching the Implementation

Before launching into the implementation, some foundation needs to be built. This foundation is less about IT than assembling the correct team and starting to build good governance procedures.

You Will Need to Pick an Implementer

An implementer for BI Applications will require a different skill set from the one used to build data warehouses—either just from data models or completely from scratch. If you have never implemented an Oracle BI Application before, resist the temptation to do it completely yourself unless several of your team members have implemented Oracle BI Applications elsewhere.

We know of very few stronger indicators of a poorly implemented project than an organization that tries to implement its first Oracle BI Application with no outside help. If nothing else, you won't be able to learn the data model on your own—this only comes from experience.

You Will Need a Governance Process

Many people look at a BI competency center as the place where report writers and other power users work. We are not looking at that type of organization, at all. Instead, we are looking for a steering committee of business people who can advise the team on what to implement next:

- Should the team add new data sources?

- Should the team add more reports?

- Should the team roll out the existing content to new groups of users?

- Should the team implement a new BI Application?

This group should be no bigger than is needed to provide good advice. As the organization achieves success, the steering committee can expand to include more stakeholders. Initially, though, keep it small enough to allow yourself to respond quickly as the organization's needs change. You need to show success and show it quickly. You need enough supervision to ensure the result comes close to meeting users' requirements, but not so much that it slows you down.

You Will Need to Pick Your Team

If you are new to BI Applications, your team will probably look different than if you have implemented several of these apps before. Although it should include the usual ETL programmers and report developers, your team will probably need fewer than you are accustomed to. After all, Oracle has built much of the content for you. We recommend you get a team that is familiar with JAD (Joint Application Development), agile development, or other similar methodologies.

Because Oracle has provided you with so much content, you will want people who can modify existing ETL, metadata, and reports quickly, not necessarily people who can build whole edifices of code from scratch.

If this is your first BI Application, you will need people who can work well with a systems implementer. Your team needs to accept the knowledge transfer that a systems implementer will provide. This way, your team can be much more self-sufficient, if desired, when it comes time to implement the second BI Application. Therefore, pick team players and insist your implementer do the same. You will also need people who are comfortable working on modifying an existing package, rather than developing things from scratch.

Because of the breadth and depth of content Oracle provides, one person has compared BI Applications to giving users "paint by numbers instead of a blank canvas." This content, then, opens the door to using more JAD and agile development techniques to speed delivery of content and set the pace for many small, incremental releases, for example, two to three months per subject area. Far too many implementations have fallen into the trap of rebuilding subject areas that already exist, due to the lack of knowledge and experience with the out-of-the-box content.

So much for the psychological makeup; let's turn to the technical skills. You will need the usual types of players one would expect in a data warehouse implementation project: ETL programmers, metadata developers, and report and dashboard developers. However, you will need fewer than you would for a build scenario. Try to find people with experience in the particular ETL tool and DBMS you will be using. And as always, you'll need resources intimately familiar with your source OLTP or CRM application data model.

Skills can be transferred from a competitive ETL tool or DBMS, but you should expect a longer learning curve. Whoever is working on the OBIEE semantic layer, however, should have at least a few years of full-time experience with the Admin tool, and someone who is also a seasoned data modeler. A common mistake is to turn the OBIEE semantic layer development (via the Admin tool) over to developers, where this needs to be left to your data modeler(s).

In fact, if there is only a small number of source systems and you are only building one BI Application, the project team for both the systems implementer and your team should probably number six or fewer full-time equivalents (FTEs), including the project manager. Even with larger, more complex implementations, having a team much larger than 12 becomes increasingly difficult to manage well.

We feel that, for an initial implementation, you should provide between 20 percent and 80 percent of the FTEs. If you have less than 20 percent from the staff, your people will be less likely to be involved in some of the critical decision making and are less likely to learn enough to be self-sufficient. If you have more than 80 percent from your staff, it is likely they will run the project the way they always have and will not learn how best to take advantage of the features Oracle has built into the BI Applications or how much of a change in implementation methodology is required when one is buying rather than building analytics.

The Implementation Itself

The key to becoming efficient and rolling out more and more (source systems, BI Application subject areas, and so on) is not to add more staff, but to approach your implementation like a factory. Each team member has a distinct role. Each role needs to perform tasks in a specific sequence. The tasks and sequences have dependencies with each other. Therefore, the key to optimizing a scheduling plan is to ensure that all resources are busy at all times.

For example, a data modeler can't verify the suitability of the out-of-the-box data model against user requirements until he or she knows what the ad-hoc subject area needs to look like. The ETL developer won't know what extension fields need to be added to existing ETL jobs until the physical data model changes are confirmed. The ETL developer is also dependent on the source system expert to identify what new fields need to be pulled from where to map to the physical data model. The OBIEE semantic layer can be updated while the changes are made, but you can't fully unit test the SQL generation until data has been loaded by the ETL process.

The cleanest way to approach an implementation is to first stand up one application at a time and use the out-of-the-box reports for testing purposes. Set the expectation with end users that they're not going to use the out-of-the-box dashboards. The initial sets of dashboards are available for them to better understand what their starting point is, and to help articulate their short-term and long-term requirements. Out of the box, the initial dashboards and reports are also going to highlight any data-quality issues that may exist in your source system(s).

Implementing out of the box first is a fast way to get feedback, such as x number of fields being missing. At that point, you can either expose the missing fields to the end users if the fields requested are contained in the semantic layer and physical data model, or you can go back to the source and acquire the data. Of course, if you've already done a fit/gap analysis, as most customers do when evaluating the suitability of the BI Applications, you should already have an initial set of requirements. Generally speaking, the important phases of an implementation and ongoing maintenance and support are

- **The initial load**   This involves all the installation and configuration steps required, at all layers. It proves out connectivity and ensures your foundation is in place.

- **The extensions**   This involves bringing in additional fields (and/or sources), with the goal of using existing tables wherever possible.

- **The subject area design**   This is mostly a drag-and-drop exercise. Out of the box, there won't be enough attributes in any given subject area. You'll need to bring in what's required to meet end users' needs, specific to your organization.

- **Dashboard development**   Ideally, power users should be collaborating with IT to first determine an analytical workflow that can overlay with a business process (for example, monitoring AR trends, backlog trends, and so on, in an order-to-cash process).

It's not within the scope of this book to cover best practices with OBIEE, Informatica, and data modeling; these are already well covered in other books. Data warehousing best practices apply to Oracle BI Applications. Any training with Kimball University would be very much worthwhile. Certainly don't allow your developers to implement if they're also learning OBIEE and Informatica technologies at the same time. Oracle University also has very good product-specific training on Oracle BI Applications.

Although as much as possible has been prebuilt, you will need to perform some extensions and customizations during the implementation. For example, consider security, multicurrency, multiple languages, analytical workflows, multiple source systems, multiple tenants, and tuning. Each of these topics requires careful planning and time allocated to your project plan. There's only so much Oracle can do in these areas because all customers implement in slightly different ways, specific to their business and technical requirements.

Security

Because multiple sources are supported and because every organization has different authorization requirements, you'll need to carefully plan out your requirements. Out of the box, there are "stubs" and a security best practices guide. You'll need to look at what application roles and initialization blocks you'll need, and what row/column level requirements you have. You also need to consider what application roles have access to what functionality (mobile, scorecards, Office plug-in, ad-hoc, and so on). With only one source (EBS), for example, you'll see more value in the out-of-the-box setup; with multiple data sources you'll need to start with the "stubs" and extend from there. With EBS you can leverage your existing Single Sign On (tradeoffs with EBS authentication, however, include challenges setting up BI Publisher, BI Office plug-in, and the Mobile client). When a user logs in, OBIEE can query the EBS FND_USER table to inherit application roles used for security. Consider implementing Oracle Access Manager to better integrate OBIEE and EBS security.

If you have too many users with completely different security requirements looking at completely different applications and source systems, then at some point you may want to consider setting up different OBIEE environments. With the growth of cloud computing and the use of virtualization technologies, setting up different environments is becoming easier to do. In some cases, you can have different OBIEE environments pointing to the same BI Applications database.

The implementation is relatively easy, compared to the challenges customers typically face in putting requirements down on paper. The largest of implementations may need to switch to a strategy of using a single (or very few) initialization blocks for performance because the queries issued to bring back security profiles when a user logs in can accumulate and take longer than acceptable. In OBIEE 11g, you can have deferred initialization blocks, but not for row-wise variables. Refer back to Chapter 3 for a more in-depth review of considerations.

Multicurrency

Out of the box, everything is presented and reported on in your primary global currency, but under the hood there's much more going on. The prebuilt ETL supports three global currencies, defined by your source system(s), the document (transaction), and local (GL posting) currency. To expose multicurrency in the BI Applications, you'll need to follow a few steps to allow for dynamic toggling between your currencies at the dashboard level on the fly. Project Analytics has this fully set up out of the box for one dashboard as an example. When looking at the local and document amounts, however, make sure you have the currency type code exposed as well, so you don't see an aggregation across multiple currencies.

It wouldn't make sense, for example, to add USD revenue and EUR revenues together, until they've been converted to a common format. A good step-by-step guide is available with Oracle Support called "Dynamic Support for Multiple Currencies in Oracle BI Applications," where you set up and configure a table called W_CURRENCY_TYPE_G. Another option is to look at the new currency prompt, available with OBIEE 11g.

Analytical Workflows

As mentioned earlier, don't expect to use the out-of-the-box dashboards and subject areas; they're really just a starting point. Encourage your team to consider "report" as a dirty word, focus on how to summarize information and look for trending and exceptions, define what a drill-down path should look like to identify root causes, and identify what corresponding actions should be taken in the source systems. Think about defining a business process that everyone should follow, and design your rollout and training around this analytical workflow. Figure 14-1 provides an example from Financial Analytics.

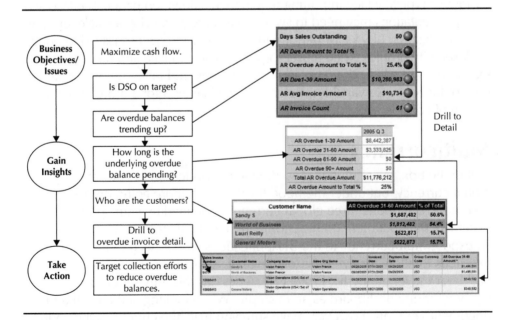

FIGURE 14-1. *Sample Financial Analytics workflow*

Far too many customers simply build an inventory of disconnected reports that don't connect the dots across multiple subject areas. Instead of starting with countless rows and pages of data, start with a summarized exception-based view that allows you to identify trends and exceptions. From there you can compare actual to plan or desired state and drill into details for a root cause analysis.

Multiple Languages

OBIEE supports multiple languages, from a technology perspective; however, should you have this requirement, you'll also need your content and possibly data translated as well. There's nothing specific to the BI Applications that are required; you can follow standard OBIEE best practices. Out of the box the dimension tables reflect the language used on the source system transaction.

Two types of customizations are available: You can externalize the metadata strings, to allow for the toggling of a dashboard and subject area between different languages, and you can set up translation tables for specific lists of values for data translation. In both cases, you can manage the data externally to the BI Applications; however you need to put in place your own means for data entry and maintenance. You can, for example, develop a shared dashboard and then have functional users translate both the content labels and underlying prompt values in an external application that would get picked up by OBIEE.

Multiple Source Systems

Ideally, you want to be on Oracle BI Applications 7.9.6.4 with DAC 11*g* to best support these requirements. The DAC 10.x version required different execution plans for each source system. This meant you could only load one source system at any given time, and each source required a different execution plan setup. BI Applications 7.9.6.4 is certified with DAC 11*g*, and it includes many recent enhancements, such as the ability to schedule multiple (mutually exclusive) loads at the same time. You still have one data source defined for an execution plan.

Keep in mind that every table in the target Oracle BI Applications data warehouse maintains the source system identifier and the source system natural keys for each transaction. The INTEGRATION_ID field maintains the source system (natural) keys concatenated by a tilde symbol (~). The DATASOURCE_NUM_ID field maintains a unique source system number.

Furthermore, there's an ETL_PROC_WID field to keep track of the specific ETL run, along with W_INSERT_DT and W_UPDATE_DT fields to track the timestamp of the insert or updates to each row. This allows you to implement the Oracle BI Applications without first implementing MDM. If dimensional values (for example, customer name, product name, and so on) happen to match, your data will naturally aggregate on your dashboards and you'll still be able to maintain your drill down to each source system.

Multiple Tenants

Each data warehouse target table in Oracle BI Applications has a TENANT_ ID field, used to separate data from a security perspective. This way, different business units can share a common database and BI Applications schema as well as maintain a firewall via OBIEE or database-level security (for example, Virtual Private Database [VPD] in Oracle Database Enterprise Edition). To leverage this functionality, ensure you're using unique IDs, as appropriate, and you'll need to set up the security for users when they log in.

Multiple Time Zones

In the case of "follow the sun" type of ETL loads, where data is trickling into your data warehouse 24/7, you may want a strategy to insulate end users from data changes as they're being loaded. This may range from a simple strategy using security applied while the ETL process is running, to more elaborate approaches offered by the Oracle Database. This should be reviewed by your Oracle pre-sales team to identify the best option for you (for example, Oracle Active Data Guard or Oracle Golden Gate replication).

Tuning

Oracle has documented a tuning and performance guide. This is available for download from Oracle support, you can search for "Oracle Business Intelligence Applications Version 7.9.6.x Performance Recommendations" (ID 870314.1). It covers an almost mandatory requirement for table and index partitioning (Oracle Database Option), for example, when using the Oracle database. Partitioning is typically done by year on large fact tables, which provides an immediate performance improvement with little effort. If all you need, for example, is data from the current year, the Oracle database doesn't scan records or indexes from previous years. This is functionally equivalent to physically partitioning your tables, from a performance perspective. This also eliminates the need to purge historical data (archiving strategy) for performance.

There is also a detailed performance and tuning guide for OBIEE, independent of custom or prebuilt BI Applications. Search for OBIEE 11g Infrastructure Performance Tuning Guide (ID 1333049.1) as an example, confirming you have the correct guide for your OBIEE version. Most likely you'll find yourself referring to these documents and tweaking your environment once you've gathered performance details and understand where your bottlenecks are. The most important configuration is setting up compression and static file caching on your web server.

EBS Flex Fields and Other Extension Fields

The challenge with flex fields is that until your company implements one (and hopefully one field doesn't have multiple purposes), you won't know if it would map to a fact table or a dimension table and which table it would belong to. Whereas a number of EBS key flex fields are mapped out of the box, EBS descriptive flex fields are not. Any additional field that's not available in the physical data model out of the box would need to be pulled over, hopefully using existing ETL mappings and placed in an existing table.

Testing and Validation

It is important for the data to be credible for users to adopt the new system. However, we all must recognize that testing and validation are never-ending chores. We should understand when the data is "good enough." Before starting on any discussion of testing and validation, we want to put forth one ironclad principle:

> Never change data in the data warehouse except as part of an ETL run. If data needs correcting, fix it in the source system or MDM system and then rerun the ETL.

Doing anything else will cause the data warehouse not to match what is in the source, which will undermine the data warehouse's credibility. Also, if data is corrected in the source system or MDM system, the revised data will have to pass all the edit checks your organization built into these systems for good reason. If you absolutely must hide source transactional data, at least try to use the soft-delete flag available on all Fact tables, to filter out the data on your Dashboards.

The Oracle BI Applications bring in transaction-level data, together with enough identifiers to tie it back to unique records in the source system. This allows people to understand whether data was brought over incorrectly, whether it was transformed incorrectly, whether it was wrong in the source, or whether it was correct in the source but represented something that should not have happened. For example, during the validation phase of building a data warehouse for a bank, it was found they were paying more for certain jumbo CDs than the bank made by lending money over a comparable term. The bankers were convinced the data warehouse was wrong. A little detective work showed that, not only was the data warehouse right, but the source system had recorded the transaction correctly. The bank had bid a little too much for those funds. Expect the unexpected.

In Financial Analytics, GL Analytics stores data—not just by the GL chart of accounts, but also in business terms such as *cash, revenue,* and *accounts payable.* The rules used to map the chart(s) of accounts to the business terms cannot be built in the prebuilt mappings because they are unique to each organization. Often, we have found these rules get misinterpreted as the mappings are built. When the balance sheet, P&L, and cash flow statements first come out, investigate these mappings first.

It's very challenging to test data when the source system is changing, so ensure you have a frozen data source when validating the data pulled into the BI Applications. You might, for example, see testing drag on for a couple weeks or more. End users will want to pull up the same transaction in a source system to compare it side by side with what they see in OBIEE during any given round of testing. For the out-of-the-box mappings, the cleanest way to test is for end users to prove if and where data isn't correct. The burden needs to be on them. The only way to truly validate the data is at the transactional level.

Either the transaction in the BI Applications matches the transaction at the source, field by field (assuming the source hasn't since changed), or it doesn't. To ensure the data at an aggregation level is accurate, the only way to measure this is to compare transaction counts from both the source and the target. This requires writing custom SQL queries to both databases to cross-foot the grand totals. The source qualifiers in the Informatica ETL mappings can assist on the source side.

Finally, don't forget about the testing of performance and tuning. Ensure you've blocked at least two to three weeks in a QA environment for this task. You won't know where any bottlenecks might be until you've run the ETL tasks, loaded a sufficient amount of data, and refreshed your dashboards. Performance and tuning can be as simple as adding some indexes, or more involved, such as deploying Exalytics (discussed in an earlier chapter). Theoretically, the tuning options available to you are the same as any custom data warehouse; the difference is that you'll likely require less time and have to expend less effort. Much work has gone into the research and development of the BI Applications, and a high degree of tuning is already in place.

Training

BI tools these days are fairly straightforward. Most people can figure out how to make minor modifications to existing dashboards and reports without very much training. They can build many simple reports themselves. There are free online courses, blogs, and videos. So why formally train?

First, we have not yet met a body of users who understood the nuances of their own data. Train the users on what their data means. We realize they may have been making decisions based on this data for years, but the data warehouse will allow them to make many more decisions more quickly. Therefore, they can make many more errors per month if they misunderstand their data. Also, if you are deploying BI Applications because they provide complex metrics the organization has never used before, you will need to train users on what the metrics mean and how to use them. If you have used BI Applications as an opportunity to enrich the data either by exposing more attributes from the OLTP system or by buying third-party data, the knowledge of what these fields mean may not have penetrated into the organization's psyche.

The concept of analytic workflows can be new. Users may not be used to thinking of analytics as a "process" with a right way and wrong way to solve a problem. Help them understand how to use these workflows to diagnose problems. Ensure there's a business process documented (for example, a flowchart or swim lane type of business process diagram) that's available as part of the training.

Help people create and use graphs and charts effectively. We find people do not understand what makes an effective graph. Instead, nonfunctional users create what is cute and flashy but conveys very little real information. We recommend Edward Tufte's series of books, particularly the original, *The Visual Display of Quantitative Information*. Oracle and others provide tools that allow for good, easy-to-understand graphics. But they are tools, and we have to use them effectively.

Your technical staff need formal Informatica and OBIEE training and need to know how to use a data modeling tool. If they've just finished the training, they're still not yet ready to touch Oracle BI Applications unless they're coached and mentored by others with BI Applications experience. For example, they can shadow and be mentored by a boutique systems integrator who specializes in the BI Applications. Although various Oracle partners provide OBIEE and BI Applications training, nothing compares to the history, experience, and quality of training provided by both Informatica and Oracle University.

At least some of the power users should take the "Oracle BI 11g R1: Build Repositories" course along with the end user training, not because they'll be using the OBIEE Admin tool, but because they'll have the language and understanding required to communicate effectively with the OBIEE developers. End users don't necessarily require formal training by an Oracle partner or Oracle University; the best option is usually to create a two-to-three-hour session that's specific to their data, ad-hoc subject area, and available dashboards.

Rollout Plan: How Big a Bang Should You Handle?

How much and how fast you roll out is dependent on the number of end users available to participate, the number of source systems, and how customized your source systems are. To stand up all the BI Applications out of the box and complete an initial data load is the easiest part. The hard part is getting feedback from end users, and getting them to sign off and be confident of the new environment as a replacement to their cherished personal spreadsheets.

As mentioned earlier, by all means implement the out-of-the-box content first before making any changes. This simply means following the list of steps very well documented by Oracle to both install and configure everything. Two documents are available online that you'll need to follow: "Installation Guide for Informatica PowerCenter Users" and "Configuration Guide for Informatica PowerCenter Users."

You can theoretically load all BI Applications for one source at one time, and can delegate the configuration tasks for each BI Application to multiple people. For example, you can run a SQL statement against a source system to gather configurations and setups made and use that information either for the domain files used by the out-of-the-box ETL process or for setting up the required variables in the DAC (Data Warehouse Administration Console).

One person can focus on what's required for Financial Analytics, for example, while another works on Order Management and Supply Chain Analytics.

Once the out-of-the-box BI Application(s) have been loaded with the initial load for one source system, you can do the data validation, add extension fields, and develop your dashboards in parallel. Keep in mind, though, that after you add extension fields on a Fact table, you may need to do another initial load, which could mean truncating your tables first. Alternatively, you may need to have a one-time strategy to update historical rows already loaded. Therefore, end user testing will need to pause and potentially have to be restarted. The same complication exists for deploying across multiple sources; at some point doing too much will result in people tripping over each other.

Dealing with a Source System Upgrade

Periodically, the vendors of your source systems will issue new versions of the source systems, and your organization will decide to implement them. As the steward of the data warehouse, you have to react because potentially the new version of the source system will break some of your ETL. Also, there may be new functionality in the source system that you would like to expose in the data warehouse.

This section is broken into two parts:

■ Why a source system upgrade is the ideal time to implement BI Applications

■ How a source system upgrade impacts an existing data warehouse built with Oracle BI Applications

Why a Source System Upgrade Is the Ideal Time to Implement BI Applications

If your organization has decided to upgrade its source system and you have a custom data warehouse, you have to decide whether to upgrade the ETL mappings to match the new data model or to scrap the custom data warehouse and put in a BI Application. Studies by Oracle and some of its partners have suggested that implementing a BI Application at this point can save time for both the upgrade of the data warehouse *and* the upgrade of the source system. We realize this is counterintuitive. "There will be enough disruption with our EBS upgrade, and you want to introduce more?" is a common reaction. Figure 14-2 is an illustration showing the types of tasks that will be needed for both upgrading the source system and implementing a BI Application. It shows that there is significant overlap in the required activities, leading to substantial savings over doing both tasks separately.

Also, you can cut down on the cost to upgrade the source system by implementing a BI Application at the same time as you upgrade your source system. When systems implementers are called in to troubleshoot performance problems on a source system, they often start by looking at what reports the customer is running directly off the source system. Often reporting from the source system is slowing down the source system. The obvious solution would be to move that reporting to the data warehouse, where a little latency is acceptable. In fact, a study by an Oracle partner found that only about

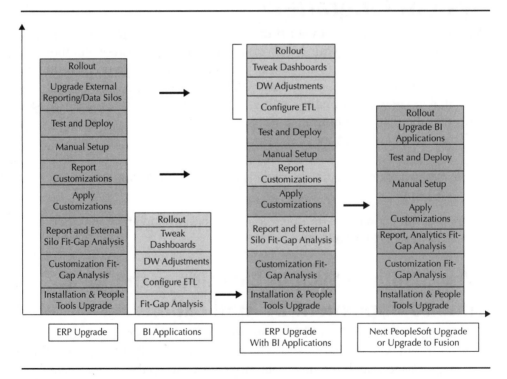

FIGURE 14-2. *Why it's best to upgrade ERP and implement Oracle BI Applications at the same time*

2 percent of the reporting typically done on a source system needed to be done there. The balance could be done from the data warehouse.

Therefore, as part of the source system upgrade, many of the reports should *not* be upgraded. They should be replaced by reports running from the data warehouse. Moreover, typically developing a report in OBIEE takes less time and skill than developing it in the reporting tool provided by the source system vendor. The money that would be spent to upgrade the reporting from the source system can be applied to implementing a BI Application.

Keep in mind the downside, though: If you require a lot of custom attributes that don't roll up in any meaningful way (for example, fax numbers), don't let those extensions become a higher priority that slows down your dashboard development. Operational and transactional reporting can be supported by Oracle BI Applications, but this should be a side benefit rather than a primary deliverable.

Figure 14-3 highlights the challenges with real time analysis against a transactional system. When you encounter these difficulties, you may find a better solution is to look at a Data Warehouse approach such as found with Oracle BI Applications, or off-load your transactional report to a replicated

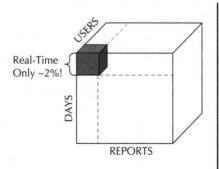

Real-Time Only ~2%!

USERS

DAYS

REPORTS

Most real-time analysis limited to
• A few days
• A few users
• A few reports

• Reliance on ERP reporting tools creates burden on ERP performance.

• Multiple reports for similar data set.

• No real BI capabilities.

• Lots of IT involvement.

FIGURE 14-3. *Why ERP transactional reporting is limited*

database or ODS (Operational Data Store). Relatively few reports will need to truly be "real-time."

Finally, as part of implementing a BI Application, you should take an inventory of the reports and dashboards currently in use. You should ask the following questions:

- Which ones are no longer used?

- Which ones can be combined using filters and row, column, and view selectors?

- Which ones are just large list reports used to feed Excel? These Excel dumps should be investigated to see whether the analysis they provide can be built directly in the data warehouse. The burden of proof should be on the people wanting to continue to work from Excel.

Oracle's systems implementers have found that, approached in this way, usually 80 percent to 95 percent of reports or dashboard panels can be combined or retired, further cutting down on the work needed to implement the data warehouse. Combining these reports also cuts down on ongoing maintenance because there are simply fewer reports and dashboard panels for IT to maintain. This is your chance to force a cleanup of clutter and get you back on a path to a single version of the truth.

Implementing a BI Application simultaneously with a source system upgrade also can speed up the validation of the new release of the source system. When there are questions about the validity of the data in the source system, it should be easier to run a query against the data warehouse to obtain the data to be validated, at least in part because a data warehouse data model is designed to be queried and because it is easier to write queries in OBIEE than it is in the query language provided with the source system.

Finally, if and when you migrate to Fusion Applications, the reports and dashboards you built with Oracle BI Applications should also migrate (not automatically, though) because the BI Applications are standing the test of time as the prebuilt data warehouse for all Oracle ERP and CRM sources. The remaining reports running against the source system can be converted to Oracle Transactional BI (OTBI), which uses OBIEE. OTBI provides real-time transactional reporting out of the box, however, you need to have Fusion Applications as your source. Figure 14-4 illustrates how this would look. For example, with an upgrade to EBS R12, you would use OBIEE for access to

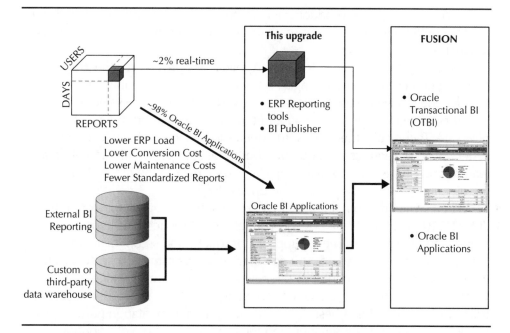

FIGURE 14-4. *BI Applications as a bridge to Fusion*

your BI Applications while using BI Publisher and other ERP reporting tools for real time and transactional reporting. In the Fusion world you can use OBIEE for both, even though the underlying architectures are different.

How a Source System Upgrade Impacts an Existing Oracle BI Application

Source system upgrades can be as minor as a technology refresh and bug fixes, or as major as a completely different business process introduced by the upgrade. Often fields are added and/or deprecated between versions. Occasionally, entirely new tables are introduced. New values can be available in a list of values on the source. Existing data could be moved from one table to another.

Occasionally, upgrades involve the consolidation of multiple source systems into fewer source systems (perhaps one). This may require Master Data Management (MDM) efforts to rationalize and harmonize key data such as customers, suppliers, products, and so on. Finally, customizations in the old source could be retired if the upgrade provides similar net new functionality to what used to be custom.

In the majority of cases, Oracle BI Applications provide for the graceful handling of these backend changes. As part of your maintenance fees to Oracle, you'll have access to the latest version of the source system ETL adaptors. Generally speaking, you can turn off one adaptor and turn on the new one. Technically there are some details to be aware of. Each source system adaptor requires a unique number to be stamped on the target data warehouse. This is used to match up the source data to the target during incremental loads for the "insert else update logic."

When switching from an older to a newer source adaptor (for example, EBS 11.5.10 to EBS R12.1.3), how do you let the BI Applications know the former source data (customers, suppliers, products, and so on) matches the new source data? Simply put, you can carry over the same source system ID (number) from the old adaptor to the new adaptor (optional). It all depends on whether or not you want to use the same data warehouse keys for transactions from two sources. This is best discussed with an implementation partner who can look at your specific situation and the pros and cons of your options.

Finally, keep in mind that while source system upgrades can set off a chain reaction of broken real-time operational/transactional reports, you in fact have many layers of insulation with Oracle BI Applications to protect you from changes. For example, the history is maintained in the BI Applications so you have flexibility in what data is or is not migrated from your old ERP to your new ERP. Oracle BI Applications are not designed specifically for one version of one ERP, but rather have stood the test of time across multiple versions and platforms (JDE, PeopleSoft, EBS, and so on).

The Role of a Steering Committee and Center of Excellence

Gartner has said multiple times that setting up a BI Center of Excellence helps a data warehousing project get off to a good start and helps the organization develop good habits. However, we see people confusing three concepts. Insofar as this confusion threatens to slow down or derail a BI Applications project, we want to address it. This brief treatment of the subject should not replace an in-depth look at a Center of Excellence. The subjects we see being confused are

- A competency center
- A Center of Excellence
- A steering committee

Viewed in the narrowest fashion, a *competency center* contains the people who understand how to make the BI Application perform optimally and understand how to build new reports more quickly and more robustly than typical power users or regular users do. In a BI Applications project, these people need to understand that their job is to modify and enhance what is provided, and to create as little from scratch as possible.

A *Center of Excellence* provides thought leadership around BI. It helps the organization understand how best to use BI and how to help the organization use analytics as a way for the organization to advance its mission more economically, more effectively, or more quickly. The training people should be tied into the Center of Excellence so that their training does not just address the mechanical aspects of querying the BI Application but also how to use analytics effectively. We recommend these people read Thomas Davenport and Jeanne Harris's book *Competing on Analytics.*

A *steering committee* provides business input into the order of implementation of new content for the data warehouse. These people should act as the internal venture capitalists or board of directors that fund the overall analytics effort.

Groups wanting to have new content added to the data warehouse should submit requests to the Center of Excellence for review that they meet data warehousing best practices and to the steering committee to ensure they align with the organization's mission. After the fact, ROI studies should be submitted to the steering committee to ensure the return is worth the effort. Finally, we believe that a council of representatives of all three groups should meet with strategic vendors annually to review and provide input into the vendor's roadmap.

We do not recommend having fully staffed versions of all three of these when starting out. By all means have a steering committee. One or two people can form the nucleus of the other groups combined together. As the project grows, one can split the two organizations. We feel it is also important for people in the Center of Excellence and competency center not to be full-time people. They need to have jobs in the rest of the organization to help keep them grounded in the organization's operational and strategic needs. Over time, you can add the following roles as required.

Recommended Roles and Responsibilities

Many roles will need to be played as Oracle BI Applications are implemented, rolled out, and maintained. The following is a list of these roles. These are roles, not position descriptions. One person can perform many roles, particularly initially. We do not want people to say, "Simon and Will advocate setting a team of 16 people before we start implementing Oracle BI Applications." Far from it. For example, a person can be borrowed from another group or contracted if not needed full time. In fact, as we have argued before, we find it useful if many of these people have outside jobs to keep them grounded in what the organization needs.

- **Executive sponsor**   Establishes high-level goals, gets funding, provides political guidance, and secures resources. Has the ability to resolve disputes—a judge, jury, and sheriff, all rolled into one person.

- **Data stewards**   Set standards for data quality, management, organization, definitions, and business rules.

- **Business subject expert and data experts**   Have innate knowledge of business processes. They can design testing plans, identify functional requirements, participate in implementation and technical reviews, design business metadata, lead data testing, and sign off.

- **Program director**   Oversees the overall DW/BI program, schedules, budgets, and deliverables.

- **Project managers and business analysts**   Plan and implement requirements gathering, manage implementation and reviewers groups, define scope and deliverables, participate in DW modeling, conduct testing, plan and oversee user testing, plan and implement metadata gathering, and plan and oversee data quality tasks.

- **Business systems analysts**   Participate in requirements gathering, investigate data sources, define data transformations, perform DW modeling, and conduct unit testing.

- **Data modeler**   Leads the overall review of the star schemas for required changes, and should be at least the primary OBIEE semantic layer developer and/or administrator. The fewer data modelers you have, the better to ensure standards and consistency.

- **ETL developers**   Develop data extractions, transformations, and loads of data mappings from source to target.

- **Front-end developers**   Dashboard development and maintenance tasks.

- **Metadata administrator**   Ensures all metadata is captured, recorded, and current; includes what is exposed through OBIEE for end users and backend ETL documentation.

- **Data quality administrator**   Enforces and monitors standards as defined by the data stewards.

- **OBIEE administrator**   Maintains environments, oversees upgrades, provisions environments, enforces standards.

- **Customer support**   Internal customer support to help with ad-hoc development and technical issues or questions. Most importantly, customer support resolves any questions around the accuracy of the data.

- **Trainers**   Development of a short burst of functional training on how to use the dashboards designed for specific roles to monitor and analyze specific issues.

- **DW architect**   Overall traffic cop who ensures technical best practices are being followed and service level agreements are being met.

- **Database administrator (DBA)**   Monitors the health of the underlying database, performance, and disk space. Also responsible for backups.

Adding New Content

In many ways, modifying the out-of-the-box BI Applications is no different from modifying any data warehouse. There are exceptions, however. For example, should you need to modify a prebuilt Informatica mapping, you need to first copy the mapping to a new folder to keep your changes isolated from future upgrades. Because you're now using this customized mapping with a new name in a new folder, you need to register the new mapping with the DAC and then update your execution plan accordingly. Also, you shouldn't modify the out-of-the-box OBIEE web catalog content; leave that alone as a baseline and instead copy what you need to a new folder and go from there. Follow the same rule for the prebuilt OBIEE subject areas.

There's a classic diagram used by Oracle for years that still applies today that differentiates the different types of backend changes you could potentially be faced with, as illustrated in Figure 14-5. Category 2 changes, by the way, require the largest amounts of effort.

It's beyond the scope of this book to document in detail every step you need to go through to modify or add to the data model, modify or add Informatica mappings, update the OBIEE semantic layer, and then update your dashboards. Oracle University covers this well with their formal training, with a few different options, for example, "Oracle Business Intelligence Applications 7.9.6 Implementation" and "Oracle BI Applications 7.9.6: Implementation for Oracle EBS." Oracle also covers this in great detail with

		Data Warehouse Modifications		
		Add Additional Column to Existing Fact or Dimension Table	Add Additional Rows to Existing Fact or Dimension Tables	Add New Fact or Dimension Tables
Data Sources	Packaged Application (Uses Prepackaged Adaptor)	Category 1	Configure Filter	Category 2
	Non-Packaged Data (Uses Universal Adaptor)	Category 1	Category 3	Category 2

FIGURE 14-5. *Categories of backend BI Applications changes*

the standard product documentation. What we will cover, however, are the key things to be aware of as a manager or project manager to be able to have an educated conversation with your team. The example we'll refer to is adding extension fields; however, the same concepts apply to adding new physical tables to the BI Applications.

Once you determine what fields you want to add to the BI Applications, you need to first determine where in the target data warehouse you should add the fields. It could be a fact or a dimension. Although you wouldn't normally use the X_CUSTOM field on any given table, it will serve as the reference and guide as to how to add your extension fields. Another example could be with Financial Analytics, where you make changes to your group account mappings in the source system, you update the domain CSV file used by Informatica, and then you update the OBIEE semantic layer metric(s) to reflect this new domain value.

Although you may not appreciate the value of the DAC at first (or were unable to fully grasp the concepts presented in Chapter 3), you will see how important this is for Oracle BI Applications when it comes time to extend your out-of-the-box (OOTB) install. As a quick recap, Figure 14-6 shows

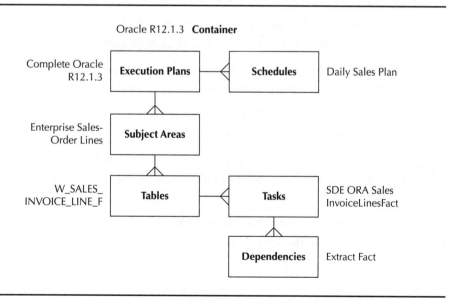

FIGURE 14-6.   *DAC metadata and sample values*

the metadata supported by the DAC, to help automatically generate the full sequence of ordered tasks required to populate your target tables. Keep this in mind when making customizations and updating the DAC, to separate DAC OOTB metadata from your customizations.

General Customization Guidelines

This section doesn't presume to cover all the specific details or replace the many pages of Oracle documentation. We will however provide you with a roadmap of major tasks to allow you to understand what to expect and to have an informed conversation with your team and implementer. Think of this as a checklist for success.

The following major areas are discussed: Informatica, DAC, and the physical data model. These are the most important areas to follow best practices, as they're where you can be affected the most during an upgrade down the road.

Informatica

1. Create a custom Informatica folder to segregate customizations.

2. Use the "safe" ETL path described by the X_CUSTOM column provided out of the box with Oracle BI Applications.

3. Be careful while editing joins in source qualifiers to prevent row explosion (for example, many-to-many Cartesian products).

4. Minimize edits to OOTB packaged (reusable) objects such as transformations and mapplets.

5. Source and target database credentials are defined in Informatica, too, not just the DAC, so don't overlook that setup in the Informatica Workflow Manager client.

6. Always keep in mind that custom modifications to existing mappings will need to be reapplied after an upgrade.

DAC

1. The OOTB container is for reference only, so create a new custom container.

2. Create a new execution plan pointing to the custom container, so your subject areas don't end up pointing to your OOTB container and therefore won't pick up your configurations. For example, in order for the ETL to use source system properties, such as INITIAL_EXTRACT_DATE configured in your custom container (for example, "Oracle 11.5.10_COPY"), you need to follow these steps:

   a. Build a new execution plan.

   b. Add all the necessary subject areas. Make sure to choose the custom container "Oracle 11.5.10_COPY" on the Choose Subject Areas window.

   c. Generate parameters and assign values to the database connections.

   d. Save and then build the execution plan.

   e. Use this execution plan for the ETL.

Data Model

1. Make data model changes directly against the original table.

2. Start custom column names with "X_".

3. Start custom tables with "WC_".

4. Add a new column rather than change how an existing column is fed.

5. Most importantly, don't forget to document all your changes as you go.

Adding New Columns End to End

1. Modify the staging and BI Application data warehouse table structures:

   a. Update DAC metadata.

   b. Update physical database schema (via the DAC).

   c. Update Informatica source/target definitions too.

2. Modify SDE, SIL, and PLP mappings to map new columns (including relevant mapplets) through end to end.

3. Modify the physical layer of the RPD. This will appear in the corresponding alias.

4. Expose the new columns in the logical and presentation layers of the RPD from the alias.

5. Use these new fields in your custom reports/dashboards.

Modifying Existing Columns

1. Don't. Instead, add new columns following the preceding steps.

Additional Tips for Category 2 and 3 Changes

1. Sync up Integration_IDs between fact dimensional references and corresponding dimensions.

2. For flat-files, use an appropriate delimiter, such as a comma.

3. Build "primary extract and delete" mappings to handle soft deletes where required.

4. For SCD2 dimensions, identify the historically significant attributes. Build additional SCD_Update mappings to support this.

5. Source necessary code/descriptions and standardize them so they're appropriate for any data source; follow the existing domain value approach as a reference.

6. Use the Currency Conversion mapplet, if required (for example, if your Document amount isn't also your Global 1 amount).

How to Set Up and Configure Multicurrency

During your implementation, you will find some configuration is required to complete the setup that's appropriate for your company. Security and multicurrency are two examples. Out-of-the-box multicurrency is set up in one location within Project Analytics as a reference point. Although almost all fact tables have the local and three global currency conversion rates stamped on each row, not all metrics in the OBIEE semantic layer are wired for the ability to toggle between rates. Simply put, this would be too much overhead (maintenance) for the customers and metrics that don't require this functionality. Other than the examples shown in Figure 14-7, almost all metrics are calculated to display the Global 1 currency.

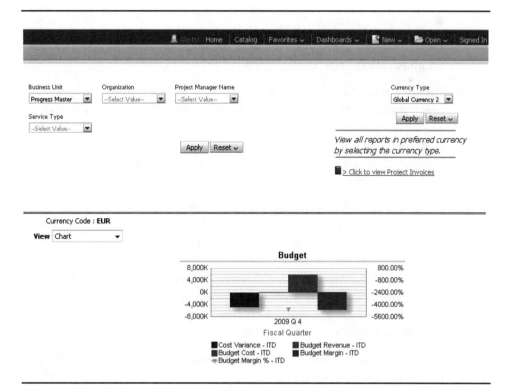

FIGURE 14-7.   *Section of the Project Executive Overview dashboard*

Multicurrency is set up using the following steps (note that steps 1–3 should already be done, depending on whether or not you're on an older version of the Oracle BI Applications):

1. Create a table as follows:

```
Create table W_CURRENCY_TYPE_G (CURRENCY_TYPE VARCHAR2(39)
NOT NULL)
```

Adjust accordingly if you're on a database different than Oracle.

2. Insert the following values (rename as required), assuming you need more than one global currency:

   ■ 'Local Currency'

   ■ 'Global Currency 1'

   ■ 'Global Currency 2'

   ■ 'Global Currency 3'

3. Import the physical table into your OBIEE semantic layer and create an alias called Dim_W_CURRENCY_TYPE_G.

4. Create a physical join between Dim_W_Currency_Type_G and any column of the fact tables you require multicurrency for in the physical layer (for example, Fact_W_GL_BALANCE_F). Out of the box, the only join is to two Project Analytics Budget Fact tables. This is a "fake" join that's required to avoid a consistency check error, but will not actually be used in SQL generation.

5. In the OBIEE RPD (Semantic Layer), create a logical dimension called "Dim – Currency Type" in the Business Model and Mapping Layer using your Dim_W_CURRENCY_TYPE_G alias table. Rename the logical column from "CURRENCY_TYPE" to "Currency Type" in this logical dimension. Set this column as the logical key and then create a hierarchy for this table. You can skip this step if you were also able to skip steps 1–3. This is also in place only to avoid consistency check errors.

6. Create the corresponding complex logical joins based on the physical joins you set up in step 4.

7. In the OBIEE Admin tool, set up three new repository variables (or modify them if they already exist), as follows, setting the value for each of them based on the currency codes you defined in the DAC before your initial data load:

   ■ 'GLOBAL_CURRENCY1'

   ■ 'GLOBAL_CURRENCY2'

   ■ 'GLOBAL_CURRENCY3'

8. Set up a new session initialization block called "Dashboard Currency" (or review it if it already exists). Set the connection pool to:

   ```
   "Oracle Data Warehouse"."Oracle Data Warehouse Connection
   Pool"
   ```

   and set the SQL to:

   ```
   "Select 'Local Currency' from DUAL"
   ```

   Create a new session variable called "REPORT_CURRENCY" (or review it if it already exists) as the target for this initialization block. Set the default to 'Local Currency'. This variable is populated in the dashboard based on user input (Global Currency 1, Global Currency 2, and so on).

9. Obtain the logical metrics you want to dynamically view in multiple currencies. Open the Logical Table Source for each metric, go to the expression builder for the metric in the column tab, and modify the expression as follows:

   ```
   CASE VALUEOF(NQ_SESSION."REPORT_CURRENCY")
   WHEN 'Local Currency'
   THEN "Oracle Data Warehouse"."Catalog"."dbo".Fact_W_{INSERT_
   TABLE_NAME}_F"."Metric"
   WHEN 'Global Currency 1'
   THEN
   "Oracle Data Warehouse"."Catalog"."dbo"."Fact_W_{INSERT_
   TABLE_NAME}_F"."Metric"
    * "Oracle Data Warehouse"."Catalog"."dbo"." Fact_W_{INSERT_
   TABLE_NAME}_F"."GLOBAL1_EXCHANGE_RATE"
   WHEN (repeat for Global 2 and Global 3 exchange rates)
   END.
   ```

NOTE
This code snippet is an example of the high-level logic, while Figure 14-8 is an example of a metric fully set up to handle multiple currencies dynamically.

10. Identify the logical fact tables where you need to support dynamic multicurrency reporting, and identify the subject areas in the presentation layer where one or more of those facts are included.

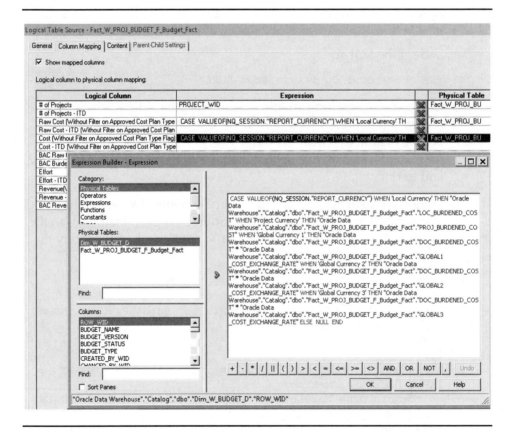

FIGURE 14-8. *Out-of-the-box example of wiring a metric to multicurrency calculations*

11. Identify the presentation table in each of those subject areas mapped to an alias of the physical table W_INT_ORG_D in the physical layer RPD (for example, Dim_W_INT_ORG_D_Operating_Unit_Org) and that defines the local currency for your facts in this subject area. Also, identify the corresponding logical dimension (for example, Dim_W_INT_ORG_D_Operating_Unit_Org). Add a logical column called "Currency Code" (mapped to CURR_CODE in the physical table in the RPD metadata) to the previously identified logical dimension, if not already mapped. You can also map it to the corresponding presentation layer table.

12. Update the expression for Currency Code with the following business rule:

```
CASE VALUEOF(NQ_SESSION."REPORT_CURRENCY")
WHEN 'Local Currency'
THEN
"Oracle Data Warehouse"."Catalog"."dbo"."Dim_W_INT_ORG_D_
Operating_Unit_Org"
."CURR_CODE"
WHEN 'Global Currency 1'
THEN VALUEOF("GLOBAL_CURRENCY1")
WHEN (and repeat for Global 2 and 3 currencies)
ELSE NULL END
```

13. IMPORTANT: In every query (report) that requires multicurrency support, include the column Currency Code so users know what currency the amounts are being represented in, and so that you don't get aggregations across multiple currencies (for example, adding USD amounts to Euro amounts). Figure 14-9 shows an example of a currency code in a subject area, the only one where it's prebuilt as a reference.

14. IMPORTANT: In every dashboard where a query with multicurrency is required, you will need a new dashboard prompt on the Currency Type column. Set a request variable called REPORT_CURRENCY. Figure 14-9 shows an example of a currency type in a subject area, the only one where it's prebuilt as a reference.

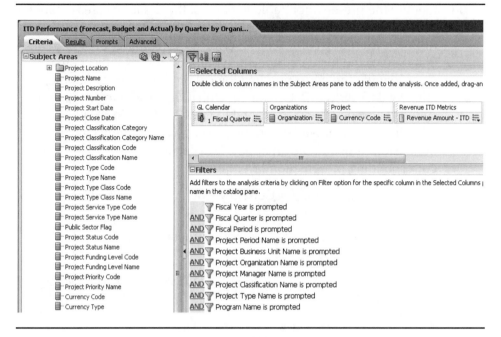

FIGURE 14-9. *Out-of-the-box report with Currency Code*

Conclusion

You will customize Oracle BI Applications—and "customize" doesn't have to be a dirty word. If you're still using the prebuilt dashboards and reports after a few months into production, then you're not getting the full value out of the solution. If you're not making changes to your environment every couple of months, you'll lose the momentum of your implementation. Either you're growing your end user base, value, and adoption rates, or your implementation is dying on the vine. Care and feeding on an ongoing basis is required so that end users have the data they need, when they need it, and how they need it. They know what to do with it and have confidence in it.

We strongly encourage you to thoroughly understand the detailed Oracle documentation on how to customize so you're protected during upgrades. Each upgrade is different, so you can expect guidance from Oracle on what steps to follow. Wherever possible, efforts are invested from Oracle Engineering to preserve your existing data.

Oracle will be available to support you, along with many integration partners. You can request a health check, discussions with Product Management, environment reviews, and product updates. You can get sponsorship during your implementation, customization, and changes to ensure your voice is heard and implementation needs are met. At a minimum, you can engage the Oracle BI sales and pre-sales consulting teams to keep the lines of communication open.

To avoid confusion when reviewing product documentation, keep in mind this book is geared toward the BI Applications 7.9.6.x versions (specifically 7.9.6.4), rather than BI Applications 11g or OBIEE 11g. This book will continue to be relevant until you upgrade to BI Applications 11g, when there is support for Applications Unlimited data sources (for example, EBS, PSFT, JDE) *with* Informatica adaptors. Alternatively, you can migrate to the ODI version. In the meantime, only Oracle Fusion Application customers will roll out (start with) BI Applications 11g. Most of the content of this book will still be relevant for BI Applications 11g, other than the specific guidance around technical constructs and examples.

CHAPTER
15

Conclusion

Having implemented the first BI Application may seem like a major accomplishment—and it is. However, the fun is just beginning. We need to help users grow their use of analytics, but to do so in the right way, for example, by building more dashboards and analytic workflows, incorporating new data, adding more sophisticated analyses, or adding more user populations. We do not want them to fall into old habits of dumping large amounts of data into a spreadsheet or local database for further analysis.

We need to establish and sustain the types of governance needed to keep the analytic system relevant and make it more valuable in the face of changes in the business climate. Ideally, we want everyone to expand the initial BI Applications deployment to cover multiple functions. This would not only satisfy cross-functional analytical requirements, but also help to serve up executive dashboards where required.

We will need to manage the change that inevitably will come when deep, rich data replaces intuition and organizational legend. Don't be afraid to extend what you get out of the box. We will have to build and guard analytics' reputation of having data of unimpeachably good quality. Finally, we will have to manage the organization's analytic roadmap going forward as the organization matures in its use of analytics and the environment in which the organization operates changes.

Going Live Is Just the Start

We have often heard that data warehousing is a journey, not a destination. This does not mean that building a data warehouse is a Sisyphean challenge. Instead, one can expect users' needs to grow as they get more used to making decisions based on data. In our experience, you can expect their needs to grow in three dimensions: more data, more users, and more complex analyses.

More Data

You can add more data in several ways, each to meet a different need. First, you can add more detailed data, in other words, more fields from the OLTP that people need to analyze. Second, you can add more history. Finally, you can add more types of data, the most common of which is third party data, from customers, vendors, or data vendors.

Chapter 15: Conclusion **371**

More Detailed Data

Ideally any extensions would follow the same design as the out-of-the-box tables, where the most detailed level transactional data is brought in and summarized from there. There's often a slight overlap in operational data store (ODS) needs and true analytics—the BI Applications shouldn't replace or fulfill the need for ODS type of operational reports, but some needs can still be met. In other words, you can slowly bring in additional dimensional attributes that serve transactional-level reporting requirements but don't assist with aggregation (for example, fax numbers and e-mail addresses), provided this is a lower priority. Don't expect the BI Applications to bring in every single field from your source ERP out of the box.

Longer History

As we said in the beginning of the book, the University of Chicago keeps stock price data back to 1926. As users get more familiar with making decisions based on data, they will want to look further back to see similar cases in the past. These may have included natural disasters, competitive dislocations, or almost any other type of black swan event. Having this history stored, even at a summarized level, will help users retain the institutional memory of what really happened, rather than the oral history that has been passed down from generation to generation.

Yes, it is permissible to keep transaction-level data for only a few years and just summarized data prior to that. Inventory balances are an example, where out of the box only three months of daily balances are kept, and after that only monthly balances are kept. Keep in mind that because disk space is becoming less expensive, and with database options such as partitioning, there are not very many cases where you need to purge ERP and CRM data from your data warehouse. Another consideration is that your snapshot tables will become more valuable over time as history is built and you can view trends over quarters and years. HR Analytics is an exception in that a full history can be built with the initial load. AR/AP Overdue Balance and Inventory Balance history, for example, is only maintained from the date of your initial load going forward.

More Types of Data

More types of data can be added. For example, you can add more subject areas and more data sources. Initially, you put up a small number of Oracle BI Applications to meet a need you identified. You reaped the benefit you had identified. Now, you and your users have identified that they can reap some of the cross-functional benefits found as well as the standalone benefits of that BI Application. Also, they may want other types of data that the Oracle BI Applications do not support directly (for example, customer satisfaction or other types of survey data, sentiment data, or third-party sales and share data).

More Users

If the data warehouse is to meet its full potential, all people in the organization should have the data needed to discharge their duties. This does not mean that everyone is building queries. Many people may have their personal dashboards. Others may just have a few BI widgets embedded in their OLTP screen. These people might not even be employees of your organization.

Some organizations, for example, publish supplier scorecards in a secure website accessed by their vendors. The most extreme example we have seen comes from the City of New York. They publish their Citywide Performance Reporting system outside the firewall. Anyone can see how long it takes to review the application for a building permit or arrive at the scene of a fire or review statistics on over 40 city departments.

With your current user base, look for adjacent populations who could use the same data as the two organizations collaborate. Fight the assumption that only managers need the data. Provide information and insights to the people closest to the action. When, for example, one of us discussed providing detailed financial data about a cost center to the manager of that cost center, not just finance people, the person responded, "It's about time operational people understood the financial impact of their decisions."

More Complex Analyses

As people get more sophisticated in their use of analytics, many of them will want more sophisticated analytics. They will no longer be content with reports comparing this period's performance with the prior period's performance or with a plan. They will want to see trends and to look for correlations. They will want to look at how and whether plans converge as one gets closer to the date when the plan becomes the actual. They will want to look at simulating or forecasting the future and deciding the optimal course of action. Figure 15-1 illustrates the natural evolution of BI maturity in organizations. Figure 15-2 illustrates how maturity usually develops over time, as you add more data, more users and more complexity into the mix over a number of deliverable phases.

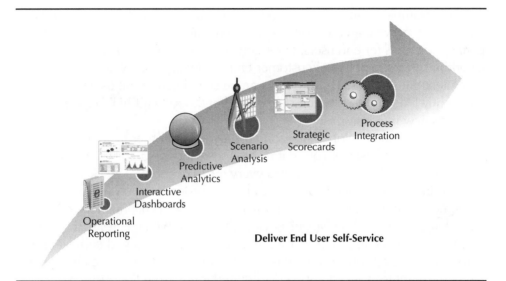

FIGURE 15-1.   *Growing complexity of analyses*

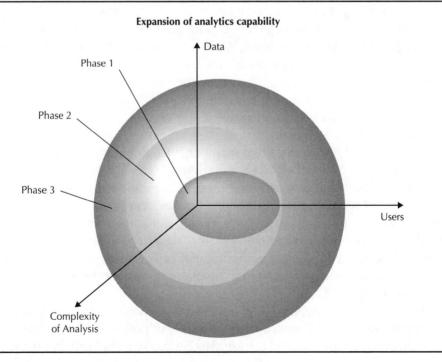

FIGURE 15-2.   *Expansion of analytics capability*

One example of an extension could be to add post-load processing (PLP) functions to provide an additional level of precalculated analyses, used to connect the dots for end users. For example, you could run data-mining algorithms to score potential customer churn, identify quality issues, or fraudulent transactions. This process can be scheduled to run as part of the nightly ETL, and results can be exposed in the RPD (OBIEE Semantic Layer) as new metrics.

Assuming you developed a roadmap showing the order in which you will implement new phases of your data warehouse and the associated types of analyses, you will want to revisit this every 6 to 12 months. Check what about your business has changed. Does this alter the order in which you will need to implement further additions to your data warehouse? What financial or other considerations drive this change? Review these possible changes with your steering committee to ensure corporate priorities have changed consistently with what users tell you. Even a change of management can drive change in the types of metrics and dashboards required to measure the business.

Managing the Change

Even more than with many other types of IT systems, Business Intelligence presents large change management challenges. We are asking people to change how they make decisions. We are asking them to use data instead of intuition as the basis for their decisions. For people who have worked in the organization for a long time, this may not be comfortable.

People will be uncomfortable having to find data to justify their actions. The president of Sara Lee used to have a sign on his desk that said, "In God we trust. All others bring data."

They may not like the fact that many organizational traditions about how the world works may not stand up to scrutiny. For example, many years ago, one of us consulted at a British shoe retailer. They felt that in resort towns, people would shop for shoes if it rained because they could not go to the beach. After we put up a data mart with shipment and point of sales data, the data warehouse team acquired weather data from the meteorological office. They merged that data with the point of sale data and isolated just the stores in resort towns. They found a 2-percent correlation between rainfall and shoe sales.

They may not accept the fact that data and the knowledge that flows from it is a corporate asset. They may see their base of power as tied to data they have that no one else has and the knowledge that derives from that data.

To combat this, the organization must have or develop a culture of making analytic-based decisions. As mentioned in Chapter 14, the best book we have seen on the topic is *Competing on Analytics,* by Thomas Davenport and Jeanne Harris. See, in particular, Chapter 2 "What Makes an Analytical Competitor?" They talk about the need to have senior management commitment and large-scale ambition as characteristics of an analytic competitor.

A BI steering committee and people on it from various lines of business can help you with the change management. They should have credibility with their managements. After all, that's one of the reasons you picked them, isn't it? They can be used to help make their organizations more analytically aware. You and they can tell stories about how the BI Applications have added value across the organization.

The Role of Trust or Credibility of the Data

As with any new system, when it goes live, people will claim to have found problems with the data in it. Any data warehouse is only as good as people perceive the data in it to be. At least with an Oracle BI Application, the mappings back to the source systems have been debugged, not only by Oracle but also by thousands of customers across industries and various versions over the years. So have the mappings used to load the data warehouse and the metadata used to calculate the rest of the metrics and build the reports, which gives you that many fewer places where errors could have crept in.

In fact, you can be confident that in the majority of cases, if you encounter an ETL failure, a quick online search either from a search engine or from Oracle support can determine if a bug or known issue exists. If you can't find a related issue documented, the odds are that you missed a configuration step in the documentation. In addition, the Oracle BI Applications data warehouse records contain enough bread crumbs that one can track back to individual records in each source system, so you can prove to your end users the data matches (assuming the data hasn't changed in your source after the ETL load).

However, particularly right after launching a new phase or major enhancement, one must aggressively address all perceived data quality issues. One should make available all bug reports and the findings, whether positive or negative. After a while, the number of valid complaints per month should fall, and the number of invalid complaints should rise. Some of the invalid complaints may arise because the data warehouse has shown that certain corporate legends are, in fact, false.

The Self-Funding Roadmap

As each major phase of your project goes live, give users time to adjust to the new content. Then, after, 3, 6, and 12 months, survey and interview them. Ask them what improvements in their business they have found. Ask them to confirm (or not) the areas of improvement you and they thought they would get when the business case for the BI Application was developed in the first place. Quantify and tabulate the benefits received. As described before, wherever possible, state benefits in monetary terms. One has to look at five types of benefits:

- **One-time benefits** The most common are inventory reduction, reduction in days sales outstanding, and increases in days payable outstanding.

- **Increases in revenue because the organization sold more products or services** These are annual benefits. However, to get a number representing the margin that the organization can take to the bank, one has to multiply these by a gross margin percentage. The benefits are typically small enough—only a few percent of revenue at most—that one can use gross margin and not operating margin percentage.

- **Increases in revenue because prices rose or discounts fell as well as all cost-cutting benefits** These, too, are annual benefits, but they drop straight to the bottom line. Also, while inventory reduction is a one-time benefit, any decrease in scrapped or obsolete inventory belongs in this category, not the first category.

- **Reductions in business expenses** These might arise because cost center managers did a better job scrutinizing expenses, because procurement did a better job procuring, or because manufacturing had to scrap less material and needed less overtime. They may arise because your organization got better at retaining the people you wanted to retain. As we explained in the chapters about many of the CRM analytics, if you think you have found a reduction in business costs in a front office activity, ask again whether the money "saved" was returned to the corporation or whether it was applied more effectively to generate more revenue.

- **Reduction in IT expenses** We deliberately put this bullet last because, if done right, the first four of these should overwhelm this benefit.

After you total the benefits, compare it to what you invested and generate a return on investment. The sooner you can show that you can deliver monetary benefits in excess of the investment plus a decent return on investment, the better shape you'll be in when you ask for more money to add to the data warehouse. As the composition of the data warehouse grows, if you have picked appropriate value propositions, the value you show should grow, building your reputation as someone who enables the organization to add value and meet its strategic objectives.

The Roadmap Going Forward

To understand the future of Oracle BI Applications, you need to first look at Oracle's overall direction. If you hear the term "Apps Unlimited," this is in reference to JD Edwards, PeopleSoft, Siebel, and EBS. Edge Products refer to a wide variety of other applications not part of the Apps Unlimited family, and are typically from various acquisitions. Fusion Applications are the next generation of applications that combine the best of all Oracle homegrown and acquired applications. The context of this book so far has been restricted to Oracle BI Applications 7.9.6.4 and earlier, which use Informatica as an ETL tool extracting data from Apps Unlimited sources.

For those of you not familiar with Oracle's general policy around discussing future products, there's a "safe harbor" statement all customers and prospective customers are asked to be aware of. Generally speaking, this section discussing future product direction could change at any time for any reason. There are numerous reasons why Oracle can't commit to a feature on a specific date—the primary one is due to a quality-driven release rather than a date-driven release. Oracle releases software updates based on when certain quality assurance checkpoints have been reached. Should a specific feature not be ready by a desired date, the choice is to release only the working functionality or delay the release until all functionality is working as expected.

BI Applications sourcing data from SAP, Apps Unlimited, and Fusion Applications all have different release versions. BI Applications 7.9.7.2 for SAP customers uses an older data model (based on Oracle BI Applications 7.9.6.1) and Oracle Data Integrator (ODI) as an ETL tool. It's limited to Financial Analytics, Procurement and Spend Analytics, and Supply Chain and Order Management Analytics. BI Applications 11.1.1.6.2 for Fusion Applications customers uses a newer data model (post–BI Applications 7.9.6.3) and Informatica as an ETL tool. The most important project right now is something called a "Unified Release," which will bring this all together—all data sources and both ETL tool options. There are no current plans to replace Informatica, but rather to offer both Informatica and ODI as an option.

Oracle has no plans to drop Informatica support in the near future. Almost all customers are using Informatica today, and it would be far too disruptive to expect customers to migrate. There are new customers, however, that prefer to implement an all-Oracle solution; therefore, Oracle is working on releasing an ODI version as well as an Informatica version. So if you're on Oracle BI Applications 7.9.6.3 or 7.9.6.4, for example, you can upgrade to the Oracle BI Applications 11g Unified release (version TBA), using Informatica for your Apps Unlimited source, sometime in the future. It should also be noted the DAC is used for Informatica but not for ODI releases, as ODI already provides this type of built-in schedule-generation functionality. There's no migration path from Informatica to ODI planned (although that could change), and an upgrade to Oracle BI Applications 11g might require a data reload. You'll need to discuss with your implementation provider and/or your Oracle pre-sales team for various strategies for maintaining historical snapshot data from Oracle BI Applications 7.9.6.X because this will be based on future releases where all the details have yet to be finalized.

You can expect the majority of new content to be available in the 11g release of the Oracle BI Applications. Don't confuse OBIEE 11g with Oracle BI Applications 11g. Most Oracle products are adopting similar version number conventions. The letter *i* stood for "Internet," *g* stands for "Grid," and *c* stands for "Cloud." Also, don't confuse OTBI with Oracle BI Applications. OTBI refers to Oracle Transactional Business Intelligence and is meant only for Fusion Applications.

OTBI provides real-time reporting against Fusion Applications using the same OBIEE semantic layer as the BI Applications. Some of the dimensions are conformed to allow for federated queries, combining real-time and historical data. Even a number of metrics are unified between OTBI and Oracle BI Applications. OTBI uses the concept of "bypass SQL," where the OBIEE requests view objects (VOs), view links (joins), and required columns to the ADF layer, similar to logical SQL in Fusion Applications. Provided in return is the physical SQL required to run; then OBIEE issues the physical SQL directly to the underlying database for the Fusion Applications.

The initial OBIEE access therefore is via Oracle Active Development Framework (ADF), which is represented through Fusion Application constructs called view objects (VOs) and entity objects (EOs). View objects and entity objects are usually constructed and defined during design time. Applications such as OTBI access their data by querying the defined view objects via the ADF APIs. In the end, OBIEE is able to bypass the middleware for data retrieval (for better performance), yet the application integrity is still preserved and business logic is enforced.

The three major themes with planned upcoming releases are broader functionality, deeper analytics, and lower cost of ownership. The goal is to allow customers to deploy a complete data warehouse within a week, which sounds like science fiction but is nearing reality. With this background information and preamble, the following areas of functional content are currently being planned for future releases of BI Applications:

■ **Shorter term** Fixed Assets, Budgetary Control, Sourcing, Time and Labor, Project Resource Management, Commitment Control (Financials), and Global Payroll. New modules for Student Information Analytics and Spend Planning are also in the works.

■ **Longer term** Talent Management, Grants, Benefits, Depot Repair and Field Service, Service Contracts, Earned Value Management and Project Scheduling, and EAM enhancements.

New adaptors are also being planned for future releases of Oracle BI Applications:

■ **Shorter term** Fusion Applications Cloud Service adapters, Procurement and Spend Analytics for JDE, Price Analytics for EBS, and Supply Chain and Order Management Analytics for PeopleSoft.

■ **Longer term** An adapter for Taleo and Rightnow (Service Analytics) as well as Manufacturing Analytics for JDE.

A number of exciting projects are underway as well. One example is a partial user experience redesign, initially planned for Project Analytics. This not only will take advantage of new features planned for OBIEE 11.1.1.7, but also will allow end users to leverage the out-of-the-box dashboards in a real-world environment starting from day one after implementation. At a high level, the project goals include

■ Refresh of the overall user experience, with a more compelling look and feel and with better business user self-service

- Support for unstructured data, such as surveys and social media, using Endeca for example

- Additional operational planning applications built on the BI Applications, such as headcount planning and project resource planning, using Essbase for example

Today, when customers request a data lineage application, Oracle provides spreadsheets in Oracle Support, which documents the source-to-target mappings through Informatica. This helps you assess what's out of the box. However, it's not always complete. It's a challenge to parse through all the SQL overrides, and you have to look at Informatica and OBIEE metadata as separate entities. Many of our implementation partners provide their version of a data lineage application using OBIEE as a front end, either as a product or as a service. Oracle is planning on releasing a scalable centralized repository of metadata, along with a prebuilt meta-model to link everything together. This will cover various sources, source databases, and will cover both Informatica and ODI. There will also be a built-in search and browse functionality.

Another important project being worked on involves ETL data validation, to assist with testing and validating the completeness of the data load. Today, this can be difficult, and the process isn't out of the box. You can run cross-foot types of queries as well as sample transactions to compare the source and the target. However, each customer needs to plan for their own testing. The planned functionality includes a comparison of the source data to the data warehouse data and the generation of data-validation reports.

A current trend in data warehousing is the notion of using change capture technologies to trickle feed an enterprise data warehouse around the clock with source systems in multiple time zones around the world. Oracle is actively planning on using Golden Gate to replicate data to an SDS (or source dependent data store) and then to the staging area. Keeping aligned with another industry trend, cloud computing, Oracle is planning on providing both cloud support and services, although partners will still be leveraged to provide adaptors to sources such as WorkDay and Salesforce.com. Finally, Oracle is also looking at leveraging and supporting unstructured and big data applications (via Endeca, for example) to allow for better analysis of unstructured text and better searching.

Around lowering the cost of ownership, BI Applications 11*g* already takes more of a wizard type of approach (than 7.9.x versions) to automate the otherwise manual tasks of installing and configuring. Today, you need to do a complete install on a Windows environment before porting to Unix. Many SQL scripts must be run to populate domain files. There are also many files to copy from one place to another, and so on. What's available today for Oracle Fusion Customers and will be grown over time includes the following:

- A single installer across Fusion Applications, OLTP, BI Applications, OTBI (Oracle Transactional BI), and underlying technology components. This helps implement both Fusion Applications and BI in parallel.

- A functional setup manager interface to manage the install and configuration tasks. The Administrative UI is meant to track and manage implementation projects and their required functional setup steps, including:

  - Assigning owners and due dates to tasks.

  - Setting up domains (source files for List of Values and mappings of List of Values across multiple sources).

  - Ensuring setups are complete and easily interrogated for auditing purposes.

- A configuration manager interface to manage detailed data warehouse configurations such as currencies and domains. The Administrative UI is meant to manage the system configuration of your BI Applications, including:

  - Global parameters

  - Language setup

  - Currency setup

  - Extract dates

  - The ability to export and import a configuration from file

- A BI extender to propagate flex field configurations into BI and ETL metadata, by interrogating the Fusion Applications setup to identify flex field setups for both key and descriptive flex fields. Some of the key features being worked on include

  - A wizard-based approach to update both BI and ETL metadata

- Shared runtime metadata for function security, data security, hierarchies, effective dating, set IDs, field descriptions/ translations, and a list of values

- Shared systems management using Oracle Enterprise Manager

The most important takeaway from looking at planned futures is to know and understand Oracle's short- and long-term commitment to this product. You can expect to benefit from enhancements over the years, above and beyond source system ETL updates. You can also contribute to future product plans by participating in customer advisory boards and by passing along feedback via your sales and service contacts at Oracle.

Case Studies

Thousands of organizations have implemented Oracle BI Applications. They have seen quick implementation times and high returns on investment. Often, they have also found something completely unexpected in their business. They have found large quantities of money "hiding under a rock" as it were, invisible until detailed analytics makes it apparent. Often, this one discovery has paid for the project. In some cases, the provision of Oracle BI Applications has helped change the company's underlying business model. This section tells some of their stories. It is divided into two parts:

- Reductions in implementation time and resources

- Business benefits

The names of these clients will be disguised. Many of them regard what they have done as part of what differentiates them competitively.

We urge you, though, to collect your own stories. Humans are a storytelling species. Having these stories will help you as you roll out more analytics to more people and help make analytics a key part of your organization's strategy because this will help people relate to what others in the organization have done before. It will also help you when you have to ask for more funds to tie in another division or another application. Finally, if you are allowed to speak about your organization's success, having a story will help make your talk more memorable. We urge you to talk about your successes at user groups of all kinds. We always find that when we have to speak about what we have done, the act of building a convincing talk causes us to learn even more.

Implementation Stories

Several Oracle partners have documented that implementing an Oracle BI Application can save 75 percent on implementation time and cost. Although it is difficult to predict what would have happened if they had tried to build this functionality, taking the numbers presented here and multiplying them by four will lead to plausible estimates. Also notice that most of these organizations have kept to the cadence of rolling out new functionality roughly every three months.

A coatings company needed to improve its supply chain. It had two instances of E-Business Suite covering different geographies. It implemented Supply Chain/Order Management, Procurement and Spend, and Financial Analytics against both instances of E-Business Suite in six months. We do not normally recommend implementing in this big a bang, but this company made it work.

A financial services company implemented HR Analytics for a workforce of over 50,000 employees across several continents in 25 weeks. This was all the more surprising because the company had 10 different HR systems. All of these were either legacy systems or non-Oracle packaged software. The company used the Universal Adapter for all of these, and estimated that to custom build this would have taken twice as long.

An industrial manufacturing company talks publicly about "Zero to BI in 100 days." It had experience with sales and service analytics from Siebel. When the company started to implement Financials and Supply Chain/Order Management Analytics, it was able to accomplish this with only five FTEs in 100 days, across 33 locations, sourcing data from 11 data sources. We do not recommend implementing your first Oracle BI Application without an implementation partner. However, because Financial Analytics and Supply Chain/Order Management Analytics were this organization's third and fourth BI Application, using all-in-house resources was certainly prudent.

A supplier to the Oil and Gas industry put in Supply Chain/Order Management and Financial Analytics at the same time as it upgraded from E-Business Suite release 11g to E-Business Suite release 12. The company went live the same day. To hear the client tell it, "We went live with EBS at 9:00 am and had dashboards by 1:00 pm." As described in Chapter 14, Oracle partners tell us there are synergies between an ERP or CRM upgrade and the implementation of BI Applications. They cite not having to redo some of the gap analyses, not having to convert custom data warehouses, moving reporting currently done on the OLTP that does not require real-time data to the BI Application, and quicker fixing of errors found as part of the upgrade process all as reasons to implement BI Applications at the same time as an OLTP upgrade.

A specialized semiconductor company had had no experience with much financial BI, relying on what came from Hyperion Financial Management, and found that while HFM was good for closing the books, it did not provide the depth of analysis needed. It implemented Financial Analytics in three months, and one person maintains the system. Many organizations find that their users often struggle to describe their requirements. This organization used the BI Application to provide an introductory set of dashboards and reports that could be modified as users became more familiar with what analytics could provide.

A manufacturer of building products implemented Procurement and Spend Analytics in 16 weeks. It had to integrate data from 14 different systems to get a full view of spend within the company. We find that many organizations have many different OLTP systems that have to be integrated to provide a complete view of a business process that an Oracle BI Application models. A fragmented architecture should not dissuade you from considering Oracle BI Applications for your needs.

A manufacturer of electrical and mechanical control components implemented Procurement and Spend, Financial, and Supply Chain Analytics in 75 days. Later, it added HR Analytics. This company grows by acquisition, and has become so adept at using the Universal Adapter that it can integrate a new acquisition's systems into the BI Applications much more quickly than it can replace the acquisition's ERP. This allows the company to deliver the synergies of the acquisition more quickly than it could before, bringing greater revenue and savings to the organization.

A health-related public sector agency implemented Financial Analytics and Procurement and Spend Analytics and had its first dashboards live within three months. It's not just commercial establishments that get this type of reductions in implementation time.

A university implemented Financial Analytics, Procurement Analytics, and HR Analytics, going live with its first application after six weeks, rather than the six months it had estimated for a build-from-scratch solution, and with 33 percent of the resources estimated for a build solution. The university estimated that the out-of-the-box solution provided about a 60 percent fit. Even though the application was not a perfect fit, the university still implemented it in about a quarter of the time it thought it would take for a custom solution. The university could spend its time working on the parts that were unique to the institution and avoid spending time on generic functions.

A European bank implemented Sales Analytics to an underperforming branch within three months and rolled it out to the rest of the bank within the next two months. It also implemented Siebel Contact Center and Contact Center Analytics in 20 weeks.

No matter what industry we study or what BI Application we study, we inevitably find that people can deliver more content more quickly to more people with Oracle BI Applications than they could if they build the functionality from scratch.

Business Benefit Stories

The building products manufacturer described earlier found that it had not taken well over one million dollars in supplier rebates it was owed. The company found this within several weeks after going live, thus paying for the project.

A manufacturer of laboratory equipment found it was not billing for over one million dollars in shipping charges a year. Supply Chain/Order Management Analytics allowed the company to see this omission. Technically, this is not a savings, but a revenue increase. Often, we see the benefit of BI as generating new revenue, not saving costs.

One week after going live with Sales Analytics, an electrical manufacturer found that it had been pricing certain products erroneously. Fixing this problem increased revenues by $500,000. The customer did not reveal how long this problem had existed, but we doubt it was a one-time occurrence.

A financial services company found that Sales Analytics increased leads by between 5 and 9 percent. This should translate into 5 to 9 percent more new accounts per year. The company had implemented Sales Analytics in 10 weeks. If you work in a company with outside salespeople, ask them what 5 percent more leads would translate to in revenue.

After the European bank described earlier rolled out to the underperforming branch, it rose from twenty-third in sales (out of 48) to third. During the next two months, as the rest of the bank was rolling out Sales Analytics, this branch rose from third to first in sales. It was doing a better job of cross-selling more products to its existing account holders. Ask your sales force what it would be worth if they could take average branches or districts and raise their performance to what the current company leaders enjoy.

A consumer goods company found that through better management of trade promotions, it was able to raise sales by between 1 and 2 percent with no increase in trade promotion spending.

A provider of IT services increased its win rate by 4 percent after implementing Sales Analytics, along with a 10-percent reduction in days sales outstanding. As this provider signs multiyear contracts, an increase in win rates today will provide dividends for years to come. It implemented Sales Analytics despite the fact that it does not use Siebel Sales.

We wish you the greatest of successes in your implementation. More than 4,000 customers have gone in front of you over the past decade and a half, so you won't be doing this alone. We'd love to hear about your success stories and get your feedback on this book. Thank you for taking the time to consider our recommendations.

Index

Reach More than 700,000 Oracle Customers with Oracle Publishing Group

Connect with the Audience that Matters Most to Your Business

Oracle Magazine
The Largest IT Publication in the World
Circulation: 550,000
Audience: IT Managers, DBAs, Programmers, and Developers

Profit
Business Insight for Enterprise-Class Business Leaders to Help Them Build a Better Business Using Oracle Technology
Circulation: 100,000
Audience: Top Executives and Line of Business Managers

Java Magazine
The Essential Source on Java Technology, the Java Programming Language, and Java-Based Applications
Circulation: 125,000 and Growing Steady
Audience: Corporate and Independent Java Developers, Programmers, and Architects

For more information or to sign up for a FREE subscription:
Scan the QR code to visit Oracle Publishing online.